Refugees and Forced Displacement in Northern Ireland's Troubles

Untold Journeys

MIGRATIONS AND IDENTITIES

Series Editors
Eve Rosenhaft, Michael Sommer

This series offers a forum and aims to provide a stimulus for new research into experiences, discourses and representations of migration from across the arts and humanities. A core theme of the series is the variety of relationships between movement in space—the 'migration' of people, communities, ideas and objects—and mentalities ('identities' in the broadest sense). The series aims to address a broad scholarly audience, with critical and informed interventions into wider debates in contemporary culture as well as in the relevant disciplines. It will publish theoretical, empirical and practice-based studies by authors working within, across and between disciplines, geographical areas and time periods, in volumes that make the results of specialist research accessible to an informed but not discipline-specific audience. The series is open to proposals for both monographs and edited volumes.

Refugees and Forced Displacement in Northern Ireland's Troubles

Untold Journeys

Niall Gilmartin and Brendan Ciarán Browne

Liverpool University Press

First published 2022 by
Liverpool University Press
4 Cambridge Street
Liverpool
L69 7ZU

This paperback edition published 2024

British Library Cataloguing-in-Publication data
A British Library CIP record is available

ISBN 978-1-80207-732-2 (hardback)
ISBN 978-1-80207-529-8 (paperback)

Typeset by Carnegie Book Production, Lancaster
Printed and bound by CPI Group (UK) Ltd, Croydon CR0 4YY

For our parents,

Phyllis and Terry Gilmartin

Marie and Paul Browne

Contents

Contents

Acknowledgements

Like most forms of social science research, the foundational basis of this book is the kindness of 'strangers' and owes a huge debt of gratitude to all interviewees who generously gave up their time, and who opened up their homes and their lives to share their stories and memories of what for many, was and remains, a harrowing and painful part of their lives. Without your testimonies and inputs, this book would not be possible. Thank you. We wish to thank the funders of the research – the Irish Research Council, the Busteed Postdoctoral Fellowship at the University of Liverpool, and the Independent Social Research Foundation (ISRF). We would like to thank the staff at the Linen Hall Library and the Public Record Office of Northern Ireland (PRONI) in Belfast, the National Archives of Ireland in Dublin, and the Liverpool Central Library for their unyielding support and dedication to assisting our research. Special thanks to Alison Welsby, editor at Liverpool University Press (LUP), for her continuous assistance. We also express sincere gratitude to the two anonymous reviewers for their time, diligence, and feedback on the manuscript.

Niall Gilmartin: I would like to thank those who generously assisted the research: Trevor Cubbon; Kenny Donaldson MBE, Brian Dougherty MBE, Eileen Jennings, John Jennings, Michael Liggett PhD, Derek Moore, Cllr Dale Pankhurst, and Cllr Mike McKee, who sadly passed away in December 2019. My research on displacement began as a postdoctoral project across two universities. I thank Peter Shirlow, Mervyn Busteed, and all at the Institute of Irish Studies at the University of Liverpool for their support, mentorship, and Busteed Postdoctoral funding. I wish to extend sincere gratitude to the Department of Sociology at Trinity College Dublin (TCD) for their friendship and support, particularly Camilla Devitt, Olive Donnelly, Andrew Finlay, David Landy, Fiona McIntyre, and David Ralph. A very special mention and thank you to the head of Sociology at TCD, Richard Layte, for his mentorship and ceaseless support of the research. I am also grateful to my colleagues at Ulster University, particularly the support of Ciaran Acton and Patricia Lundy. The process of transforming what was in late 2015 a very basic idea about displacement and the Troubles into a robust and feasible project primarily came about through many conversations with Colin Coulter at Maynooth University. At every stage of designing, researching, and writing, Colin provided continuous encouragement, support, and interest. Thank you, Colin. A final and special thank you to my wife Ann Marie and our girls Beth, Anna, and Clara for supporting me in the researching and writing of this book.

Brendan Ciarán Browne: There are a number of individuals I would like to thank for their generous time in helping to facilitate various aspects of this work, including: Seamus Magee, Ciaran McLaughlin, Danny Morrison, Isshaq Al-Barbary, Michelle Teran, Sarah Pierce, Kate Turner, and Olivier Martin. Thank you also to Colin Coulter and Peter Shirlow for providing a platform to initially reflect on conflict-related displacement in their co-edited volume in Capital & Class. At Trinity College Dublin, I am most grateful to my Head of School, Siobhán Garrigan, for her mentorship and continuous support throughout the life span of this project. Thanks to my mum, Marie, for always supporting, encouraging, and publicising the work, and to my sisters Catherine and Maeve for their interest, support, and honest appraisals. Thanks to my brother Niall for always providing uncensored feedback during late night conversation.

    A special thanks is reserved for my good friend and collaborator Casey Asprooth-Jackson who has been a mainstay in this research journey. Throughout every iteration of the work, Casey's insightful critique helped to sharpen its focus, and by exhibiting our work through artistic installations in Belfast and Oxford, he helped to push the boundaries of how to present the story of conflict-related displacement during the Troubles. For that, and so much more, thank you. A special thank you is reserved for my wife Emma for her unwavering support, for critical feedback, and most importantly, for reassurance throughout the duration of this project. Thank you. Finally, to my dad Paul, for your never-ending patience and the willingness to be so transparent and forthright about your and the family's experience of being 'burned out'. Your guidance, reflection, and interest as this project has evolved has been crucial for me. Beyond thank you, for my part, this book is for you.

Maps

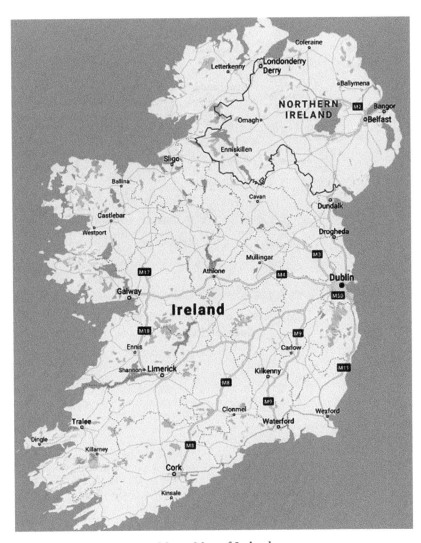

Map 1 Map of Ireland
Source: PRONI

Map 2 Map of Northern Ireland
Source: PRONI

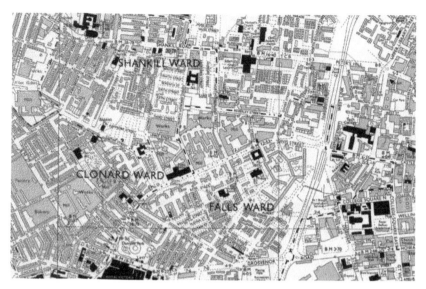

Map 4 West Belfast showing Falls Road and Shankill Road, *c.*1969
Source: PRONI

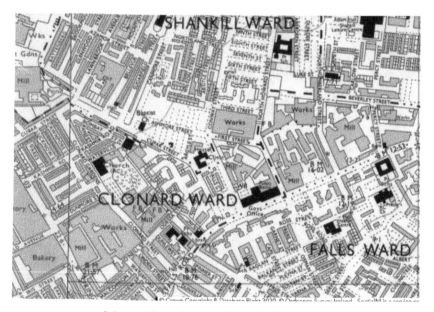

Map 5 Clonard area of West Belfast, *c.*1969
Source: PRONI

Map 2 Map of Greater Belfast area

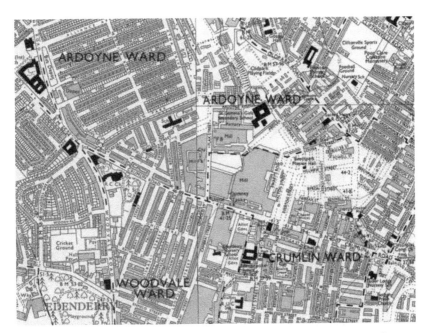

Map 6 North Belfast showing Woodvale, Ardoyne, Crumlin Road,
and Oldpark Road, *c.*1969
Source: PRONI

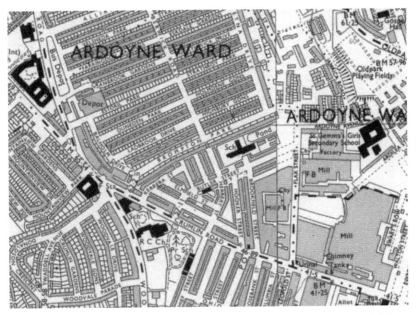

Map 7 Ardoyne, North Belfast, *c.*1969, showing Hooker Street, Brookfield
Street, and Butler Street in the lower, centre part of the map. At the top left
are Cranbrook Gardens, Velsheda Park, and Farringdon Gardens
Source: PRONI

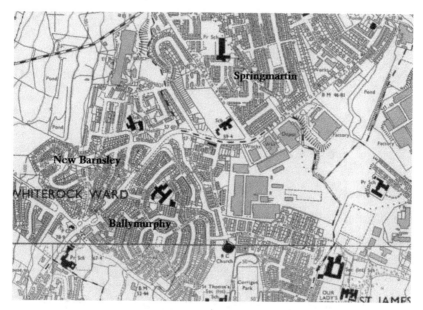

Map 8 New Barnsley, Springmartin, and Ballymurphy, West Belfast, *c.*1969
Source: PRONI

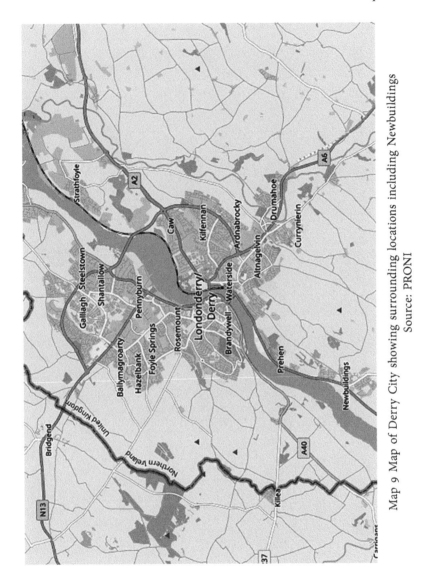

Map 9 Map of Derry City showing surrounding locations including Newbuildings
Source: PRONI

Chapter One

Introduction: The Silence of War

Exile is strangely compelling to think about but terrible to experience. It is the unhealable rift forced between a human being and a native place, between the self and its true home: its essential sadness can never be surmounted. And while it is true that literature and history contain heroic, romantic, glorious, even triumphant episodes in an exile's life, these are no more than efforts meant to overcome the crippling sorrow of estrangement. The achievements of exile are permanently undermined by the loss of something left behind for ever.

Edward Said, *Reflections on Exile*, 180

You can talk about buildings; you can talk about jobs but this thing is just beyond description. I can see a generation being blasted into bitterness; youngsters growing up, they'll never forget this. They'll never forget the homes they've lost. The people they've lost. I just can't find words to describe the agony of this week.

Rev Eric Gallagher, Belfast, 19 August 1969

Accounts and narratives of war often give powerful expression to the death, loss, and harm associated with political violence, vividly communicating the noise, chaos, and destruction of lives, families, and communities. Within prevailing accounts, our attention is, understandably, drawn towards what are presented as the 'key events', the 'watershed moments', or 'turning points' considered to signify important transitionary junctures in the trajectory or de-escalation of armed violence. In the case of all conflicts,

1

however, such accounts are also replete with multiple silences – voices, experiences, and perspectives typically occluded or muted by the predominance of certain events, actions, and actors deemed to constitute the sole representations of conflict-related violence and harm. Northern Ireland's conflict from 1968 to 1998, often dubbed 'the Troubles', is certainly no exception, where despite a vast and extensive body of research and study,[1] there remain layers of violence, harm, and loss that have yet to be recognised, much less acknowledged and addressed.[2] This book seeks to 'end the silence' with regards to forced displacement during the Troubles, a neglected and, as this book demonstrates, ubiquitous aspect of the conflict. Based primarily on in-depth interviews, the purpose of the book is two-fold: first, it seeks to capture the unique perspectives of those forcibly uprooted over the course of the 30-year conflict and place on historical record their unique stories and experiences; and, second, in considering these narratives, we seek to challenge and broaden prevailing understandings of conflict-related violence, harm, and loss in Northern Ireland so as to demonstrate the centrality of forced movement, territory, and demographics to the roots and subsequent trajectory of the Troubles.

The dearth of attention to displacement during the Troubles is curious and perplexing when we consider the centrality of land, people, and identity within the historical divisions that imbibe Northern Ireland.[3] The roots of Northern Ireland's 'recalcitrant antagonisms' lay in the plantation of Ulster during the early seventeenth century, which 'produced a demographic pattern where the native Irish were concentrated in different areas from those of the colonising Scots and English…differing in religion, language, social customs and economic status' (Darby 1986: 9; Patterson 2013). Moreover, the extent of forced movement is a well-established practice going back to the mid-1800s continuing right up to the present day. As early as 1857, segregated forms of residential housing based on ethno-religious identities were an increasing feature, particularly in urban settings such as Belfast. Although sectarian violence and displacement were perennial features of life in the North before and after partition in 1921 (and remain so to this day), the outbreak of ethno-sectarian violence during the late summer of 1969 gave rise to a refugee crisis that, at the time, represented the largest involuntary movement of a population in Europe since the end of the Second World War. Unlike previous periodical outbursts of inter-communal violence and mass movement in the 1920s and 1930s, the deliberate targeting of homes, streets, and communities for demographic purposes was not an ephemeral outburst confined to August 1969. While thousands of displaced Catholics crossed the border into the Republic of Ireland, particularly during the years 1969 to 1974, and hundreds of Protestants evacuated to Liverpool and Glasgow, the 30 years of armed conflict also generated considerable levels of internal displacement whereby people increasingly fled their homes and sought safety within their own ethno-religious group and residential areas.[4] The importance of forced movement is further underpinned by both its immediate impact and long-term consequences. The traumatic events considered in this book caused profound demographic changes within some of Northern Ireland's delicately balanced residential settings. While the traditional sites of inter-communal violence located along interface fault-lines in places such as Belfast were eventually regulated and contained by the erection of large boundary structures, dubbed 'peace walls', those deemed a minority living among a majority community were increasingly targeted and, in many instances, forcibly expelled. Forced displacement effectively signified the end of mixed residential housing in many working-class districts across Northern Ireland as well as in rural hinterlands close to the border, thus creating unprecedented levels of residential segregation, demarcated territories, and enclaves. The existence of homogenous communities was central to solidifying and mobilising collective identities and interpretations of violence, which were particularly favourable to the growth of militant republicanism and loyalism, leading to the unprecedented direct involvement of the British Army and RUC[5] personnel in social housing policy from the mid-1970s onwards (Coyles 2017). For those living in highly segregated communities, the reality of fear, suspicion, and attack drove a purposeful bonding of experiences into strategies for reaction and community cohesion, conjoined with notions of secureness and the appreciation that community space was insecure, violated, and symbolically constructed around the identification of a threatening 'other' (Shirlow and Murtagh 2006).

The symbolism and visual significance of displacement, that being the arresting and discommoding images of blazing and scorched homes in Bombay Street, Hooker Street, and Farringdon Gardens, were essential to the 'defenderist' logic that underpinned the embryonic development of armed republicanism and loyalism, directly leading to a surge in supporters and recruits.[6] Embedding images of mass displacement and attack within the discourse of 'defenderism' allowed the creation of similar but opposing narratives of 'state failure' within republicanism and loyalism. For the former, mass displacements were understood as a recurring feature for Catholics and emblematic of the inherent sectarianism within the Northern Ireland state; in their analysis, the state was, at best, a reluctant bystander, while thousands of nationalists were displaced, and in some instances, the state stood accused of aiding and abetting attacks on Catholic homes.[7] For the latter, attacks on Protestant homes and businesses, as well as individual targeting of RUC and UDR[8] personnel, furnished firm evidence of the state's inability or unwillingness to adequately deal with the growing threat from republican violence. As a result of the failure of the state to protect each community and ensure the rights of all citizens within Northern Ireland, non-state military groups thrived and fed the cycle of displacement, drew upon segregation, and the lack of police protection or mistrust in state security services, allowing them to act as de facto community defence forces and, in such a position, provide legitimacy for them to attack the other community (Moffett et al. 2020). Furthermore, we scarcely need reminding that the roots of the recent conflict resided not in constitutional preferences, sovereignty, or self-determination but within the more banal though no less important issue of housing – from Caledon to the Derry Housing Action Committee, the Civil Rights Movement to Lenadoon Avenue in July 1972, to the Torrens estate in 2004 – housing, territory, and people were both cause and symptom of the entire conflict, furnishing the ideological and physical space where fear, vulnerability, and attack could flourish and endure. Though predominant accounts of the Troubles tend to afford displacement little more than a footnote of history, the direct role and downstream consequences of forced movement were significant and hiding in plain view; we therefore contend, that to fully understand the eruption and outplaying of the Troubles, we need to engage with and understand displacement.

Beyond these important issues, there is of course, a human cost. As this book demonstrates, forced movement engendered specific forms of loss, dislocation, and insecurity that are not addressed by resettlement in new homes and communities, nor are they considered an issue of redress with its fragmented approach to the past under the auspices of 'Legacy'. With regards to their individual experiences of displacement, all research participants spoke of the pain, loss, distress, and 'heart-break' of losing their family home, their communities, their friends, social networks, their sense of identity and security, their places of employment, family farms, places of worship, and education, among many others. The idea of 'ontological security' concerns self-identity and confidence derived from a sense of stability, security, and familiarity in an often-unconscious understanding of place and belonging. As primary foundational blocks, 'home', 'community', and attachment to place are broadly understood as spatially defined locations that are emotionally invested with a sense of familiarity, continuity, and belonging, providing us the context within which we have the confidence, stability, and security to go about our everyday lives (Mitzen 2018). Forced movement entails more than the material loss of home and possessions; the acute obliteration of an established way of 'being' in the social world furnished a visceral sense of liminality, where 'one finds oneself cut off from the past, unsettled in the present, and unsure of the future' (Ghorashi 2005: 182). The often-violent uprooting of families and communities produced, for many, a legacy of dislocation and unease that remains potent and unresolved. Despite the propensity of conventions depicting war and peace as two distinct temporal forms of social and political action, the emotional impact of violent uprooting and loss is clearly deep-seated and present. The visceral sense of being silenced, ignored, or marginalised are the outcomes of reductive discourse and policy outputs that continue to frame loss, suffering, and victimhood solely as those acts associated with conventional forms of physical, armed violence, thus cultivating a hierarchy of harms and victims. Furthermore, the dearth of recognition by scholars and wider society is exacerbated by a silence imposed from within. The violation of the home, a place of individual and familial safety and security, for many, was just too painful, too raw, too surreal, and in some instances, too shameful to speak about. For most research participants, their testimonies contained in the pages that follow is the first time they have spoken publicly and at length about their experiences of forced exile. Even within close-knit families, the narratives and memories of displacement were bounded by walls of silence; at individual, familial, and communal levels, for the most part, the story of displacement remained unspoken. Therefore, the silence we speak to in this book is not just the occlusion within academic and non-academic accounts of the conflict, but also to the silence that enclosed many individual, familial, and communal experiences and memories of displacement. Whether we term such silences as 'gaps', 'inadvertent oversights', or simply 'blind spots', the widespread neglect of forced displacement is often interpreted by those who experienced it as a denial or trivialisation of their loss. Though it is relatively easy to recognise the presence of conflict and the presence of armed groups and actors, less tangible and discernible, however, is the presence of silence and absence.

Throughout the book, we have endeavoured to disaggregate the violence and intimidation that led to displacement into its various constituent formations, and our research extrapolates a plurality of forms of displacement and a range of factors that explain decisions to flee. While the notion that displaced persons are motivated by a concern for safety and well-being in the face of overt violence and intimidation is logical and self-evident, there are, nevertheless, important disparities and contexts that existed. The violence and mass movement of persons in the early years of the Troubles certainly resonates with explanations linked to acute forms of social and political flux generated by an eruption of political violence and armed conflict. While there are clearly instances of the classic 'push' and 'pull' factors, in all cases, respondents expressed reluctance and sorrow to uproot themselves and their families and therefore the 'push' factors of fear, intimidation, and vulnerability consistently preceded the 'pull' factors of employment, housing, and familial networks. While the messy and complex reality of armed conflict often means that many of these competing factors overlap and blur, the overriding priority for those who fled their homes in Northern Ireland was safety not social mobility. Therefore, the underlying commonality across all respondents was fear and vulnerability, and the anticipation of attack. Fear and mistrust are linked to understandings of risk, doubt, and behavioural responses that are influenced by continuous assessment of threats. Feelings and perceptions of fear and insecurity may not be directly related to violence; however, they are invariably shaped by attitudes towards the 'other community' via the history and reproduction of collective memories (Shirlow and Murtagh 2006). This book, and the perspectives of those contained within it, does not seek to dissolve or diminish the significance of the physical 'conventional' forms of armed conflict that characterised the Troubles. Our intention is to provide for readers a critical encounter with a range of narratives and experiences that bring to light a set of perspectives typically precluded from the transitional justice agenda. The significance of the stories and experiences contained in this book derives from their ability to denote a plurality of forms of violence, fear, and harm that are typically less tangible within conventional understandings of conflict-related violence. Therefore, we are not advocating that displacement be 'added' to and subsumed within canonical narratives and texts; rather, we argue for the need to broaden the spectrum of what is considered conflict-related violence and harm and, therefore, challenge what are considered to be axiomatic subjects of security and redress within processes of conflict transition.

Context and Extent of Displacement

The vexed and often antagonistic political history between Britain and Ireland is essentially a struggle for power connected to religion, politics, and nationalism (Cochrane 2013: 8). In the aftermath of the Protestant reformation in England in the seventeenth century, religion became the primary marker of in-group identity and out-group identity amid increasing efforts to colonise and Anglicise Ireland. Ireland served two key purposes in terms of its strategic value; first, land was given in reward for service by the English Crown to its soldiers and, second, Ireland was viewed as a potential security weakness for England against potential invasions by the Spanish and others. The largest transfer of land and resources was the plantation of Ulster. Although a previous plantation attempt in Munster in the 1580s failed primarily due to the issue of absentee landlords, the plantation of Ulster in the early seventeenth century saw more than 170,000 English and Scottish settlers given land in Ulster from dispossessed 'natives', leading to the establishment of 23 new towns in the province (Cochrane 2013; Stewart 1997). More than any other historical event, the Ulster plantation copper fastened the tenacious links between land, identity, and power and, furthermore, furnished a powerful and enduring historical narrative transmitted from generation to generation (Stewart 1997). According to Darby (1986), the broad outlines of the current conflict in Northern Ireland had been sketched out within 50 years of the plantation: the same territory was occupied by two hostile groups, one believing the land had been usurped and the other believing that their tenure was constantly under threat of rebellion. They often lived in separate quarters. They identified their differences as religious and cultural as well as territorial.

The growth of Belfast as an industrial powerhouse in the 1800s witnessed an increased influx of Catholics from rural areas, thus increasing sectarian tensions, often culminating in outbreaks of violence. While often associated solely with the Troubles, ethno-sectarian violence and forced displacement were endemic features of everyday life in the north-eastern counties of Ireland prior to the creation of the Northern Ireland state in 1921, with inter-communal riots recorded in 1835, 1857, 1864, 1872, 1886, 1898, 1920–22, and 1935 (Darby and Morris 1974). Even as early as 1857, segregated forms of residential housing based on ethno-religious identities were an increasing feature, particularly in urban settings such as Belfast. Although synonymous with the violence of 1969–72, house burnings or the destruction of property were long-standing methods used to enforce physical and social segregation in Belfast (Boyd 1969). Rioting in 1872 saw 872 families forcibly displaced from their homes, a pattern repeated with regularity for the remaining years of the nineteenth century (Boyd 1969). The abiding and foreboding shadow of history is a constant feature in Northern Ireland and these historical instances of displacement embedded a legacy of constant fears and threats within what were deemed to be vulnerable communities. The birth and formative years of the new Northern Ireland state witnessed intense episodes of sectarian violence, primarily inflicted upon Catholics, with hundreds rendered homeless, leading to the establishment of the Catholic Relief Fund and White Cross Collection groups. By the mid-1930s, relationships between the two communities had deteriorated to the point where 1935 saw the worst sectarian riots since the formation of the state. In the run up to the annual twelfth of July Orange Order parades in 1935, growing sectarian violence in various parts of Belfast resulted in the killing of eight Protestants and five Catholics, while 514 Catholic families – some 2,241 people – were displaced from their homes (Liggett 2004). The practice of targeting and forcibly displacing people based on their ethno-religious identities was not confined to the north-eastern part of the island. In the lead up to partition and the years and decades afterwards, the Protestant population throughout the South suffered significant decline. The causes of Protestant decline and exodus has provoked significant debate and contestation, with explanations ranging from 'voluntary migration' (Bielenberg 2013) to deliberate strategies of IRA 'ethnic cleansing' (Hart 1998).

The exact scale of displacement during the Troubles is unknown. Given the chaos and confusion in the early years of the Troubles and, moreover, the frenetic and disparate forms of displacement, it is simply not possible to put an exact figure on levels of forced movement (Shirlow 2001). The scale of the task of quantifying movement is further complicated by the fact that many did not liaise with the Northern Ireland state, particularly those from the Catholic community, as detailed in Chapter Four, and so any formal record will invariably be incomplete. However, the figures that do exist are sobering. We know from the Scarman Tribunal that examined the violent events of 12 to 15 August 1969 that at least 3,500 families were displaced during these tumultuous days (McCann 2019; Walsh 2015). As the violence intensified, between 30,000 and 60,000 people were forced to evacuate their homes in Belfast from 1969 to 1973, comprising 11.8% of the population (Darby and Morris, 1974). The city of Londonderry[9] saw the Protestant population in the city centre's West Bank decrease from 8,459 in 1971 to 1,407 in 1991. The causes of Protestant movement have been the subject of visceral debate and contestation within the city and beyond. A recent report commissioned by the Pat Finucane Centre caused much anger when it suggested a myriad of factors for Protestant movement, such as jobs, housing, re-development, and sectarian intimidation (Hansson and McLaughlin 2018). It is clear, however, from existing research (Burgess 2011; Kingsley 1989; McKay 2000; Ó Dochartaigh 2005; Shirlow et al. 2005; Southern 2007; Smyth 1996) and from our own research presented here that while issues of housing and employment were clearly factors for some, the overarching reasons for many Protestants were various forms of intimidation and fear. Given that Belfast and Londonderry were the epicentres of the conflict, it is unsurprising that much of Northern Ireland's displacement occurred in these urban settings, though not exclusively so. The experience of mass displacement in 1969 was not limited to Belfast, with 150 Catholic families forced out in Dungannon, and a further 35 Catholic families living beside the city walls in Derry, fleeing after being subjected to regular attacks from the other side. During the same period dozens of Protestants in Derrybeg in Newry were forced out of their homes (Moffett et al. 2020). In April 1974 the Catholic population in the town of Newtownabbey (just north of Belfast) had been reduced by 95 per cent since 1970 (180 families down to 16) due to intimidation, with the number of Catholic children at school in Rathcoole having dwindled from 1,000 to 350 during this time. In the same period about a third of the Catholic population had departed Carrickfergus. Indeed, the census data supports this decline of Catholic families in Carrickfergus from 16.2 per cent in 1971 to 8 per cent in 1981. There was a forced 'exodus' of dozens of Protestant families from the Suffolk area of West Belfast in July 1976 while on the border with the Republic of Ireland, hundreds of Protestant families fled South Armagh and Fermanagh as a result of a violent campaign of intimidation and murder. In Newry, Protestant school attendance fell 37.2 per cent (1,614 to 1,014) from 1973 to 1998 with a similar 40 per cent trend in the decline of Presbyterian congregations in the area (Moffett et al. 2020). According to the Northern Ireland Census, although the overall population of Newry increased by 32 per cent from 1971 to 2001, the Protestant community decreased by more than 50 per cent.

Given the significance and extent of forced displacement, both historically and throughout the Troubles, it has nevertheless constituted little more than a footnote or fleeting reference in most academic accounts. Notwithstanding, within the extensive literature on Northern Ireland, some welcome and notable exceptions have either explicitly incorporated displacement and movement as part of their overall thematic analysis or, in some instances, alluded to its importance. The role of housing, segregation, territoriality, and identity in the perpetuation of ethno-sectarian antagonisms is well established and remains a feature that has endured despite the advent of the 1998 peace accord (Boal 1969; Coyles 2017; Poole and Doherty 2010; Power and Shuttleworth 1997; Shirlow and Murtagh 2006; Shuttleworth and Lloyd 2009; Shuttleworth, Barr, and Gould 2013). Providing one of the first major studies of ethno-religious division during the Troubles, Boal's (1969) work demonstrated the importance of framing political and religious antagonisms regarding space and territory within a historical prism, highlighting the consequences for contemporary forms of urban segregation in a place such as Belfast. Also noteworthy is Shirlow and Murtagh's (2006) ground-breaking examination of place and territoriality in post-Good Friday Agreement (GFA) Belfast, cogently demonstrating the role of segregated places in the reproduction of violence (and its mutation from armed violence to everyday forms of sectarianism) and the consequences for residents, not only in terms of deepening communal polarisation, but also social exclusion, fatalism, and economic truncation. Until very recently, John Darby's research on intimidation, violence, and housing in the early to mid-1970s and again in the mid-1980s was effectively the lone academic in-depth account of forced displacement. Although limited to the greater Belfast area only, nevertheless, his 1974 and 1976 studies examined a variety of forms of intimidation and their cyclical patterns, the immediate effects on individuals and communities, the importance of housing shortages in patterns of resettlement, and the role of various agencies in dealing with intimidation and its consequences.

As a contested and sovereign frontier, the border, and its ubiquitous military structures along its hinterland, were the focus for much violent attack, differentially experienced and interpreted by those living within the northern side of the border (Patterson 2013). Though many enactments of violence during the Troubles were relatively confined to the six counties, inevitably, 'spill overs' into the South, including the perennial influx of thousands of Catholic refugees from the North presented the Dublin Government with a series of civil, political, and security challenges, as well as provoking points of nadir in Anglo-Irish relations (Hanley 2018; Mulroe 2017; Patterson 2013). Hanley's (2018) and Mulroe's (2017) accounts are particularly detailed in their analyses of the Dublin Government's changing attitudes and actions towards the Northern refugees as the conflict evolved. In border areas like south Armagh and Fermanagh, narratives of dispossession, intimidation and violent attack abound and were embedded in wider Protestant fears regarding a broader, terminal decline in Protestant culture, influence, and power (Dawson 2007; Donnan and Simpson 2007; Patterson 2013).

Despite the ubiquitous reference of 'defenderism' within the gargantuan body of work on republicanism and loyalism, very few accounts afford more than a passing reference to those displaced or their role as constituent communities on which they claimed to act on behalf of. Matthew Whiting's (2019) analysis of the embryonic period in the Provisionals development cites the ability to shoehorn the perceived or actual social context of disadvantage and repression among new recruits into the framework of the national question, where Irish self-determination was presented as the solution to their ills. The ability to combine everyday forms of 'defenderism' within the larger framework and objective of a united Ireland marked the Provisionals from previous forms of republicanism, thus functioning as the central modality of recruiting and sustaining the movement across the decades. Ian Cobain's (2020) compelling and thoroughly researched *Anatomy of a Killing* provides one of the few informed accounts of the Troubles that 'connects the dots' between social class, poverty, housing, forced displacement, and decisions to engage in political violence. Richard Reed's extensive research with loyalist combatants consistently highlights the deeply localised nature of the response of many working-class Protestants to the onset of the conflict. For Reed's respondents, their role in the conflict as loyalists were overwhelmingly understood in solely localised terms, as defenders of streets and estates against republican aggression (Reed 2015). Moreover, the facilitation of communal exodus stemmed from the collective action of citizens with hijacked lorries and vans from the Shankill used to transport furniture and family belongings (Mulvenna 2016). According to Mulvenna, it was the nascent networks of loyalist paramilitaries that were instrumental in the movement of Protestant families during the early years of the Troubles.

The 50th anniversary of the Troubles in 2019 fomented some new appraisals of the period in question, with some notable contributions focusing on the importance of displacement. Michael McCann's thoroughly researched *Burnt Out* (2019) examined the mass burnings of August 1969 and offers a detailed analysis of these seismic events, challenging many of the assertions and claims within existing accounts, firmly placing culpability for the violence at the actions of John McKeague and Ian Paisley and an inept and indifferent Stormont Government. Those communities disproportionately affected by displacement, such as Ardoyne, also generated informative and detailed local historical outputs, giving voice to displaced individuals and the impact on the local district (Liggett 2004; McKee 2020). While this diverse body of work has explored forced movement to varying degrees, nevertheless, with the notable exception of Darby and Morris (1974) and Darby (1986) there existed few in-depth studies solely focused on forced movement. In recent times however, a small but burgeoning body of work has begun to address the relative paucity of attention. The report *All Over the Place: People Displaced to and from the Southern Border Counties as a Result of the Conflict 1969–1994* (Conroy, McKearney, and Oliver 2005) contains a great deal of valuable information, themes, and perspectives, and represented the first post-Troubles endeavour to shed light on the extent and impact of movement. It is, however, limited in certain crucial respects. In particular, the research that informs *All Over the Place* involved an impressive though relatively small number of informants (32) and, furthermore, focuses excessively perhaps on former members of non-state militaries – while Katherine Side's (2015, 2018) work on displacement included visual representations of displacement across a range of diverse outputs, while also examining the efficacy of the Scheme for the Purchase of Evacuated Dwellings (SPED).[10] Additionally, both authors also published articles based on their initial batches of research, arguing for the necessity to shift the harms and losses of displacement from the margins to the centre of scholarly approaches to Northern Ireland (Browne and Asprooth-Jackson 2019; Gilmartin 2021). Based on focus groups across a wide geographical spread, the 'No Longer Neighbours' (Moffett et al. 2020) report continued these increasing endeavours, documenting the sentiments of displacement, the impact of violence on land tenure, as well as housing and redress schemes during and after the conflict in and around Northern Ireland. More recently, experiences, memories, and the long-term consequences of displacement regarding loss of identity, place, and belonging have featured in richly descriptive personal memoirs and reflective prose (McAleese 2020; ní Dochartaigh 2021), alongside a relative flurry of media and public interest on various aspects of the displacement story (McClements 2021; Sheeran 2021). While such works provide a range of insights, nevertheless, the occlusion of displacement from the Troubles' narrative and lack of academic engagement is conspicuous and perplexing. Our research presented here builds upon and adds to these important works; our unique contribution, however, is a book that represents the first comprehensive and in-depth analysis of forced displacement during the Troubles, both in terms of its geographical scope and the diversity of perspectives within it.

Definitions

Undertaking an in-depth examination under the broad auspices of 'displacement' in the context of a deeply divided society requires some conceptual and definitional clarity as well as some dedication to the language and titles used throughout. We define displacement as a social process involving the communication of intimidation, fear, and threats, or the perception of intimidation and threats, which provokes either an immediate or long-term sense of insecurity and vulnerability that compels an involuntary flight, either permanently or temporarily, for the purpose of securing refuge and safety. Such a definition has the capacity to encapsulate all degrees and formations of forced movement by emphasising, first, the presence or perception of fear and insecurity, second, the primacy of *forced* flight, and lastly, by dispensing with the state-centric categorisation of 'refugees' as simply those who cross international borders in favour of a more encompassing application of the term to all those who were forced to flee and seek refuge. Furthermore, the scope of our research design invariably had limitations and we focused solely on forms of displacement from homes caused by threats and fear, emanating from the 'other community', thus precluding those displaced by internecine feuds and conflicts, of which there were many throughout the Troubles. Given our focus on homes and communities, we are also conscious that our research design does not specifically focus on those forced from their places of employment, the loss of businesses, and in some instances family farms, although the targeting of businesses and livelihoods are weaved in throughout some of the narratives.

Our constructivist approach to social identity, particularly with regards to religious and ethno-national division in the context of Northern Ireland, rejects foundational understandings of identities as fixed, durable, and immutable. Although the Troubles are often erroneously described and/or explained as a 'religious' war, enactments of violence were not motivated by differences in confessional status or theological divergences; rather, religion primarily functioned as both a marker of ethnic identity and the block foundations on which ethnic identity is constructed and formed (Coulter 1999; Coulter et al. 2021). While ethnicity in Northern Ireland is typically viewed as 'fixed' by familial religious denomination, there is greater fluidity and agency with regards to issues of citizenship, national identity, and constitutional preference (Coakley 2007). Given this, any scholarly endeavour that reifies or suggests the idea of fixed, homogenous ethnic groups is misleading and disingenuous. Moreover, the reification of the 'two communities' invariably neglects the growing portion of the population who do not identify with one or two of the identity categories they are assumed to fit (Coulter et al. 2021). Despite the complexity of ethnic and political identity formation in Northern Ireland, it is hard to deny the reality of two readily discernible blocs, 'Protestants and Catholics' (Smithey 2012). The boundary division between 'Protestant' and 'Catholic' in Ireland is composite, incorporating religion, ethnicity, nationality, history, and – in Northern Ireland – politics (Todd 2018). Given this, we draw on the work of John Coakley (2007) and use the terms 'Catholic' and 'Protestant' as the primary formations of identity, as they are typically determined by parents or guardians and as they provide an initial 'world view' of identity and belonging and function as a formative site of socialisation with regards to norms, values, and symbols on which individual and communal identity is subsequently derived, though not pre-determined. While in many instances religious identities do align with ethno-national identities and constitutional preferences, we have deliberately eschewed the temptation of applying broad acronyms such as CNR (Catholic, Nationalist, Republican) or PUL (Protestant, Unionist, Loyalist). Our use of the terms 'Protestant' and 'Catholic' therefore does not signify or suggest on our part the existence of homogenous, unified communities; differences of class, gender, location, and political affiliation all contribute to the complexity of identification in Northern Ireland society. Moreover, across the cohort of research participants was a panoply of identities reflecting the fluidity of identity formation regarding ethnicity, national identity, political and social standpoints and constitutional preferences, among others. Our use of the terms 'Protestant' and 'Catholic' is therefore a means of using a common category of identity while simultaneously respecting the diversity within and across them.

Within mainstream parlance, terms such as refugees, asylum seekers, and immigrants are deployed and used inter-changeably. Matters are further complicated by motivations for movement; for instance, terms such as deportation, internally displaced, economic migrants, environmentally displaced, and ex-patriates, among many others, have added to the debate and discourse. Over the course of recent years, and particularly with the moral panic in Europe regarding what was dubbed the 'Mediterranean refugee crisis', terms such as migrant, economic migrants, and illegal migrants have been used interchangeably in public discourse with a distinct and conspicuous absence of the term 'refugee'. Regardless of the endless semantics, the key definitional issue here is, of course, 'force' and 'choice'. Theoretically the migrant is positioned as the archetypal rational choice person, weighing up the 'push and pull factors' before making an informed choice whether to uproot and move. In contrast, the refugee is *forced* into movement, not seeking a 'better life' elsewhere but motivated by the sole purpose of survival. The issue at stake here ostensibly is a distinction between voluntary and involuntary forms of movement. Refugees are of course concerned primarily with 'push factors'. As is the case with many dichotomous classifications however, the reality of life, particularly in the realm of armed conflict, is far more complex and disordered. The decisions to uproot against one's wishes, as will be demonstrated in this book, are subjective, context-specific, and shaped by numerous factors, including but not exclusive to levels of threat, gender, social class, pathways available, and social networks. What do we mean when we say 'forced' or 'involuntary'? Moreover, how do we measure it in a valid and reliable way? The research contained in this book reveals the complex and conceptually ambiguous realities of displacement in times of conflict. While much theoretical analyses of refugees and those forcibly displaced focus on either the breakdown in relationship between citizen and state or as members of minority groups facing imminent danger, the case of Northern Ireland does not fit within such prescribed models. While of course the displacement of Catholics and nationalists in Northern Ireland does reflect the archetypal depiction of a minority group suffering at the breakdown in the relationship with the state, the displacement of Protestants defies the state-centric explanations. More often than not, displaced persons in Northern Ireland did not seek safety across a sovereign border but within what were perceived as 'safer communities' comprised of their own political community. As a result, the terms 'refugee' or 'internally displaced persons' become more complex and nuanced, dare we say irrelevant, when we consider the views and perceptions of those who experienced forcible displacement during the Troubles.

Drafted in the aftermath of the Second World War, the 1951 Refugee Convention notes that the term 'refugee' shall be applied to any person who

> owing to well-founded fear of being persecuted for reasons of race, religion, nationality, membership of a particular social group or political opinion, is outside the country of his [sic] nationality and is unable or, owing to such fear, is unwilling to avail himself [sic] of the protection of that country; or who, not having a nationality and being outside the country of his [sic] former habitual residence as a result of such events, is unable or, owing to such fear, is unwilling to return to it.[11]

The language of the 1951 Refugee Convention was crafted in such a way as to focus primarily on issues related to European refugees, however the enhanced definitional protection afforded by the Additional Protocol of 1967 recognised this inherent bias and subsequently broadened the language to be more international, thus widening its scope of applicability. One of the core components of the convention is that to be considered a refugee under international law and therefore entitled to the subsequent protections therein, an individual or group of individuals must cross an international border in the midst of fleeing persecution. In addition, and in highlighting the distinction between a refugee and a migrant, the language of refugee applies to those who are forced to leave their home for fear of being persecuted for the reasons listed above, namely, a well-founded fear of being persecuted due to reasons of race, religion, nationality, membership of a particular social group, or political opinion. This fear of persecution was due to a belief that the individual and/or group would not be afforded protection from their own state/country.

Owing to a perceived need to expand upon the definition of refugee to include those who are fleeing their country due to the 'general effects of armed conflict and/or natural disaster' several non-binding regional instruments have been implemented to widen the net of protection. (See in particular the Cartagena Declaration on Refugees and the Convention Governing the Specific Aspects of Refugee Problems in Africa.) With reference to the principles underlying these non-binding regional instruments (particularly the latter, drafted in 1969 at the outset of the Troubles) it would be reasonable to argue there would be little doubt that any individual or group who fled their home due to the 'general effects of armed conflict' would be considered a 'refugee' if they crossed an international border. Importantly, those who left as refugees would therefore be entitled to support from the state from which they are fleeing for repatriation or, in the event that repatriation is not possible or indeed desirable, some form of reparations (a point we return to later in the book). Similarly, the host country (in most cases of displacement in Northern Ireland, this would be the Irish Republic) would, according to the principles above, be bound to provide support for those 'refugees' as noted below.

However, given that the vast majority of those who experienced forcible transfer in Northern Ireland remained displaced within the borders of the state, and would therefore be considered definitionally internally displaced persons (IDPs), there exists a need for greater understanding of the differences between rights, responsibilities, and protection for IDPs when compared to those of refugees. In contrast to the significant protection provided for refugees under international law, IDPs are not subject to protection under a binding legal convention that applies at the international level, and up until relatively recently the status of IDPs remained relatively underdeveloped. However, in 1998 the United Nations drafted its 'Guiding Principles on Internal Displacement' that sought to provide some definitional clarity on the status of refugees, defining them as

> [p]ersons or groups of persons who have been forced or obliged to flee or leave their homes or places of habitual residence, in particular as a result of or in order to avoid the effects of armed conflict, situations of generalized violence, violations of human rights or natural or human-made disasters, and who have not crossed an internationally recognized state border.

Whereas the rights afforded to those who attain refugee status directly extend to those who are outside their country of origin, there is less protection provided for those who are classified as IDPs. The primary difference between refugees and IDPs concerns the state-centric issue of crossing an internationally recognised border that subsequently triggers a further level of international protection as noted above (as noted in the 1951 convention, the AP, and other regional instruments). However, by virtue of being human, IDPs are entitled to protection afforded by other internationally binding conventions, including rights enshrined under International Human Rights Law and International Humanitarian Law. However, in recognising that there existed a discrepancy pertaining to the support given to IDPs, the 'Guiding Principles on Internal Displacement'[12] were drafted in 1998 in an effort to '[c]onstitute the key international standard on internal displacement worldwide, restate and compile human rights and humanitarian law relevant to internally displaced persons'.

The conceptual construction of refugee identity is therefore constituted by the interplay between sovereign political borders and notions of citizenship. Invariably, the boundary construction around citizenship is premised upon processes of inclusion and exclusion. Refugees therefore are forced into the gaps between states (Haddad 2008). With the sedentary citizen and sovereign state as the key reference points, conventional refugee identity is consequently a negative construct, whereby the constituent parts are composed of what the refugee is not or what the refugee lacks. The

1951 Convention cites individual persecution as the sole causal factor behind the acquisition of refugee status. The inclusion of 'a well-founded fear of violence' allows enough flexibility to allow for degrees of subjectivity. The emphasis on crossing sovereign borders remains problematic and difficult in the case of Northern Ireland, not least because of the political and symbolic contestation regarding the border's legitimacy, therefore complicating matters further. So, while thousands of Catholics who crossed the border into the South legally qualified as refugees, many in this research rejected the label on the grounds that they did not recognise the legitimacy of the border, and therefore one 'cannot be a refugee in your own country'. Therefore, a state-centric focus on border crossings as the primary reference point obscures the meanings ascribed to displacement by those who have suffered and survived it.

In the case of Northern Ireland, the issue of transgressing borders appears an irrelevance to experiences and meanings associated with displacement. In addition to the widespread 'internal displacement' within the state, there is much evidence of instances of informal house-swaps between members of opposing communities. Evidence of squatting is equally ubiquitous. Of equal importance are the ways in which the violence of conflict for some intertwined and overlapped with other factors such as employment, housing allocation, and urban redevelopment. Despite both the complimentary and contradictory factors offered here, the key definitional issue is that decisions to leave and seek refuge were forced upon respondents and inextricably related to the conditions created by violence, whether the source of that violence were members of opposing political communities, state forces, or paramilitaries. Although the vernacular among the general population and interviewees to describe their displacement was the simple epithet of being 'put out', the forms of intimidation and movement were disparate and often defied categorisation: some fled across borders; some returned to their original homes; others did not; many were internally displaced within Northern Ireland; in some instances, some resettled a very short distance from their original home. While international law, policies, and discourse seeks to analytically differentiate the degrees of movement with a panoply of terms such as refugee, evacuee, internally displaced persons, asylum seekers, migrants, and economic migrants, in the case of Northern Ireland, such terms are arbitrary, disingenuous, and wholly inept for capturing the complexity of forced movement experiences. If the true meaning and spirit of the refugee category is to 'protect the unprotected', then surely it is both logical and morally correct to extend that same level of protection and humanitarian aid to others such as internally displaced persons, who are in qualitatively the same predicaments as 'refugees' (Haddad 2008). We follow the contention of Haddad (2008) and Loescher (1992) that there is no conceptual difference between the 'refugee' and 'internally displaced persons' and therefore propose that a working definition of a 'refugee' appropriate to many contemporary conflicts should include all persons who have been forcibly uprooted because of violence and persecution, regardless of whether they have left their country of origin (Loescher 1992). We have therefore applied the term 'forced displacement' as an all-encompassing term designating the entire process of movement while also applying the term 'refugee' to all those who forcibly fled their homes to secure refuge and safety, regardless of the distance, geographical spread, or the transgression of the border.

Methodology

The book sets out to examine the lived experiences of forced displacement during the Troubles; the scale, nature, and sensitivity of events under examination therefore required a considerable level of thought and planning. The research adopted an interpretivist methodological approach using semi-structured, narrative-based interviews with 88 people. While one-on-one interviews were the main form of primary research, a small number of focus groups were used at different times, principally to reflect and compare the two datasets for themes, consistencies, and anomalies. In addition to our extensive field research, we drew from a comprehensive range of secondary sources from both Northern Ireland and international contexts, including academic research and reports, policy documents, official reports, memoirs, film documentaries, and diaries. Qualitative forms of research have long been championed by critical scholars for their ability to explore subaltern voices and experiences that invariably produce new forms of knowledge and standpoints that often challenge and disrupt the accepted orthodoxies within dominant accounts and approaches. Interviewing, particularly non-hierarchical interviewing, is cited as an important method that places emphasis on personal experiences within transitioning societies, while reducing the exploitative nature of the researcher–researched relationship (Oakley 1981). Moreover, it creates the conditions to discover realities by generating data that provides an authentic insight into people's lived experiences (Silverman 2010).

Methodological considerations within the field of refugee studies have led many to concur that qualitative interviewing, specifically narrative approaches, are an important and effective way of learning from refugees because it permits a fuller expression of refugee experiences in their own words. A narrative-based data collection method is grounded in the belief that meaning is ascribed through experiences, and furthermore that we can only know about other peoples' experiences from the expression they give to them (Eastmond 2007). Analytically, it distinguishes between life as lived (the flow of events that impact upon a person's life); life as experienced (how a person perceives and ascribes meaning to what happens); and life as told (how experience is framed and articulated in a particular context) (Eastmond 2007). While the politics of 'storytelling' is of course subjective and reflects particular perspectives and standpoints, its strengths reside in the ability of research participants to structure a narrative that signifies events and experiences in a particular order. In the case of displacement, the use of personal testimony challenges erroneous assumptions regarding the homogeneity of experience among refugees, thus displacing generalised analytical accounts in favour of a more nuanced understanding of the diversity and complexities within those groups forcibly displaced. Far from being a matter solely of individual experience, memory is a social phenomenon. What and how we remember is shaped and moulded by our experience and interaction with significant others, our participation in social discourse, and our interactions with meaningful symbols, surroundings, and landscapes. Nor is memory purely a record of the past. While memory is indeed about the past, perhaps its defining feature is its presentism (Misztal 2003). As an active and dynamic process, recalling and narrating past experiences is shaped and filtered in light of the present and, moreover, the content of what is recalled or not is situational and contingent on the audience and narrator and the power relationship between them. Testimonies of tumultuous and violent 'life experiences' such as forced displacement should therefore be considered constructions and products of active agents and 'experiencing subjects' seeking to make sense of violence and turbulent change, paying particular attention to the ways in which experience is framed and articulated (Eastmond 2007). Thus, the caveat here is that stories and recollections cannot be seen as simply reflecting life as lived through some rational, objective, value-free lens; on the contrary, narrations should be seen as creative constructions or interpretations of the past, generated and shaped in specific contexts of the present (Eastmond 2007).

In the context of a region transitioning from protracted armed violence, recollections of the past are also embedded in a wider, adversarial framework of 'memory politics' as the social action of collecting and recording stories become sites of struggle and resistance regarding legitimacy, morality, blame, and culpability. Ruti Teitel (2003) contends that recollective accounts generated in transitional times are never autonomous and are often anchored in national narratives; therefore, 'transitional truths are socially constructed within processes of collective memory' (70). Notwithstanding, the opportunity and ability to narrate one's own story, as a means to secure recognition, have become associated with a transition from the condition of being a (passive) victim into that of an (active) survivor (Dawson 2007). In our research design and conduct, we were sanguine that the large cohort of research participants from a variety of backgrounds and locations, coupled with the extensive body of secondary literature, provided a robust and holistic vision of forced movement and its many after-effects. Importantly, our decision to avail of qualitative methods reflects our training, our epistemological positioning in the constructivist tradition, and our fervent belief that narratives on the social world are constructed as part of a discussion between interviewer and respondent (Gubrium and Holstein 2001; Miller, Kulkarni, and Kushner 2006; Silverman 2006, 2010).

To transform the interview transcripts into meaningful data, we used an inductive thematic analysis approach using a grounded coding system, otherwise known as open coding (Strauss and Corbin 1990). Open coding essentially entails scanning each line of transcript, taking note of the essence of portions of data and seeking key events, critical events, and themes. Grounded theory research develops analytical categories and theories from the data rather than adhering to preceding concepts or theories; theory is derived from the data and meaning is achieved through reflection upon the data. In other words, it is a specific area of study in which the relevant concepts and theories subsequently emerge. Applying this technique and using NVivo coding software, we then employed a 'focused coding' where recurring codes were reviewed and forged into 'Nodes', that is, discernible themes and recurring patterns. Linkages between themes and emerging concepts were developed and thus formed the basis of the findings within the book.

Field Research and Ethical Considerations

As is the case with any form of research design, our research and the perspectives generated were shaped by design decisions regarding the inclusion and exclusion within the study. As stated above, our research focused solely on those forced from homes and communities as a consequence of fear and threat from persons of opposing religious and/or ethno-national identity. Therefore, our purposive form of sampling sought out those forced from their homes and communities because of direct or indirect forms of intimidation during the conflict. Both authors already had existing networks of contacts with a range of community organisations and activists in Belfast and Derry and sought to initiate contact with potential interviewees via gatekeepers in community organisations and then proceeded with and sustained our research using a snowballing technique. Our ability to access individuals initially is indebted to representatives across civil society who assisted in gathering individuals (and groups) interested in sharing their views and experiences. Once we commenced our field research and built significant trust, rapport, and relationships, much of the remainder of the field research was based on chain referral. As part of the reflective process, upon the conclusion of each interview (detailed in the next sub-section), several research participants then recommended other persons to interview and passed on our contact details or the contact details of potential interviewees, leading to more participants. The more interviews we conducted, the more we validated our commitment, sensitivity, and authenticity as researchers; given the tight-knit nature of society in Northern Ireland, particularly in working-class communities impacted by conflict, reputation was invaluable.

Though we consistently sought to ensure gender and ethno-religious identity representation in our purposive approach to seeking interviewees, our use of snowballing and various outreach methods to potential gatekeepers meant that we had limited input and control in identifying and locating interviewees with regards to their individual biographies, gender, and geographical spread. While we consistently endeavoured to locate interviewees from diverse locations and backgrounds, invariably our highest response rates emanated from those in urban settings, and so most of our interviewees originally lived in an urban or suburban area. The urban–rural divide among interviewees was also exacerbated by the pandemic. Like so many aspects of life, our field research was severely impacted by the Covid-19 pandemic, which halted all interviews from February 2020 to May 2021. Due to time constraints with regards to both funding and publication deadlines, our original plans to conduct extensive research with rural forms of displacement in the latter stages of the project were significantly impacted, leaving only a short time period of August and September 2021. It is therefore important to signpost that much of the analysis within the book reflects largely urban forms of displacement. Nevertheless, our research with rural interviewees, particularly with the Protestants in Fermanagh, South Armagh, and South Down, offer invaluable insights and highlight a tangible rural–urban difference in experiences.

Field research was conducted by the authors from June 2017 to September 2021, collecting 88 in-depth interviews with those who suffered displacement. The interviews occurred in a range of locations including Belfast, Londonderry, Liverpool, Shannon, Fermanagh, Armagh, Roscommon, Down, Dundalk, Glasgow, Southampton, and Lanzarote.[13] Of the 88 interviewees, 56 were male and 32 were female. 46 of the interviewees self-identified as Protestant, while the other 42 self-identified as Catholic. The vast majority of interviews occurred in interviewees' homes, which were ideal settings for participants to feel secure and relaxed in order to speak of their past. A small number of interviews were held in other locations, such as coffee shops or bars in city or town centre locations, primarily to suit the schedule of interviewees, particularly when interviews were conducted during working hours. Other locations such as community centres were also used for a small number. Most interviews were akin to an informal conversation and lasted anywhere from 30 to 90 minutes; most interviews were approximately 40 minutes in duration. After interviews, time was spent reflecting on the interview and on certain issues that were raised during the process, as well as general chat about political developments or personal stories about our own families, and this formed an essential part of the transition out of the interview.

The research methods, accessing participants, data storage, and safeguards fully adhered to established international good practice and were compliant with Irish and EU law. Conducting any form of social research can often be complex and challenging, presenting an array of potential risks and harms. This is particularly pronounced in the case of displaced persons in armed conflict, where there is clear potential for trauma, pain, and vulnerability. We envisaged several key ethical considerations, including issues of consent, power, confidentiality, trust, and rapport, harm and benefits, issues of representation and analysis, possible benefits, and, finally, the outcomes of the research. Despite the passage of time since their displacement, we were cognisant of latent or continuing forms of psychological and emotional harm derived from their displacement experiences. Another key concern is that displacement was embedded and often enveloped by other forms of violence, and so we were also mindful that displaced persons were likely to have been impacted by other forms of violence before, during, and after their forced movement. We adopted an iterative model of consent, which assumes that ethical agreement and truly informed consent can be best secured through a process of negotiation that develops a shared understanding of what is involved in the research process (MacKenzie and McDowell 2007). We utilised several strategies that sought to mitigate the risks of emotional distress and increase the power and capacity of the interviewees.

In most cases, contact with potential interviewees began with introductions and a general conversation regarding the purpose and objectives of the research through several mediums, including face-to-face meetings, phone calls, and/or email. Information sheets and broad research themes were also exchanged. To reaffirm their capacity and participation, we sought to reduce perceptions of rigidity and formalities, and instead framed the interview processes as a mechanism and opportunity to 'share their story' of displacement as opposed to constituting a formalised, structured interview. While interviewees were aware that we would ask some questions during the course of the interview, at all times we foregrounded their control over the relaying of their stories and memories. The purpose of this process was two-fold: first, to establish trust and rapport between the researchers and potential interviewees and second, it functioned as a mechanism to allow potential interviewees to reflect and decide if they wished to contribute their story. In some cases, persons, or their immediate family members, decided that the risk of revisiting distressing memories would be too much and kindly declined our research invitation. In other instances, elderly persons were encouraged to have a family member present with them, typically a son or daughter. While some interviewees were emotional during the process, they insisted that the interviews continue, and their emotions be noted on the transcripts.

Most interviewees offered generous hospitality involving tea, coffee, and other refreshments during and after the interviews, creating the necessary time and space for post-interview conversations. Some conversations related to displacement, sometimes to wider political issues, and in other instances about more pleasant aspects of life, such as families and holidays. It was not uncommon to spend several hours in an interviewee's home. With regards to follow-up contact, all interviewees were offered a full transcript of their interview. While a small number declined and were happy to conclude the relationship with the recorded conversation, most wished to receive a copy, which presented an opportunity to 'check in' with interviewees some weeks after the interview. Research participants were invited to read the transcript and provide any feedback they may have. Some interviewees also wished to read chapter drafts, which were provided. In these instances, issues of accurate representation were raised in certain aspects and a process of re-drafting and consultation with interviewees continued until all parties were content. While these procedures were laboursome and time-consuming, given the subject matter, both researchers were cognisant of the importance of interviewees' input as 'experts in their own lives and experiences' and the importance of accurate representation. Given the absence of displacement experiences from the narratives of the Troubles, we were committed to working with those interviewees who wished to contribute to the project.

Over the duration of the project, all interviewees were contacted and apprised with any updates regarding the research and particularly the production status of this book. Beyond this text and its important contribution, we also committed to organising a series of public talks and events right across Northern Ireland, Liverpool, and beyond to highlight the overlooked stories of forced displacement, something most interviews expressed a keen desire for. We intend to invite some interviewees to participate in panels as a platform to tell their stories. We also held some meetings with Dr Irene Boada Montagut who is currently endeavouring to establish a Museum of the Troubles and Peace in Belfast city centre and we expressed the importance of including the displacement stories in the museum and our willingness and that of our interviewees to contribute to that project. We hope that the strategies adopted throughout this process and those envisaged for future outputs have genuinely provided some tangible benefits to those who participated in the research and that, overall, the research constitutes a form of mutual benefit and reciprocity for both the interviewees and the researchers.

Notes

1   The breadth and scope of academic commentary on and accounts relating to all aspects of the Troubles is vast. For debates regarding the roots of the conflict, see Colin Coulter's *Contemporary Northern Irish Society* (1999), Brendan O'Leary and John McGarry's *Explaining Northern Ireland* (1995), and Jenifer Todd and Joseph Ruane's *The Dynamics of Conflict in Northern Ireland* (1996). For an entire overview of both the Troubles and the peace process, see Feargal Cochrane's *Northern Ireland: The Reluctant Peace* (2013).

2   As is typically the case in any deeply divided society, terminology and discourse are politically loaded and Northern Ireland is no exception. Considering this, it is important to clarify our use of terms. Throughout the book, we use terms such as 'the North of Ireland' and 'the North' as well as the official title of 'Northern Ireland' to refer to the geographical area of the Six Counties that constitute Northern Ireland. We also use the term 'the South' at times in reference to the Republic of Ireland. We do not seek to cause any disrespect or offence by using these terms and we are cognisant that the use of interchangeable terms may cause confusion or inconsistency for some readers. This book, however, is based on a large quantity of diverse perspectives and narratives from a variety of backgrounds and so, as a mark of respect to them, we have endeavoured to use a range of terms that reflect this diversity.

3   It is not intended that this book be an exhaustive account of the Troubles; there already exists an overabundance of textbooks that fulfil that purpose. For a comprehensive account of the conflict see Feargal Cochrane's *Northern Ireland: The Reluctant Peace* (2013) and David McKittrick and David McVea's *Making Sense of the Troubles* (2001). For further reading around the roots and escalation of the conflict see Thomas Hennessey's *Northern Ireland: The Origins of the Northern Ireland Troubles* (2005) and *The Evolution of the Troubles 1970–72* (2007).

4   Additionally, it is important to note that people were also 'displaced' or intimidated out of workplaces. Furthermore, many persons were 'ordered' into exile by paramilitaries for alleged transgressions such as 'fraternising with the enemy' or 'anti-social behaviour'. Also, many buildings were the target for violence, particularly public houses, which were deliberately earmarked in 1969, as well as buildings linked to religious and cultural identities and practice.

5   The Royal Ulster Constabulary (RUC) was formed alongside the partition of Ireland and the creation of the Northern Ireland State in 1921 and drew its recruits and personnel largely from the Protestant community. While the force was viewed by Protestants as a vital safeguard against any potential threat, those within the Catholic minority saw it as a partial and coercive force of unionism. Accusations and evidence of police mistreatment of Catholics throughout the history of the state only served to exacerbate these tensions. Furthermore, the unionist government also recruited an all-Protestant force called the Ulster Special Constabulary ('B-Specials'), which acted as an auxiliary to the RUC. For a full and detailed analysis of the origins of the RUC and its role in the Troubles see G. Ellison and J. Smyth's *The Crowned Harp: Policing Northern Ireland* (2000).

6   A cursory examination of the sociological profiles of some of those who participated in armed loyalism and republicanism, once again underscores the centrality of forced movement. One of the most well-known 'refugees' was IRA leader, MP, and hunger striker Bobby Sands, who was displaced from the family home in Rathcoole. According to Denis O'Hearn's comprehensive account, Sands's life was relatively ordinary and certainly apolitical until his experiences of intimidation and those of other Catholics living in Rathcoole, leading to his family's eventual forced exile and relocation to Twinbrook on the outskirts of West Belfast. Andy Tyrie was the 'Supreme Commander' of

the Ulster Defence Association (UDA) throughout the 1970s and into most of the 1980s. Andy and his family fled their home in New Barnsley in West Belfast in 1970. Ian Cobain's thoroughly researched and compelling account of the 1978 killing of RUC officer Millar McAllister, *Anatomy of a Killing. Life and Death on a Divided Island* (2020), again underscores the importance of displacement. The person convicted of the killing, Harry Murray, was a loyalist forcibly displaced from Tiger's Bay in North Belfast after he married Kathleen Kelly, a Catholic from the Cliftonville Road area. Re-housed in Lenadoon in West Belfast, Harry was overwhelmed at the warm reception afforded to him by the residents of Lenadoon and was increasingly sympathetic to the republican analysis of the conflict. His eventual decision to join the IRA resided not in far-reaching concerns regarding self-determination, sovereignty, or socialism but in his desperation to 'get back at the prods' for his forced exile and the legacy of animosity of losing home, community, and his sense of identity and belonging.

7   Definitions and analyses of the state are diverse and deeply contested. Rather than viewing the state as a self-evident, material, and centralised object, throughout this book we view the state as encompassing a vast array of institutional sites and structures with dedicated personnel, including governance, police, judiciary, civil service, and local government. While Northern Ireland does not technically constitute a state, historically, it has claimed political authority over the defined territory of the six counties, and unquestionably embodied the Weberian contention regarding a monopoly over the legitimate use of violence and authority within that territory.

8   The Ulster Defence Regiment (UDR) was established in 1970 as an outcome of the Hunt Report, which recommended the disbandment of the B-Specials, deemed to be a paramilitary and coercive arm of the state. The UDR was effectively a replacement for the B-Specials, absorbing many of them into the ranks of the new regiment. While the B-Specials were essentially part of the Northern Ireland state apparatus, the creation of the UDR was an attempt to attract Catholic recruits, precisely because the regiment did not answer directly to Stormont, but to the hierarchy within the British Army. The regiment was the largest in the British Army and was recruited solely from within Northern Ireland. Although open to all, the UDR overwhelmingly comprised of members of the Protestant community. While Catholics did initially join in relatively significant numbers, by 1972, they comprised a mere 3.7 per cent of the regiment. Many factors account for this, including the presence of former B-Specials in the command ranks, a growing discontent among the Catholic community in the aftermath of Internment and Bloody Sunday and the targeting and killing of Catholic UDR members by the IRA. Narratives and perceptions of the regiment are polarised; for many unionists, the UDR represented a formidable form of protection against republican violence and intimidation; for nationalists, they were viewed as a partisan and coercive part of the British state, augmented by accusations that the regiment was infiltrated by loyalist paramilitaries and that it actively colluded in the killings of Catholics throughout the conflict. It was disbanded in 1992 and replaced with the Royal Irish Regiment.

9   According to the city's Royal Charter of 1662, its official name is 'Londonderry'.
    Although the city council changed its name from Londonderry City Council
    to Derry City Council in 1984 and was subsequently replaced by Derry City
    and Strabane District Council in 2015, the official title of the city remains
    Londonderry. For those from a nationalist background and certainly for most
    people in the Republic of Ireland, the city and county is referred to as Derry
    and County Derry, respectively. While some Protestants in the city also refer
    to it as 'Derry' in their everyday talk and conversation, many unionists across
    Northern Ireland refer to the city as 'Londonderry'. All Protestant research
    participants expressed their preference for the term 'Londonderry', which is
    used widely throughout the book where pertinent to their stories and experi-
    ences. In other instances, we use the term 'Derry'. Again, it is not our intention
    to cause confusion or inconsistency for the reader, but our approach in using
    both Londonderry and Derry was guided by a respect for the diversity of
    perspectives contained in the book and we have endeavoured to use 'their
    terminology' where appropriate.

10 SPED, a British Government funded programme, was established in 1973 to
    provide 'limited financial compensation' to homeowners and residents who
    lost their homes due to the conflict. However, the SPED process was deemed
    complex and onerous, with tight eligibility criteria, the requirement of 'evidence'
    of displacement, and long, bureaucratic processes involving solicitors, the RUC,
    and the Northern Ireland Housing Executive. Complicating this further is the
    fact that many Catholics were reluctant or unwilling to deal with the RUC,
    deemed by many Catholics as a partial and coercive police force. A compre-
    hensive exploration of SPED is contained in Chapter Five.

11 The United Nations Convention Relating to the Status of Refugees was adopted
    in 1951 by a conference of 26 states including the United Kingdom and later
    ratified by Ireland. The text of the convention and the subsequent 1967 protocol
    are available at https://www.unhcr.org/3b66c2aa10.

12 The 'Guiding Principles on Internal Displacement' (E/CN.4/1998/53/Add.2). Other
    international frameworks have sought to provide guidance on frameworks for
    durable solutions to internal displacement, including those considered under
    the African Union Convention for the Protection and Assistance of Internally
    Displaced Persons in Africa (Kampala Convention (23 October 2009)). See: https://
    www.ifrc.org/docs/IDRL/-%20To%20add/AUConventionProtectionIDPs2009.pdf.
    And also the Inter-Agency Standing Committee (IASC) Framework on Durable
    Solutions for Internally Displaced Persons (IASC Framework) IASC. Available:
    https://www.unhcr.org/50f94cd49.pdf.

13 Like so many other aspects of life across the world, the research process was
    significantly impacted by the Covid-19 pandemic; field research was suspended
    in March 2020 and resumed on 17 May 2021. While there was some discussion
    on whether to continue interviews over the medium of an online platform,
    we judged that conducting the interviews online would have a potential
    adverse effect. We therefore held off and waited for restrictions to lift and the
    widespread inoculation of the population through the vaccination programme.
    Notwithstanding, four interviews were conducted online with those living in
    Britain and further afield.

Chapter Two

Formations of Intimidation, Fear, and Flight

Introduction

Though there exists a voluminous body of work examining conflict-related forced movements, many of these tend to focus on processes of human-itarian aid, re-settlement, host communities, long-term integration, and the pursuit of a 'just return' home (Ager and Strang 2008; Davenport, Moore, and Poe 2003; De Vroome and van Tubergan 2014; Heimerl 2005). Relatively less explored and understood are the multi-causal factors and determinants that force persons and families to abandon their homes, lives, and communities. Moreover, the small but burgeoning body of research examining causes of displacement are primarily quantitative, drawing upon large-scale datasets and statistical models (Czaika and Kis-Katos 2009; Moore and Shellman 2004; Steele 2011). While the presence and intensity of armed conflict is often understood as the logical and axiomatic causal factor of flight, this chapter offers a more nuanced understanding of the circumstances and factors that shape decisions to flee homes and commu-nities. The predominance and disproportionate focus on structural factors such as the magnitude of armed violence or the role of the state furnishes a vision of displacement that often omits or precludes the actions and voices of those forced to flee. Many accounts of the Troubles, particu-larly the early years of 1969 to 1974, are actor-centric, delineating a set of narratives and experiences that reflect the perspectives of those deemed the primary protagonists to the conflict. The significance of the perspectives and experiences contained in this chapter derives from their ability to denote a plurality of forms of violence, fear, and harm that are typically less tangible within conventional understandings of conflict-related violence.

By categorising displacement in Northern Ireland in this chapter, not only by its temporal and spatial dimensions but also by highlighting the plurality of forms of violence and intimidation that led to forced movement, we not only eschew the pitfalls of viewing forced displacement as a singular and immutable phenomenon but we also highlight the complex and layered 'push and pull' factors that impinge upon decisions to leave. The objective of this chapter is, first, to offer unique insights into the first-hand narratives of fear, violence, and displacement that have hitherto been largely side-lined from the history of the Troubles, and second, to provide understandings of plural determinants that cause flight in times of armed conflict. The depictions of displacement we share in the chapter portray similarities and specificities, sketching out a mosaic of narratives and experiences that contain both overlaps but also considerable divergence. Notwithstanding their heterogeneous lives and experiences, the common thread linking most testimonies is 'forced' movement, persistently precipitated and triggered by a threat, or perception of insecurity. The communication of that threat, as this chapter demonstrates, came in many forms and complexions.

Formations of Fear

Conventional understandings of displacement in Northern Ireland tend to depict the astounding mass movement of persons as an insidious and irrational by-product of the escalating violence of 1969 and early 1970s. While the arresting and discommoding footage and images of rows of terraced houses burning in Bombay Street, Hooker Street, and Brookfield Street in 1969 embedded particular understandings of forced displacement in the public consciousness, our research contends that forced movement in Northern Ireland was rarely linear or consistent.[1] In many ways, predominant interpretations of forced movement are tied to what is understood as an archetypal or 'standardised' form of displacement, typically involving direct, physical attacks on homes, individuals, and communities. While such acts of violence and intimidation were of course commonplace, particularly in the early years of the Troubles, they were, however, one of many complex patterns of fear and intimidation. The primacy of what are considered 'conventional' modes of displacement therefore tends to obscure the complex nature and reality of forced movement in Northern Ireland, which often involved more subtle, though no less effective, forms of intimidation and threats. Based on our research, Displacement in Northern Ireland is schematically aggregated into three broad categories: 1. Direct intimidation, 2. Indirect intimidation, and 3. Mutual Arbitration.

Direct Intimidation

According to Darby, intimidation is the 'process by which, through the exercise of force of threat, or from a perception of threat, a person feels under pressure to leave home or workplace against his or her will' (1986: 53). As the most prevalent reason for exile throughout the Troubles, direct intimidation broadly included direct assaults on homes through gun attacks, smashed windows, petrol bombs, arson, physical assaults on persons, and verbal and written threats. Drawing upon the work of Kunz (1973), we make the important distinction here between 'acute' and 'anticipatory' forms of movement because of direct intimidation – the former referring to mass movements triggered by a moment of rupture while the latter indicating a series of incremental events, typically over a longer period, that culminate in a decision to flee. Initial episodes of forced displacement in the Troubles, such as the harrowing events in Bombay Street, Ardoyne, New Barnsley/Moyard, Percy Street, Conway Street, and Clonard, are what Kunz (1973) terms 'acute refugee movements' (131), which tend to arise from great moments of political and social change. In these instances, persons either flee en masse, or if their flight is obstructed, in bursts of individual or group escapes. Of fundamental importance here is the immediacy of danger, attack, and insecurity, compelling those to seek safety with little or no preparation. Given the extent and primacy of the mass burnings and forced movement of August 1969, many interviewees were directly affected by these distressing and momentous events, and it is therefore logical and appropriate that we commence our analysis with these events and provide some important background context.

Though the eruption of inter-communal violence in August 1969 is understandably perceived as the self-evident starting point of the Troubles, tensions had been unfolding and developing steadily from January 1969 onwards, leading to small-scale movement and the establishment of citizens defence committees[2] across Northern Ireland.[3] Instances of violence between residents and the police in Hooker Street and Crumlin Road in North Belfast led to the establishment of the Citizens Action Committee on 25 May 1969, an umbrella group comprising an eclectic mix of nationalists, trade unionists, socialists, and republicans, among others. Prior to this, on 1 May 1969 the Shankill Defence Association (SDA) was established by John McKeague. Before the eruption of violence in mid-August 1969, evidence abounds of instances of involuntary movement based on fear and intimidation. By July 1969, there was already evidence of forced movement; the RUC reported that several Catholic families left their homes after receiving threats including letters containing 9mm bullet rounds, purported to come from the Ulster Volunteer Force (UVF). The *Belfast Telegraph* reported on 5 August that two dozen Catholic families were forced out of Protestant neighbourhoods while seven of the seventeen Protestant families living in Hooker Street had already applied for re-housing (Prince and Warner 2019). From January 1969 onwards, Protestants living in Hooker Street began to flee their homes, some of whom were directly attacked. By August 1969, all 24 Protestant families living in Hooker Street had fled (Hennessey 2005). Though simmering tensions and antagonisms were clearly evident, events in Derry and Belfast from 12 to 15 August 1969 were significant turning points, both in scale and their long-term repercussions.[4]

The annual Apprentice Boys' parade in Derry on 12 August 1969 brought tensions in the city to a head when local Catholic youths threw stones and clashed with Apprentice marchers and their supporters at Waterloo Place, at the edge of the Bogside. The importance of territory and defence from attack was already a stark reality with the declaration of 'Free Derry' in January 1969, the creation of the Derry Citizens' Defence Association (DCDA), and the constant need for 'local defence' (Ó Dochartaigh 2005). When RUC officers charged into the Bogside, they were met by a crowd of hundreds determined to 'defend the area' and prevent the police from entering. A pitched battle between the RUC and residents, known as the Battle of the Bogside, raged for two days and three nights. While the RUC flooded the tight-knit residential area with CS gas, locals armed with stones and petrol bombs erected multiple barricades around the Bogside and called for protests elsewhere in Northern Ireland to stretch RUC resources and 'take the heat off Derry' (Prince and Warner 2019). Inevitably the repercussions of events in Derry exacerbated inter-communal antagonisms in an already tense Belfast, leading to large-scale violence, primarily erupting along some of the main communal fault lines in the west, east, and north of the city.[5] Over the course of the next three days and nights, various parts of Belfast witnessed intense and extensive violence, resulting in widespread destruction and the deaths of eight people, culminating in the deployment of the British Army onto the streets of Northern Ireland on 14 August. Many interviewees were directly caught up in these painful and decisive events. Their gritty and richly descriptive testimonies convey the fear, chaos, and destructiveness of this period.

'Anna' married in 1967 and had a young family living in Hooker Street in August 1969. She recalled the sense of foreboding around the community, cognisant that the emerging trouble in Derry would have repercussions in Belfast. She describes her experiences of forced exile:

> I remember the houses in Hooker Street, wee small houses, kitchen houses and I remember we all settled down [for the night], and I was feeding my daughter and then the windows were smashed all round us and it was loyalists from Crumlin Road and B-Specials and they were coming in and smashed all the windows with their batons and we had to hide, going up the stairs and I had two kids and a wee baby and my husband and I were sitting on the stairs trying to keep them quiet because they [attackers] were running by the door but ours was an end house so everybody had back doors and so they ran out the back into the district but because we were an end house, we had a side door and so we couldn't get out into the alleyway. We just sat there all night and I remember them all shouting 'burn everybody out' and we were terrified for the kids or that the kids would be crying. I really don't know how I

went through it all. So we went over to my mammy's who lived nearby and the next day our house was just riddled with gunfire ... my house was smashed up. So the women and the children were evacuated over to the Falls Road and there was a school but we were all put into the school into the school assembly and so we slept there for the first night. The next night loyalists burnt the next street, Brookfield Street – burnt the whole street.

Some accounts documenting the beginning of the Troubles tend to frame these events as an opportunity-driven scenario whereby loyalists and in some instances, aided and augmented by the B-Specials and RUC, were simply reacting to what was perceived as an increasing threat from the nationalist community. There is an abundance of evidence indicating that protest marches and 'mini-riots' were being organised by nationalists and republicans to 'take the heat off Derry' by overstretching the RUC, as noted above. A recurring feature in the dynamics of loyalist violence correlates to times of crisis and uncertainty, typically where the state is deemed either unwilling or incapable in dealing with what is perceived as a growing 'threat' from the Catholic community (Reed 2015; Spencer 2008). While some respondents spoke of the spontaneous nature of the violence of that fateful period, many such as Agnes and 'Anna' also described a sense of foreboding in the general atmosphere of that year. Others spoke of major planning involved in mounting the attacks. Historian Michael McCann has extensively researched the period in question and, along with his family, was put out of their home in North Howard Street, Lower Falls. He recalled:

On the 14 [August] my father and I were standing on North Howard Street at the gate and a Protestant man came up to my father and said, 'Joe, I don't want to frighten you but they're making hundreds, thousands of petrol bombs up in fourth and third street' and that was it, he walked on. So, my father went in and rang his boss, and asked for sheeting to go over the windows of our house and he came in and said to my mother and said she'd be better off taking herself and the kids off to my grandmother's house in Garnett Street, and so we went there. Garnett Street was about four streets away, you cross over the Falls and down the Albert Street side and then cross Raglan Street, and that's where we went and heard the gun fire of that night.

In the preceding months of August 1969 many respondents were cognisant of a building and relentless tension, thus accelerating polari-sation between both communities, and yet it is also clear that the scale and level of violence and destruction was precipitous and erratic. While the statistical evidence documenting this particular period indicates that the majority of those forcibly moved were Catholics, a significant number of Protestants were also attacked or intimidated from their homes. Though many prevailing analyses suggest the IRA[6] was unprepared and/or incapable of engaging in armed actions at this time as a consequence of a deliberate run-down of their military capabilities by its left-leaning leadership based in the South, nevertheless, evidence suggests small and sporadic forms of republican armed actions particularly in the Lower Falls area of Belfast (Hanley and Millar 2009; Prince and Warner 2019). Although situated in close proximity to the Catholic Falls Road area, the southern side of the Grosvenor Road, which connects the Falls Road to the city centre, was home to a sizeable Protestant population who lived in and around Blackwater Street, Linden Street, and Distillery Street. Betty Morrison was a young woman at the time planning her forthcoming wedding and living with her family when violence broke out:

> These big police vans came in, something like a big water cannon; so we were right facing Leeson Street and as I said, my Dad closed the shutters and next thing was gunfire. The bullets were coming into the room walls where we were, and we had to hit the floor. It was terrifying as they [republicans] were firing at the police; the police had the water cannons going and CS gas but the bullets were coming from the other [republican] side. Then we heard this massive bang and then the police were at the side-door and we opened the wee side door and the police were there saying, 'C'mon we have to get ye out.' So, they loaded us all up into this police van and [we were] taken up the Shankill and we were spread out among two friends and two sisters; my brother was with an aunt; my mam and dad were with another aunt.

The rich descriptions of the chaos, suffering, and intensity of violence as a backdrop to displacement invokes critical questions regarding the (in) actions of the state. According to Brian McCargo's recollections of the violence of August 1969, the 'police couldn't cope with the mayhem … the police were undermanned [*sic*]', citing the fact that many police officers were confined to desk jobs while others on the streets had not been trained for the purposes of containing and quelling civil disorder (McKee 2020) Other appraisals of the actions of the police cite a shortage of numbers and overall levels of exhaustion among rank and file officers as opposed to any partisan policing or a lack of professionalism (Ryder 1989). According to the Scarman Report, which examined the events of August 1969, the police on the ground lacked clear direction from senior ranking officials at key points in the disturbances, in a number of incidents the police fired on civilian targets in a reckless manner, at least in part because 'many of the police, including senior officers, [believed erroneously] that they were dealing with an armed uprising engineered by the IRA' (1972: np).[7] Other assessments cite the nature of the street violence and disorder, which made it difficult for the police and emergency services to access the local areas affected, particularly in working-class Catholic neighbourhoods where the police were viewed as a partisan and often repressive arm of the state. At the other end of the spectrum, eyewitness accounts suggest that uniformed members of the B-Specials were active participants in identifying and setting fire to Catholic homes, particularly in Ardoyne (McKee 2020: 81). The role of the state, or lack thereof, generated a mixture of perspectives that generally adhered to ethno-religious identities. Most Catholic participants contend that the state, at best, stood idly by and allowed mass burnings and intimidation to occur; some accused state forces of aiding and abetting loyalists in doing so. Many Protestant respondents believed that over the course of the Troubles, the state was unable or in some instances unwilling to provide protection to Protestants, particularly in IRA strongholds such as Derry city, Ardoyne, the Lower Falls and the rural hinterland that housed the contested border with the Irish Republic. Betty's testimony resonates with many other Protestant respondents who described some level of police action in assisting the evacuation of vulnerable Protestants living in what was deemed 'hostile territory'. For those in the Catholic community, the RUC and the auxiliary B-Specials either participated in or facilitated what was interpreted as a mass form of coercive violence targeted at an entire population.

Joe Doyle lived all his life in Conway Street in the Lower Falls and, as was typical of the time, had a large family circle who lived nearby in the close-knit streets of West Belfast. Conway Street adjoins the Protestant Shankill and Catholic Falls Road and was completely destroyed in a single night on 13 August 1969 by loyalists. After losing his home, Joe was taken to a school in Turf Lodge and was eventually rehoused in Andersonstown. Now aged in his late 70s, Joe still finds it difficult to comprehend the ways in which a single night of violence destroyed an entire neighbourhood forever:

> As the night went on, I met a policeman at the corner of David Street and I said, 'You see that [Catholic] crowd down there, they are offering you no opposition whatsoever' so I turned into Norfolk Street and within seconds the first [loyalist] attack took place. And this crowd were throwing whatever they could, and I remember the first house getting attacked; this big fella with dark hair, he must have been over six foot. And he did a direct hit on No. 1 Conway Street and that's when the first of the houses started burning. The attacks went on for a couple of hours and later that night when it got dark the police brought in Shortland armoured cars with machine guns, and they were circling Cupar Street and Conway Street and the crowd on the Falls and firing rounds. So the whole lot [street] was gone, and I had to get out of there because it was too dangerous. We knew an attack was going to happen and we lost everything; we lost 240 photographs, clothes, furniture was all in a heap; all gone.

While many understandably highlight the exceptionalism associated with these early mass burnings and movements, outbreaks of inter-communal violence and the physical segregation of communities represented a recurring feature of life, particularly in places like Belfast., as we note above. Indicative of the historical legacy of forced movement, many respondents expressed the importance of locating the displacement of the Troubles, particularly the events of August 1969 within the wider historical narrative of forced population movements that constituted a perennial feature of life in the North long before partition and the creation of the Northern Ireland state. Michael McCann contends that the mass burnings of Catholic homes in 1969 was a re-run of previous patterns of inter-communal tensions, and that August 1969 was simply 'the state and loyalist response to the demands of Civil Rights – uppity fenians that needed to be put back in their place'. Michael Liggett has lived all his life in Ardoyne, and like many other interviewees from that part of the city, the events of August 1969 were also interpreted not as a discrete starting point for violence, but as another event on a continuum of fear, violence, and vulnerability for Ardoyne:

> So this run of burnings in '69 and early 70s is just another fuckin re-run of whole years and years. So, it's not like Syria which just erupted – 'Where did this come from?' – but this conflict, especially around Ardoyne, has to be set against the context of fear, constant fear … since the 1860s. You see where I live, in Ardoyne and the Bone and those places like that, and they have been subject to displacement since the 1920s and I have records and photos. Sure, the whole of Ardoyne in the 1920s and 1930s was based on displacement. When Catholics were burnt out of Lisburn they all came to Ardoyne. So the Bone was all burnt in the 1920s … then in the 1930s the docks were all burnt … Catholics moved out of streets off the Shankill.

Given the deeply held antagonisms and suspicions within many parts of the Protestant community, events during the early period of the Troubles were interpreted in the context of an eternal cycle of threat and violence from republicans and others seeking to destabilise the constitutional position of Northern Ireland (Reed 2015). Furthermore, on the evening of 13 August 1969, the Irish Taoiseach Jack Lynch gave a televised address concerning the spiralling events in the North, concluding that the Irish Government would not 'stand by' and watch as persons were injured. The consequences of the speech were two-fold; for Catholics it was interpreted by many as a commitment to send Irish troops into places such as Derry, thus adding succour to the morale of rioters in Derry; for Protestants, it exacerbated their fears regarding the constitutional position of the state and intensified their sense of anger and peril.

Though it is tempting to interpret these egregious early episodes of mass burnings, violence, and displacement as simply irrational violence and outright hostility, at this early stage, discernible spatial dimensions are clear. The formations and locations of this initial episode of displacement are undoubtedly shaped by the overall intensity of violence and inter-communal antagonisms, but also primarily determined by place, thus indicating the importance of geographical factors and territory. Vulnerable homes and populations located on the peripheries and traditional fault-lines between ethno-religious communities became the primary frontlines and focal points for escalating violence, intimidation, and displacement. As with previous instances of inter-communal violence in the 1920s and 1930s, the onset of political uncertainty or general increases in sectarian tensions has tended to result in the frontiers separating ethno-religious residential communities becoming sites of violent enactment and border demarcation (Shirlow and Murtagh 2006). While the initial solution involved erecting barbed wire fencing and concertina-type barriers by the British Army and the creation of semi-permanent barricades operated by a mixture of persons including vigilantes, citizens defence groups, and paramilitaries, the realisation of conflict as a long-term feature of daily life in Northern Ireland, however, demanded more robust and durable forms of separation, most clearly expressed in the creation of large-scale separation walls: high concrete and steel compositions dubbed 'peace-lines'.

Though the numerous peace-lines dotted across Belfast and other urban settings were persistent sites of violence throughout the Troubles and remain so to this day (Shirlow and Murtagh 2006), their presence significantly decreased the capacity of individuals and groups to launch the type of widespread attacks and violence that gave rise to the mass displacement synonymous with the early years of the conflict and effectively served as the state's primary mechanism to manage and contain inter-communal hostilities along interface fault lines. As the white-heat intensity of conflict in the early 1970s abated into the relatively diminished, though no less lethal configurations of the 'acceptable level of violence' from the mid-1970s onwards, forced displacement also modified its symptoms and formations and migrated slowly outwards from inner-city settings to more suburban regions in Belfast and Derry and rural locations particularly along the Border.

Notwithstanding, the mass house burnings and direct physical assaults on homes and persons that were distinct features of the early years of the Troubles have, understandably, come to represent something of a popular archetype that dominates popular perceptions of displacement. Consequently, there is a propensity to conflate displacement solely with mass burnings and physical attacks, which we suggest draws attention away from other forms of what perhaps could be termed more prosaic, though no less common-place forms of attack and intimidation. Formations of direct intimidation also involved houses being daubed with threatening or sectarian graffiti, anonymous letters and phone calls threatening attack or orders of expulsion, and physical assaults of persons in proximity to the home.[8] The outcomes of these instances can be broadly categorised as direct forms of intimidation resulting in anticipatory displacement. The idea of anticipatory displacement, though triggered by similar feelings of insecurity and vulnerability, take place in times when freedom of action, safety of movement, and planned departure are still possible (Kunz 1973), though not always guaranteed. Jeanette Warke lived in Londonderry city centre, close to Bishop Street. Despite being situated close to the Catholic Bogside, Jeanette's neighbours were mixed, although Catholics made up the majority of those living in her residential area. Up until the early 1970s, she and her family lived a happy and relatively quiet life with her husband and young children. From 1970 onwards however, both her home and members of her family were targets for violence and attack:

> A neighbour was watching Deborah [baby daughter] for me while I went out to the grocery store and I remember I was walking along and then I was set upon; and I can still see this girl's face. She raced across the Abercorn Road, grabbing me by the hair, pushing me out onto the street shouting, 'You Orange bastard; orange scum'[9] and I ran into Johnny's grocery store and I was shaking and really scared, and they brought me round to my house but it is still so vivid in my mind; I can still feel her, I can still feel her trailing me; she was a horrible woman; a horrible person. So, what happened, David was on night shift at Du Pont and the doors were getting banged. 'Get out! Get out! You're being told now to get out.' And so I got the three kids and blankets and we all sat at the bottom of the stairs because I wouldn't go upstairs because I was afraid of them throwing petrol bombs. So, David came in and the kids were all lying sleeping, actually lying on stairs and we were scared of our lives to move, and he came in from his work and said, 'Right well that's that, we can't do this anymore.'

In contrast to the intensity associated with mass house burnings and evacuations, much of the direct forms of anticipatory intimidation were akin to a slow grind – months and sometimes years of smaller incidents that culminated in a decision by families to leave their homes for fears of safety and vulnerability. Victor Wray's family were from the Northlands area of Londonderry; his father was a member of the RUC, and the family home was targeted on many occasions:

> My father was a policeman, and we were shot at; our house was shot at, at least two or three times through the front door; and on other occasions then they tried to break into the back and they tried to get in through the backdoor and it was just intimidation. But my father was determined that he was not going to move. But it ended up with the police saying to my father, they couldn't do any more in terms of security and so we had to move.

Despite the tendency to depict the Troubles as a conflict that engulfed the entire region over a 30-year period, the reality is that there was a geographical unevenness with regards to the violence, with much of it confined to very specific locations. The inter-communal violence of August 1969, often understood as marking the beginning of the Troubles, was very localised and involved specific forms of targeting and violence. Niall Ó Dochartaigh (2021) correctly highlights the importance of local cleavages and networks and their interactions with national projects in shaping the violence of intrastate wars. The 'local turn' within conflict and peace studies challenges the idea of highly centralised and structured organisations driving violent conflict and instead highlights patterns of violence and mobilisation in terms of alliances between local actors and centralised leaderships. As is the case with most intrastate conflicts, the violence of the Troubles was unevenly spread across the six counties and therefore generalisations depicting 'two communities' both engaging in and suffering displacement belies the importance of locality and place in shaping and determining levels of threat against individuals and their families. Though conventions tend to homogenise large-scale territories and residential areas as 'Catholic' or 'republican', 'Protestant' or ''unionist', such accounts often neglect the parochial dynamics, tensions, and relationships that exert a significant local influence over the nature and trajectory of violence. Our research indicates a symbiotic relationship between displacement and the wider armed conflict; the plural configurations *and* locations of forced movement shaped both by the general dynamics of the conflict at the time but also by localised boundaries of spatial demarcation and patterns of intercommunal relationships, particularly as the epicentres of displacement migrated from locations of traditional boundaries between Catholic and Protestant communities to the new locus of mixed residential settings. For example, mass displacement in central Belfast in 1969 was both quantitatively and qualitatively different from the forms of intimidation and movement that occurred in the suburban settings of Whiteabbey in the mid-1970s, or that which took place in suburban areas of outer East and West Belfast. Formations of displacement in Northern Ireland are therefore relative to and contingent on the territorial environment and parochialised spatial relationships of coexistence, integration, and animosity derived solely from ethno-religious identity and affiliation. The array of burnings and displacement in 1969 and 1970 effectively map directly onto residential areas and fault lines deemed to be de facto interfaces and boundaries – lines of clear demarcation that were understood and mostly adhered to in terms of residential segregation. The erection of numerous, large-scale separation walls in Belfast and to a lesser extent in Derry effectively mollified this previously fertile source of mass displacement, leading to a reconfiguration of both patterns and locations of subsequent forced movement. Additionally, the years of 1971 and 1972 marked the apogee of violence with regards to both intensity and levels of fatalities. The shift in formations of violence from overt street battles and confrontations to more clandestine, actor-based activities, particularly post-1973, militated the enabling conditions that shaped the scale, frequency, and symptoms of forced movement in the Troubles.

Accordingly, many subsequent episodes of displacement shifted from largely urban, residential settings situated on the boundaries separating 'two communities' and began interspersing within what were considered 'mixed residential settings'. Historian Michael McCann, who himself was tempo-rarily displaced from his family home in the Lower Falls in August 1969, describes manifestations of displacement over the course of the Troubles as akin to a pebble dropping into a pond – with the initial, intense episodes occurring in Ardoyne, New Barnsley, Clonard, and Lower Falls and subse-quently having a ripple effect. As the violence of the Troubles intensified, Michael contends that the 'ripples' of the initial burst of burnings of 1969 began to reverberate beyond the 'front line' urban communities towards mixed housing communities and out to the suburbs including Whiteabbey, Rathcoole, Suffolk, Cregagh, Lenadoon,[10] Sydenham, and Dundonald. Therefore, the consistent foregrounding of mass forms of violence and intimidation within popular framings of forced movement distorts our understandings of the multi-layered nature of displacement, and often precludes the lived reality of those forced to flee due to more subtle and indirect forms of intimidation. Unlike the acute forms of displacement caused overwhelmingly by imminency of firebombs, violence, and attack, anticipatory forms of movement are a mixture of 'push' and 'pull' factors, the latter typically related to employment, housing, and social networks and familial connections to other, 'safer' places of residence. Christina Bennett's family were forced from their home in Whiteabbey on the outskirts of north Belfast in 1975. The family re-settled in Shannon in the Republic of Ireland. She described the lead up to and the final moments before her family left their home:

> I remember the UWC [Ulster Workers' Council] strike [of 1974]. I didn't really understand it at the time but our street was under martial law and I don't know who it was, whether it was the UVF or the UDA[11] but they all wore masks, sunglasses, you know, but I know from my mum talking about it a lot and I remember when we were all sitting in the living room and there was a bit of a commotion and a bit of panic and group of UVF or whoever they were came marching down the street in formation … like an army … and they stopped at every Catholic house and there were about three Catholic families in our street and they stopped at every Catholic house and they would stop and do their drill or whatever bullshit that made them feel fucking important; they stopped and done that outside every Catholic house and I remember being fascinated by it but I remember my mum being beside herself panicking and we were all told to get away from the windows and to

get back and all of our doors were daubed in paint to like single us out – the mark of being a 'taig' I suppose.[12] And apparently the priest came up; so, the word went round the Catholic community that if things got bad, and the Catholics were getting attacked, that the convent down on the Shore Road, on the way to Carrickfergus, they would ring the bells and that would be a signal for us to leave and head towards the convent which was behind the walls.

The experience of Christina and her family, with the strong sense of constant fear and anxiety, is typical of the many cases of displacement of Catholics in Rathcoole, Monkstown, and Whiteabbey and similar to forced movement of Protestants from Suffolk, parts of the West Bank in Londonderry, and also along the border. The specific targeting of persons deemed to be non-co ethnics, that being those who constituted a minority population in a particular territory, has been termed a strategic process of 'displacing the disloyal' (Steele 2011: 432). Marie McNally's (née Keenan) immediate and extended family were impacted severely by forced displacement on several occasions throughout the conflict. In August 1969 Marie's Aunt Lizzie's home on Conway Street was torched and destroyed. Marie's own family originally lived in Longlands Road in Newtownabbey, North Belfast, a predominantly Protestant area with a mixture of Catholics interspersed. As the conflict increased, Marie stated, 'There was lots of intimidation at our house in Longlands Road, against my brothers and my parents; threatening letters to the house from the UVF, and so my mother had to leave her house and the house was just left lying there unused.' Two of Marie's sisters, Rosaleen and Fionnuala, were married to two brothers, Mervyn and Billy. Billy and Fionnuala's home was located between Monkstown and Rathcoole. While enjoying a drink with workmates in Carrickfergus, Billy was abducted by the UVF and received a brutal physical assault in a local hall in Carrickfergus. His life was only spared when word came through that the UVF had just announced a Christmas ceasefire. Before dumping Billy from a speeding car, Billy was warned to leave his home and the area immediately.

> So they [UVF] told him if he went back to their house, they'd shoot them, so Billy and Fionnuala lost their house. It was just outside Monkstown, between Monkstown and Rathcoole so it wasn't the best place to be living anyway, at the best of times. But then we got them a house in the New Lodge, and I was saying to them, 'Why are youse living in mixed areas? It's just too dangerous' … and then next thing Rosaleen married Mervyn and she asked Mammy for the house [abandoned family home in Longlands Road] and we begged her not to take the house; [Mammy] said, 'That house is marked, you're putting yourselves in danger.' But she [Rosaleen] was saying, 'I'm not involved in politics' and Mervyn was saying, 'I'm from that area, born and lived there all my

life, know everyone, and have friends who are Protestant and Catholic, so we're safe enough.' Anyway, they took the house. So they [UDA/UFF] went in and shot them dead in front of their children, and so another family displaced, and we were left to raise those two children, one was 6 months old and the other 18 months old. The oldest wee boy was in the garden playing and they [gunmen] lifted him into the play pen and then shot Mervyn at the front door and then they took the baby out of my sister's arms and they put a machine gun into her ... [pause] ... so there was another family gone.[13]

After the horrific killings of Mervyn and Rosaleen in 1976, none of the Keenan family ever returned to the home. Marie's parents owned their house in Longlands Road and were subsequently offered £70.00 for it by the Housing Executive, which the family refused. A vesting order was eventually place on the house by the local government, and the original house, what Marie termed a 'house of horrors', was levelled and a new house rebuilt on the site. Although Marie is explicit in stating that Rosaleen and Mervyn McDonald were targeted as innocent Catholics, she is sure that it was also part of a campaign by loyalists to drive the small Catholic population out of the area. The violence of forced displacement is clearly embedded in the overarching framework of competing ethno-nationalist claims regarding national territory, self-determination, and the constitutional position of Northern Ireland. However, the ebb and flow of displacement is also contingent on local dynamics of territory, tension, and engagement. Drawing from Steele's (2009) distinction between selective, indiscriminate, and collective targeting, from 1972 onwards there is a distinct mutation at the level of targeting with a discernible shift from the communal to the individual; from wholesale acts to a more methodical and selective targeting of individuals and families.

Just as the risk of exposure to the armed violence of the Troubles was significantly determined by place of residence and ethno-religious identity, there exist equally discernible patterns with regards to displacement. While much analysis understandably focuses on the dynamics and importance of ethno-religious identity and sectarian violence, the perennial 'white elephant' in the room in the urban and suburban settings is of course social class. Forced movement occurred almost exclusively in working-class districts and overwhelmingly occurred in public forms of housing. Despite the intensity of the violence from 1969 to 1974, middle-class parts of Belfast and Derry experienced little to no disturbance at all (Darby 1986). In many of the initial episodes during 1969 and 1970, those living along or in proximity to the boundaries or ethno-religious fault lines were significantly more likely to be targeted. As patterns of targeting and intimidation moved from urban, interface ground between largely homogenous territories, those deemed a minority living among a majority community were also more likely to experience increased levels of fear, vulnerability, and attack.

The study of intrastate conflicts has consistently highlighted the need to foreground how the spatial variations within a territory or state influence the characteristics and the durations of armed conflict (Cederman and Gleditsch 2009). While the issue of territory has long been identified as a salient mobilising factor in explaining the emergence of intrastate armed conflict and conflicting groups (Demmers 2017; Horowitz 2000; Weidmann 2009; Wolff 2007), many accounts of the conflict in Northern Ireland have understandably focused on the disputed six counties of the state at a macro-level, often neglecting the importance of local territory and identities in explaining and understanding the formations and trajectories of violence. While places such as Belfast do contain some vast concentrations of single, homogenous communities, it was also home to a patchwork of residential enclave settlements, often in proximity to the 'other' community. The deliberate and selective targeting of civilians because of their alleged ethnic identity and not their behaviour or participation in political activities constitutes a form of 'group-selective' violence (Straus 2015) as it targets at the level of groups, but is individually indiscriminate within those targeted groups (Guti´errez-San´ın and Wood 2017 cited in Cederman and Gleditsch 2009). John Darby's (1986) extensive work and research concluded that there is little evidence of a consistent paramilitary involvement in direct organised intimidation, although individual members were undoubtedly involved. The reason for this, Darby contends, is not due to a lack of interest but rather that their direct involvement was rarely needed; forced movement was fuelled by fear and was often accepted and approved by paramilitaries, who only intervened when the situation threatened their interests, such as in Lenadoon in July 1972. Notwithstanding, Darby and Geoffrey Morris's detailed research from 1974 contends that 'organised groups, including the IRA Provisionals and the UDA, have on various occasions, encouraged intimidation for tactical reasons', creating territories and populations that are more easily controlled (1974: 63). The essential prerequisite for protecting 'their communities' was the ability of paramilitaries to maintain internal control and unity, coupled with the perennial existential threat from the 'other community' that engendered an ideal setting for paramilitaries to flourish (Darby 1986: 159). Mary McAleese (née Leneghan), her family, and large extended family all lived in the greater Ardoyne district and Mary recalled a very happy childhood and home-life, although always aware of 'sectarian undercurrents'. The eruption of the Troubles obliterated that family life where family, friends, and neighbours were continuously forced from their homes. Living on the upper Crumlin Road where Catholics constituted a minority, by December 1972 the family were increasingly fearful and vulnerable to patterns of loyalist attacks on Catholic homes:

> Our neighbours, one after the other were shot, evicted from the houses around us; we never felt protected and increasingly felt more and more vulnerable ... and little by little, they picked off the Catholic neighbours,

murdered them; intimidated them; looking back it was obvious that we were next on the list and it was obvious to me because the night our house was shot up, I begged my mum not to stay there. My father had not been able to stay in the house at all and so he was staying with a cousin over on the Falls Road so he stayed over there ... and I remember the year before we lost our home, it was a year of pure misery; crowds gathering at the door, putting stones through windows, an attack on my brother John who is handicapped, profoundly deaf and an attempt to kill him. So they did that and bit by bit, our house changed from being a home to a place where you felt like you were a hostage and you were a hostage to forces that you simply did not know how to cope with; we didn't have the wherewithal to cope with them or fight back against them. So we had all these episodes and we had screens put up on our windows to prevent petrol bomb attacks on our house; we never even dreamed that they would come and empty two machine guns in through our house ... because it was the 8th December and she [Mum] left the lights on in two bedroom windows and loyalist gunmen shot in through the windows and riddled the bedrooms with bullets. But thankfully they were so ignorant of Catholic Liturgical commitments that they were unaware that my family were out at first mass.

Having survived some of the worst episodes of violent displacement in the early years of the Troubles, the experiences of Mary and her family were more akin to individualistic attacks on isolated minority families located in increasingly hostile territories. Localised territorialisation, spatial factors, and group concentration are significant geographic aspects that deserve particular attention in the study of intrastate conflicts and civil wars. Expected changes in territorial control creates fear and disrupts feelings of security, often leading to forms of forced movement. The mass movement of Protestants from Ardoyne in the aftermath of the introduction of internment on 9 August 1971 and the flight of Protestants from New Barnsley/Moyard certainly display the key characteristics associated with a shift, or anticipated shift, in territorial control that influenced individual and collective interpretations of fear and insecurity. In New Barnsley[14] in West Belfast, Protestants there believed that their housing was a 'target area' for moving Catholics into, and so a process of encroachment ensued after August 1969 (Reed 2015). The immediate days and weeks after the introduction of Internment on 9 August 1971 was the catalyst for another round of mass population movement and evacuations, particularly in Ardoyne,[15] the Oldpark district, and the greater Belfast suburban area, taking in Rathcoole and Monkstown, as well as the evacuation of thousands of Catholics from Ballymurphy and Ardoyne, among others, across the border into the South once again (as discussed in detail later in the book). One of the largest population movements was in the Farringdon Gardens, Velsheda Park, and Cranbrook Gardens in Ardoyne, where in a single day, the entire Protestant population fled their homes. Many respondents spoke of upper Ardoyne as an integrated area, a tight-knit community, describing a relatively happy, stable, and content area prior to the conflict. For Protestant interviewees, from August 1969 onwards Berwick Road effectively functioned as a residential boundary between the mostly Protestant residents of Farringdon, Cranbrook, and Velsheda and the other predominantly Catholic streets. Many Protestant interviewees stated that, from mid-1970 onwards, the environment deteriorated and became discernibly more hostile and dangerous, where the most ordinary and mundane tasks were drenched in fear and intimidation. Many recalled being attacked on their way to Everton School on the Ardoyne Road, eventually requiring an armed guard by the British Army for school journeys every day.

Pheme Browne recalled that from 1970 onwards, 'the bottom end past the Berwick Road was a no-go area for us. You weren't allowed down near it and that had been going on a lot of years before we actually moved out. By 1971, people couldn't stick it no more but there was a vigilante group who would have met daily, and I'd imagine that this would have been discussed, you know, that our families are in danger and no longer safe here anymore.' Pheme's sister June recalled a toxic and febrile atmosphere that ruptured their entire social lives: 'What annoyed me was that you couldn't go round to the shops at night; we used to walk round to the shops. So we would have walked past the bus depot to get to the first shop in Ardoyne but you couldn't do that then because you got stoned, got beat up but something always happened to you.' All respondents described months of sleepless nights, particularly for parents. For many, the night-time quiet was frequently pierced by gunfire, rattling bin lids, verbal threats against Protestants, and houses being attacked. Many recalled their parents placing mattresses in front of windows to protect from attack. During intense periods of violence, respondents recounted endless nights of sleeping on the floor or under stairs. Ken Hefferon recalled:

> There were these committees, these joint committees that were trying to keep a lid on things and keep things quiet. But they were fighting a losing battle because once the Official IRA and Provisionals split, the Provisionals took control of the area around Northwick Drive. And then after that, when you went up to the shops, people that you had known for a long time [pause], they started giving you a hard time. And it got to the stage that you didn't want to go to the shops so that stopped. So the whole atmosphere after August 1969 changed and people were more hostile but it gradually got worse until that tipping point. [Internment 9 August 1971]

Kate Rankin (née Hefferon) came from a large family of ten children and lived in Cranbrook Gardens. Although the Hefferons were a mixed family with grandparents of different religions, she and her nine siblings were brought up in the Protestant faith but had many friends from the Catholic community. In August 1969 when inter-communal violence broke out in 'old Ardoyne' Kate recalled a sense of detachment and remembers many Catholic neighbours coming to their home telling them that 'we'll all have to stick together to make sure this doesn't happen or spread up here'. Kate recalled an 'initial "trickle" of Protestant movement out of the area as the situation deteriorated but these were mainly the elderly who were increasingly fearful. But rather than sticking together, every time a Protestant home was vacated, a Catholic family moved in.'[16] Ken Hefferon recalled:

> After Internment, there were some really bad nights of rioting and shooting, really bad and the feeling among Protestants was bad, every-one's nerves were tingling. And after about three days and nights of that I remember a lorry pulled into our street and this family was moving out. But then it was another lorry, and then another lorry and another one and there was a big guy who lived facing me, you called him Billy Rankin and so I called into him and said, 'Billy, are you staying?' and he says, 'Oh aye, I'm staying' and so I said, 'Well I'm staying too.' An hour later, I see a lorry pulling up outside Billy's door [laughs] and so here I am with my wife and young kids and so what was I to do? And I didn't know anyone with a lorry but lucky enough there was this guy in a lorry who said, 'I'm away to take these ones out but when I get them away, I'll come back for you.' There were lorries organised down on the Shankill and I mean things were getting pretty hairy. You can imagine hundreds of families moving out and loading furniture onto lorries and then there was all this shooting going on and coming up from the other side of the Berwick Road. It was unbelievable, actually shooting up at us as we're all trying to leave.

Kate Rankin recalled the panic and chaos of 9 August 1971 in her home street:

> It was like a war zone – people had stuck it out since 1969 and they couldn't take it anymore, and then you had, 'I'm going, I'm going, I can't take this anymore', and then others started leaving. There were many families that had nobody to help move them or their furniture; it was chaos, complete chaos. If you didn't know someone who had a van or lorry then you weren't getting anything out; and even if you did, you weren't getting everything out anyway. You'd only be getting bits and pieces of furniture. Some people's furniture was getting thrown out the top windows into the garden because they couldn't get it out down the stairs quick enough because the shooting had started and you were dodging bullets and it was really hard, hard for everybody but really hard for the older people. The day we were moved, there was shooting

coming up from the bottom end of the street. We were all trying to get into the car but my dad could not get into the car because my father was a Dunkirk veteran and this is how he ended his life, by getting thrown out of his own house. And we were trying to get him out but he had arthritis and so he couldn't sit, and so trying to get him down that path and trying to get him into the car, he was squealing because we had no choice because there was shooting coming up the street and eventually we ended up in a flat in Glencairn.

Other accounts by displaced Protestants from Ardoyne contended that during the introduction of internment, 'insanity seized the city. Hundreds of vehicles were hijacked, and factories burnt. Gun battles raged and in north Belfast … Protestant families began to realise that their days in certain parts of north Belfast in particular were numbered' (East Belfast Historical and Cultural Society 2000). Protestant accounts of this period frequently described increased IRA sniper fire and the open movement of IRA gunmen roaming the Ardoyne area, threatening the Protestant population to leave (East Belfast Historical and Cultural Society 2000).[17] Asked what the motivation was for the displacement of Protestants from Ardoyne, most interviewees contended that it was about control of areas and increasing power through the control of populations. By 1971 the population patterns in Belfast were increasingly regarded in a territorial way – the Provisional IRA pressure in Suffolk and the UDA pressure in Rathcoole appear to have been aimed at producing areas that are more easily controlled by the organisations (Darby and Morris 1974). Fear and considerations of flight, therefore, arise as civilians anticipate a possible shift in territorial control and the resulting implications for their safety and well-being.

Instances of what could be termed a 'scorched earth' policy became an increasingly prevalent characteristic of anticipatory forms of direct intimidation and movement. The practice of 'scorched earth' can be dated back as far as the Boer War and American Civil War; in more contemporary times, it was widely used during the Second World War. Scorched earth consists of a strategy of warfare whereby retreating armed forces destroy or devastate whole towns, villages, facilities, agriculture, transport routes, and general infrastructure in order to deprive advancing enemy forces or the opposition population of food, shelter, fuel, communications, and other valuable resources that may be useful for them. Although often solely attributed to armed actors, there is significant evidence of the deliberate destruction of homes by those forced to flee to render them obsolete and inhabitable for members of the 'other' community. 'Robert' was in his late teens when the Troubles broke out and lived with his family in the predominantly Catholic New Lodge area of North Belfast. After being intimidated from their homes, 'Robert's' father and uncles returned to the house to retrieve as much furniture and belongings as possible.

The boys [B-Specials] in the car just stood there in front of the lorry ... but when I looked into the car there was a machine gun in the car, but the boys sitting in were pointing it up the street and I was thinking, 'Jesus!' So, we filled up the car with possessions we could – couple of wardrobes and that, filled up the coal lorry and went back into the house and my father was the quietest man you'd ever meet. And he is sitting there and says, 'I'm not leaving this house like this for them' and Tony [B-Special] says, 'We'll burn it' and I said, 'No daddy because there was an old pensioner attached to our house, so we can't burn it; don't even consider it.' So, he said, 'Right we'll wreck it' and he went out to the backyard and got a sledgehammer, and he wrecked the house – top to bottom; every single thing; the rafters. To me this wasn't my father. I'd never seen him like this, never. It was like watching another person. But he wrecked that house from top to bottom to make it uninhabitable.

Paul Browne, who was raised in a Catholic/nationalist family in an overwhelmingly Protestant area of East Belfast, recalled the moment that his family were forced from their home on the Garnerville Road. He described in detail the highly charged atmosphere and noted a rare outpouring of anger from his own father before they left for good:

My father had a wee VW Beetle, which he was absolutely in love with, and it was a red beetle ... and when we were leaving the next day after clearing the house, he left it there ... he was completely destroyed by it. The car was damaged; I think they'd done something to the car, probably danced on the bonnet or something like that. And I remember my dad, just as he was getting into the van, he turned, and it was his first sign of anger ... And he lifted a brick, or he kicked the headlight and smashed the headlight in, which was totally out of character. My father would never have done anything like that ... the beetle was sitting there ... . and he just ... smashed the light.

Lynn McLernon had just turned nine years old four days prior to the introduction of internment and lived in Upper Ardoyne. Like other Protestant residents of the area, she vividly recalled the trauma and upheaval of that day, including the destruction of homes by residents as they fled:

I remember a lot of crying and a lot of panic and the smoke, the smell of smoke and then, my granny and grandad had the key to the house across the street because the family there were away to Canada to see their son and so they had the key to the house, so they had to try and get their furniture out as well their own. And I remember my grandad sitting on the stairs with his head in his hands and this man came in, and he recognised my grandfather from the army but he had a hammer and broke the gas meter and took the money out. My grandmother says, 'No you can't be doing that' but we had a gorgeous new lemon bathroom suite and that was wrecked – took the hammer to it, smashed it to pieces. Anything they couldn't take was wrecked. And I remember the lorries coming up the street, lemonade vans, milk floats, and there was a man carrying me out and putting me in the front of the van on the floor because they were shooting [pauses with emotion]. When I think about it now, I could cry ... because, you would not expect any child to have to go through that, you know. But it was just terrible, and I never saw my friends ever again, none of them. My grandfather set fire to our houses. A lot of Protestants set fire to their own houses. And we had nowhere to go, and I remember my mum panicking, saying, 'We've nowhere to go; we have nowhere to go.'

According to an account from a Protestant who fled their Ardoyne home in August 1971, the rationale for destroying their own property was that 'we will not allow our homes to be used by IRA gunmen or their sympathisers'. As much furniture and valuables as possible was lifted before many chose to set fire to their homes (East Belfast Historical and Cultural Society 2000). Alan Simpson was a detective in the RUC during these times, based in Tennent Street police station, which covered Ardoyne, the Shankill, and Crumlin Road district. He recalled the horror of witnessing the deliberate destruction of homes and properties as Protestant families fled Ardoyne in the face of increasing fear, intimidation, unrest, and the escalating violence between the IRA and the British Army.

The lucky ones managed to arrange all sorts of lorries and vans to shift their belongings; the less-fortunate only had cars – at best. As over-stretched police officers (and in spite of the assistance of the army), we found it incredibly frustrating to be unable to offer much assistance to these refugees, other than to keep a presence. Then, as the houses were vacated, I heard what must be one of the most distressing sounds imaginable, as the former occupants began to smash the interiors of what had been their homes, so as to make it as difficult as possible for families from the opposing side to occupy them. Gun battles between the IRA and the army raged all day and throughout the night, which I could clearly hear from my bedroom in Tennent Street police station. When I reported for duty on August 10, 1971, we were informed that, during the night, 200 houses had been burned-out in Protestant-held Farringdon Gardens and Velsheda Park, in the area behind Ardoyne shopfronts. I could so easily imagine myself in somewhere like Berlin or Dresden at the end of the Second World War – such was the level of destruction. I was amazed to learn that some of the occupants had burned the houses themselves to prevent them being taken over by Catholic refugee families.

Members of the police and army and their families also found themselves as victims of displacement. RUC officers and the locally recruited British Army regiment, the UDR, as well as prison officers were often targeted and killed at close quarters by the IRA, including in their family homes, at their leisure activities, when out shopping, or visiting places of worship. Incidents such as these again pressurised them, their families, and other serving members to reassess their residential location, with many moving to what were deemed 'safer' parts of the province.[18] The daily reality of policing in Northern Ireland, its associated dangers for its members, and the close-knit nature of the 'policing family' also meant that the losses sustained and their impact were closely felt, particularly on immediate family members (Lawther 2014). 'Jenny's' father joined the RUC in the early 1960s and despite the threats and tensions that accompanied the increasing violence of the Troubles, 'Jenny' recalled a very happy home and community life in her village in County Armagh in the early 1970s. That sense of safe and secure family life was shattered on Christmas Eve when the entire family was permanently evacuated from their home.

> The next thing is I remember packing up to go; Dad wasn't there. I later found out that we as a family had been targeted, Dad specifically but also our home, by the IRA. In those days that was it, you were just told, 'You're under death threat and good luck' because there was no real experience of it and the pressure was just starting to build from paramilitaries. Today families under threat have the SPED scheme (Scheme for the Purchase of Evacuated Dwellings), advice and help to get out, to find a safe house. So, there we were in 1972, all happily living in [County] Armagh, then Christmas Eve, Christmas tree up, presents under it, and suddenly we were in the back of an RUC Land Rover – me, my brother, and my mum and we're being driven to [named town in County Down], no sign of Dad. He was in the riot squad, and we wouldn't have seen him for long periods of time and that night we had to flee without him. We were literally on the run bundled into the back of this Land Rover, screeching down the road towards [named place] where my grandfather had a wee holiday home. It was normally only used for annual holidays and fun, and we landed in to this dark, cold house on the verge of Christmas Day. It was strange, frightening, miserable. Yet looking back on it, we were lucky: we had a place to go, a safe home.

'Jenny' and her family never returned to their home in County Armagh. The family were forcibly moved from their home on two further occasions due to security threats to her father, experiences that left devastating impacts on all family members, as will be detailed in Chapter Four.

The IRA's targeting of both UDR and RUC Reserve in the border areas commenced in the early 1970s; given that many were part-time and therefore had other forms of occupation, this meant that many of the killings were in close quarters, such as the home, places of worship, and places of work when many were off-duty. The targeting and killing of off-duty army and police officers was consistently interpreted by interviewees in the Border hinterlands as a widespread communal attack upon the Protestant population. Some interviewees were former members of the RUC or the UDR in the 1970s and 1980s, and described the years of stress and constant vulnerability living in places like Newry, Warrenpoint, and Kilkeel. Some of those we spoke with had relatives, fathers and brothers, killed by the IRA, all off-duty at the time. Accompanying this immeasurable loss and suffering were the decisions by some to flee their homes and communities for their own safety. In many instances, the forced uprooting also included members of extended family who had no connection whatsoever to the police or army, such as parents, parents-in-law, and siblings. Leslie Long, whose father was in the UDR, outlined the fact that there were very few Protestant families in Northern Ireland who did not have a family member or knew of someone who was in the RUC, RUC Reserve, or UDR, and therefore their killings were consistently interpreted as the killing of fathers, mothers, brothers, and sisters and, by extension, an attack on the wider Protestant community.[19]

Although much of our research and analysis concerns urban and suburban settings and the importance of social class, there is a tendency to think of ethno-religious division and territoriality as a largely urban phenomenon. Certainly, the absence of large walls of community segregation and instances of inter-communal violence in rural settings is interpreted by some as an indication of comparatively reduced levels of division. Rural segregation, however, mirrored that of urban settings whereby persons would significantly alter their social lives, shopping in businesses owned by their co-religionists, even in instances where such activities meant undertaking longer journeys and where the cost of products may be greater. Even in areas of proximity between different communities, mixing and contact was, and despite the peace process, remains limited (Murtagh 1996). Rural social life is therefore characterised by segregation along sectarian lines. Not only do Catholics and Protestants obviously belong to different churches, but they also are likely to be residentially segregated, to be educated in separate schools, and to marry endogamously (Donnan 2005; Southern 2007). Additionally, and unsurprisingly, they also tend to occupy segregated social, sporting, and associational life in the community.

Unlike Armagh and Down, Fermanagh Protestants were particularly vulnerable to IRA attacks as it bordered four counties with the Republic (Patterson 2013: 42). John McClure was born and reared on a small family farm in the village of Garrison in Fermanagh; the family farm ran to the border with County Leitrim. John was also a member of the B-Specials and after their disbandment in the aftermath of the Hunt Report in October 1969, he joined the newly commissioned UDR. From late 1971 onwards however, Richard and his family were increasingly targeted by the IRA.

> My house was about 400 metres from the border. In September 1971, about this time of the evening [6.30 pm] a bomb went off up a nearby lane and there were bits of clay everywhere, and a big hole in the bank and ditch but no obvious target. And then, about a month later, we were sitting down another evening, and then bang – off goes another explosion. A bomb had been left in some pipes that the council were laying down. And that was the start of it because at that stage, police were not seen in our area and so we were basically living in a war zone … now there were the odd army patrol which went by in Land Rovers but you were on your own, and that was the start of it.

A significant turning point for the Protestant community in Garrison was the IRA killing of Thomas (Johnny) Fletcher in March 1972. Richard McClure and Leslie Long lived on neighbouring farms and knew Johnny and his wife Edith very well. Like many Protestants in the area, Johnny lived on a small, isolated farm and was also a member of the UDR, having previously served in the Ulster Special Constabulary (B-Specials). Four masked IRA persons held Johnny and his wife Edith at gunpoint, searched their farmhouse home for weapons before leaving with Johnny on the pretence they were using him as cover to reach the safety of the border. Within minutes Johnny Fletcher was shot dead in a nearby barn and found by his wife. The impact and horror at the killing reverberated throughout the Protestant community. Leslie Long's family also had a small farm in Garrison and, for them, after the killing of Johnny Fletcher,

> the writing was on the wall; if you were going to stay, then that meant putting your life and the lives of your family at serious risk. And the army hierarchy told my father that they couldn't protect him or the family and Protestants were being pinged all along the border: South Armagh, South Tyrone, South Fermanagh … and within a week of that, the animals were all sold, and we were living in Enniskillen. And that was very traumatic, especially for my parents.

For John McClure, and others, the Fletcher killing and escalating IRA attacks signified a tipping point in terms of the exile of border Protestants in Fermanagh:

> We were in the very same position as Johnny; we had a young family, aged from 5 to 12 and so we started to panic, I suppose you could call it … after Johnny Fletcher was shot, we chatted and talked about it and we went to speak to the police and then eventually a policeman came to me, called to the door, an undercover fella and he said to me 'the

IRA has your name and somewhere down the line, you're going to be a target' and so we were living in a war-zone anyway, so we decided to leave and we left and moved the whole family 10 miles inwards. And my mother and father were living nearby because I was reared just up the lane and when I got married we built our own house a little down the lane. So when we left, my mother and father didn't want to stay and so there were two houses left vacant.

While the McClure home in Garrison lay vacant for the next two years, an elderly couple, recently retired from Belfast, rented the house from the McClure family. One night the IRA placed a bomb at a gable wall that collapsed in on top of the elderly couple killing the woman. Leslie Long and the McClures have always viewed and understood these attacks and killings as part of an IRA strategy to drive Protestants away from the border and create 'buffer' or 'liberated zones' (Dawson 2007; Patterson 2013). In addition, business owners and premises were increasingly targeted by the IRA in places such as Derrylin, Newtownbutler, and Rosslea. Though IRA attacks in border communities were in existence since the early 1970s, many respondents noted a discernible increase from the late 1970s onwards. The communal sense of isolation and vulnerability was heightened by the attacks on what were termed by republicans as 'economic targets'. 'Anne' and her family ran a successful business in a village near the Fermanagh–Cavan border and recalled great relations with her Catholic neighbours. The family home was also located above the business. From 1978 onwards, the business, and by extension their home, was attacked six times with various forms of explosive devices. 'Anne' is in no doubt the family were targeted because they served members of the police and army in their business and also because they were one of the few Protestant businesses left in the village. The point of forced departure came in the late 1980s when a bomb attack on their business killed a young British soldier. The experience of 'Anne' and other Protestant businesses were commonplace, again augmenting the argument that such actions were viewed by members of the Protestant community as being strategic and systematic. After several previous attacks on his shop in the predominantly Catholic village of Rosslea, Douglas Deering was shot dead in his shop on 12 May 1977, the last remaining Protestant business in the village. Johnston's Drapery in Newtownbutler was destroyed by incendiary bombs in April 1979; it was the tenth attack on the premises (Patterson 2013: 130). Interviewees from Newry and South Armagh all spoke of the IRA killing of Robert Mitchell, then a retired businessman, Justice of the Peace, and Vice-Chair of the South Down Unionist Association, which for them crystallised their contention that this was part of a deliberate strategy to force Protestants from the district. Beyond the immeasurable human loss and suffering, deteriorating community relations followed as suspicions grew regarding the possibility of information and assistance to the IRA from Catholic neighbours (Patterson 2013).

As is the case with many intrastate conflicts, Davenport, Moore, and Poe (2003) contend that state-led actors often target individuals and their families for their support of participation in organisations that challenge the authority or legitimacy of the state. In these cases, individuals might choose to flee from government persecution after having voiced their opposition to a government, in expectation that retribution by the regime is forthcoming. Others choose to flee when they perceive themselves to be in danger because a family member, friend, or acquaintance was the recent victim of government violence, anticipating that they would meet the same fate should they stay put. What the people in each of the above predicaments hold in common is the perception that their security is at risk in their country of origin, and the expectation that their situation would be improved when they reached their destination (Davenport, Moore, and Poe 2003). Active republicans and their families were also forced to move. Some were 'on the runs' or 'runners' who were evading security force harassment, arrest, or prosecution by fleeing to the South across the border. Many towns, including Dundalk, Clones, and Monaghan, saw a significant influx of republicans during the Troubles. Due to deliberate targeting by loyalists and harassment by state forces, many family relations of active republicans were also forced to flee despite being wholly unconnected to the conflict. 'Kay' came from a republican family in West Belfast and eventually resettled in Shannon in County Clare. 'Kay' was keen to stress that it was primarily her mother and father who were actively involved in the republican movement while she and her siblings were not. Nevertheless, 'Kay' and her entire family circle were persistent targets for state harassment, searches, and house raids among others. She described the process and factors that determined their departure for Shannon.

> My mum was arrested for 'doing something' but was released on bail and as soon as she was, she skipped to Dublin to stay with a friend but then she had a brother and a cousin who were living in Shannon … and had got jobs that way and so there were family connections already in place. So my father then escaped internment, and my mother was already in Shannon and the younger ones [siblings] were already sent down to Shannon, although I was still in Belfast because my husband was interned and my sisters were still living in the house but the house was constantly getting raided, getting wrecked and the disruption to our kids. So my sister kept saying to me, 'Come on and we'll get a house in Shannon' and then in 1977 we came down for a visit, I think it was just before Christmas, and we just decided 'no we can't go back'. Our kids couldn't get out to play, because Saracens were always about. Now we had been down here [Shannon] for holidays so we knew what it was like. The kids could run about, plenty of green places; you could go to the shops without getting searched, or bombs going off. All my family was down here – brothers, sisters, aunts, and

uncles – were all here so we had the family connections to the town but we still had and have plenty of family still in Belfast and so I still go up and down regularly.

Though the idea that active protagonists to the conflict might be considered 'victims' of displacement seems incongruous for many and will likely generate much debate and contestation, nevertheless, the voices of republicans, loyalists, and state forces and their families highlights a heterogeneity of displacement experiences that signify the often less-tangential layers of forced movement. In many instances such as those described by 'Kay' in relation to her own family, the existence of 'push' and 'pull' factors exerts significant influence over decisions to either stay or leave. Perceptions of fear coupled with the availability of housing, employment, and familial links to new sites of resettlement represented crucial factors for many who fled their homes and communities, particularly those affected by indirect forms of displacement.

Indirect Forms of Intimidation

Like direct forms of anticipatory displacement, indirect forms of intimidation and flight typically occurred in instances where Catholics or Protestants lived as a minority within certain residential areas or rural territories. Drawing upon John Brewer's (2010) work on 'communal violence', members of the ethnic group were often targeted not as 'enemy combatants', but by virtue of their tokenism as symbols of the ethno-religious community. Though it is important to foreground the heterogeneity and malleable boundaries associated with the seemingly solid ethno-religious blocs in Northern Ireland, violence and fear did, however, have the capacity to create a more unified sense of mistrust through the representation and/or perceptions of ethno-sectarian assault as an attack upon the 'home' community (Shirlow and Murtagh 2006). The targeting and killing of co-ethnic or co-religionist persons in close quarters was interpreted as particularly threatening, piercing the safety of the family home and community and distilling a communal sense of fear and vulnerability. The violence enacted against individuals functioned to solidify a communal sense of identity and was therefore interpreted collectively as an attack on the entire community, thus creating a mutually reinforcing relationship between collective identity, space, and fear. With regards to displacement, a direct attack on one family home was interpreted as an attack on all minority, co-ethnic residents. In addition to attacks, there were also more subtle incidents of exclusion and tension as the conflict persisted through the decades. In contrast to the intensity associated with mass house burnings and evacuations, many of the indirect forms of intimidation mirrored the dynamics of anticipatory forms of movement, that of a slow grind – months and years of smaller incidents, targeting minority groups that culminated in a decision by families to leave their homes and communities.

Direct forms of intimidation and violence are relatively clear and often self-evident, in that they typically encompass observable forms of harm and threat. Moreover, they encompass a process involving the communication of a threat, causing a discernible (re)action from recipients. Indirect intimidation and its resulting forced movement, however, are often less tangible, and typically involved layers of intimidation, often subdued and banal, but that, nonetheless, eventually culminated in forced flight. According to Darby (1986), the perceptions of the victims are central in understanding and assessing the level and extent of threat and danger, which contains a wide spectrum of conditions. For the purposes of this research, we draw on Darby's concept of 'environmental threat', which may be considered in two main groups: specific environmental pressures and general environmental pressures. Specific environmental pressures include a variety of conditions within one's immediate community, which create a feeling of unease or an impression that intimidation might occur, even though no specific threat has been made: neighbours becoming unfriendly; children finding it more difficult to find friends; an increase in the number of political or sectarian slogans on pavements or walls. In their mildest forms these changes can convince parents that their district is no longer suitable for rearing their children. They can, however, also take forms that, while not directed at individuals, are symptoms of a more general violence in the community – families caught in crossfire between paramilitaries and the army; houses in areas subject to frequent bombings. The desire for a more peaceful neighbourhood can therefore be a powerful motivation for a family to leave its home.

General environmental pressures result not from changes within a community, but from pressure on the community itself. These pressures have been strong enough to produce enforced population movements, not because individuals have been attacked or threatened, but because the communities to which they belonged have themselves become isolated and vulnerable. There are many examples of communities becoming detached from their broader religious heartland through gradual demographic changes. The Catholic enclave of Willowfield in East Belfast, the Protestant community in Newry, or Protestant New Barnsley surrounded by Catholic estates, provide three instances where communities eventually disappeared as the result of perceived vulnerability within the broader urban setting. Similar patterns of communal movement among rural Protestants in border regions in Fermanagh and Armagh are equally discernible. There is evidence that Catholics and Protestants have regarded their communities in such strategic terms since the 1835 riots and have carefully monitored the shifting patterns of religious demography (Darby 1986).

Much of our research with members of the Protestant community in Belfast, Londonderry, and the Border region reflected an awareness of growing separation between themselves and what is often perceived as the 'other community'. The increasing violence of the Troubles, and particularly the actions of the IRA, were consistently interpreted as mechanisms to mobilise collective fear as part of a deliberate strategy to forcibly move Protestants. Colloquially known as the Exodus (Burgess 2011), the Protestant population in the West Bank of Londonderry decreased from 8,459 in 1971 to 1,407 in 1991, a reduction of 7,052, indicating an overall trend of Protestant movement out of the city area completely (Smyth 1996: 53). Jonathan Burgess's family left the West Bank in the early 1970s due to increasing violence and fears for safety. He recalled:

> From speaking to nationalists, who lived in Creggan, they went to bed one night with their neighbours, woke up the next morning and they [Protestant neighbours] were gone, just moved out. So, it was real evacuation type stuff, and it was bred through fear and fear was a big part of that, in my opinion. You see, people didn't differentiate; if you and I lived in the same street, and went to the same church, and kids went to the same school, and went to the same clubs, and you happen to be a policeman and I don't, and someone comes to shoot you, well then, I'm thinking, 'I'm going to be next', because fundamentally I am the same as you. And wearing that uniform doesn't make a whole lot of difference to me – civilian targets, commercial targets in the city centre, which led to this utter sense of dis-enfranchisement within the Protestant community in the city centre, so you have this shrinking Protestant community here.

Terry Wright was a life-long member of the Ulster Unionist Party in Londonderry and he visited Protestant families in Creggan when the violence of the Troubles increased. It is important to state that, at the time, Creggan would have constituted a central part of the territory known as Free Derry, which for all intents and purposes was a territory largely administered and controlled by several organisations, including the Derry Citizens' Action Committee, as well as the Official and Provisional IRA. Much documentary evidence from the period in question shows armed men and women patrolling Free Derry and operating multiple checkpoints within the area. Terry states:

> Certainly from 1969 onwards there was a distinct movement [of Protestants] that coincided with the Troubles. I remember when the Scarman Tribunal was set up and I was in the Unionist Party and was sent into what was called Free Derry to speak to Protestants who were living in Creggan, which was a mixed area; my brother who passed away lived up there. But we went up through the barricades and we were stopped and asked where we were going, and I had some football jerseys in the car and I said I was going to a football match and so they let us

go on. I met this family – no street lights, completely dark. So I called to this house, introduced myself and the place was dark, blinds were shut, completely dark and it was a very intimidatory situation because you had [IRA] gunmen in the streets, patrolling around, you had frequent gun attacks, attacks on Rosemount Police Station. And so many people were finding this situation very intimidating. By this stage, the IRA was active and people wondering about their future here for Protestant families living in Creggan ... and there were families that received threats, notices in their doors telling them to move. And so that sense of fear begins to spread, and it spreads throughout the community that 'we're not safe here' and that begins to spread throughout the community.

Interviewees from Newry, the Mourne region, and South Armagh all spoke of the impact of IRA killings and attacks and the correlating demographic displacement of the Protestant minority in these areas. Like the patterns of indirect intimidation in Londonderry, the targeting of Protestant businesses and/or business owners led to the closure of many shops and businesses in the commercial centre of the town while simultaneously inducing an anxiety and reluctance among Protestants to conduct their shopping and recreational activities in the town. Protestants have consistently expressed their anger and disappointment at the blasé way in which the declining Protestant businesses and population is consistently framed as simply 'disappearing'. Jean Bleakney expressed to researcher and author Susan McKay her frustration that the nationalist newspaper *The Irish News* wrote about 'Protestant businesses disappearing' from Newry, either deliberately ignoring or overlooking the obvious links between the fate of business people such as Robert Mitchell at the hands of the IRA and the decline in Protestants in Newry, concurring that 'our stories are just going to go unrecorded and forgotten' (McKay 2021: 278–79). By way of another example, one interviewee described the Irish National Liberation Army (INLA) shooting of David Wright, the headmaster of Model Primary School, in October 1981 and its downstream outcomes. An ex-UDR member, David had left the regiment six years previously and was teaching religious education to a group of 10- and 11-year-old students when a single gunman entered the classroom and shot him. While David Wright was seriously wounded, the impact on the children present in the classroom, their parents, and the wider Protestant community was incalculable. The enrollment and attendance at the Model Primary School steadily declined due to the attack on David Wright and other patterns of republican violence. In 1973, the school had a population of 275 students; by 1996, the school was closed.

Official census figures, as well as the documented declining school and church attendance, all demonstrate a mass movement of Protestants from Newry during the 1970s and 1980s. While IRA killings and bombing attacks were identified by interviewees as a prominent source of Protestant displacement, alongside these were attacks on Protestant culture and symbolism, particularly attacks on Orange Halls, places of worship, and opposition to Loyal parades, among others. Though this research is concerned with those forced to flee, interviewees from Newry stressed the importance of also examining those 'who stayed' within a declining Protestant population, where the overall environment became what interviewees termed a 'cold house' for Protestants. While the direct violence of the gun and bomb attacks have largely ceased, other forms of threats and intimidations have continued, engendering the 'specific environmental pressures' whereby Protestants feel physically and culturally isolated from the wider community. A recent example of the environmental hostility experienced by Protestants was the naming of a a children's playground in Newry after IRA hunger striker Raymond McCreesh. While flags, graffiti, and symbols were also mentioned, there remains a distinct physical threat. Interviewees were particularly fearful for the safety of their own children, stating that while the overall situation today has improved in comparison to the 1970s and 1980s, most younger Protestants do not socialise in Newry and instead frequent towns such as Banbridge where they feel safer, a feature that resonates with existing research on isolated Protestant communities around the border (Southern 2007). Although the attacks and violence synonymous with the Troubles have ended, nevertheless, the population decline among Protestants has continued despite the peace process and the passage of time since the 1994 ceasefires.[20] Though the overall population of Newry increased by 32 per cent from 1971 to 2001, during the same period, the Protestant population decreased by more than 50 per cent. From the perspective of Protestant interviewees, the cumulative effect of violence and intimidation via a range of direct and indirect manifestations led to the displacement of the Protestant minority in Newry.[21]

Martin McAleese and his family experienced both direct and indirect forms of intimidation. In the immediate aftermath of his family's forced eviction from their East Belfast home in August 1971 by loyalists, the state allocated the family a new house in the loyalist stronghold of Rathcoole on the outskirts of North Belfast. Like Terry's description of IRA patrols in Free Derry, Martin, and his brothers and father had to negotiate at least two UDA checkpoints daily to exit and re-enter the estate for work and university, engendering high levels of anxiety. As a minority living in Rathcoole, Catholics such as Martin were also aware of the intimidation and forced movement of other Catholic families in Rathcoole and had already accepted that their time in their new home would be short-lived. As the violence of the Troubles increased in 1972 and the strength and presence of the UDA in Rathcoole grew, Martin's family reached a point of critical mass where feelings of fear were replaced by feelings of an existential threat and were once again rehoused, this time on the outskirts of Andersonstown in West Belfast.

Although distinctly different from the direct, communal attacks on homes and streets synonymous with the beginning of the Troubles,

nevertheless, the common thread linking these experiences are perceptions of actions as constituting a substantial and tangible threat. Many
depictions outlined above adhere to Darby's (1986) idea of psychological
insecurity in an 'environmental sense', where the everyday lives of families
are enmeshed in a general 'intimidatory' situation as opposed to being
directly targeted. Episodes of mass evacuation such as those from New
Barnsley in 1970 and 1971, and that of Ballymurphy and Ardoyne in August
1971, were on the 'orders' of those who deemed the intensity of the violence
as reaching an apogee of becoming widespread and therefore posing
immediate danger to all residents. In coordination with authorities in the
Republic, many women and children (and some men) were packed onto
buses and trains and taken to pre-determined refugee centres, typically
army camps.[22]

Furthermore, according to Avila Kilmurray (2016), the power of rumour
and the attendant fear factor fed perceptions of intimidation for those
people still living in 'mixed' areas. An early study cited by Kilmurray's
research records the feelings of a Catholic housewife: 'When you lived in
a Protestant area after '69 and you went into a shop, all the people would
be having their heads together and whispering, and when you entered they
stopped and there was dead silence. And nobody spoke a word till you went
out.' Similarly, Mary McAleese (née Leneghan) described silences and 'chill
factors' in some shops on the Woodvale and Shankill roads in the aftermath
of the beginning of the Troubles. The wearing of school uniforms also
significantly increased levels of fear, threat, and attack during the conflict
with many interviewees recounting stories of verbal and physical attack
as they made their way to and from schools across Northern Ireland. As
noted above, these 'environmental pressures' (Darby 1986) helped induce
real psychological insecurity amounting to fear. 'Mixed' areas increasingly became uncomfortable for whichever denomination slipped below the
majority watermark, resulting in a constant reconfiguration of community
space (Kilmurray 2016). Many Protestant interviewees forced from Ardoyne
in August 1971 described a significant downturn in the general atmosphere
after August 1969 onwards, particularly when they went to local shops, were
on daily school trips, or generally travelling in and out of their particular
residential streets.[23] Similarly, two Protestant respondents who lived in the
Rosemount area of Londonderry recalled similar experiences of hushed
silences and whisperings when entering local shops, something they had
not experienced prior to 1969.

Compelling theoretical and empirical works on ethnicity and identity
consistently highlight both the malleable nature of ethnic boundaries
(which are fluid and constantly re-negotiated through social processes of
interaction) and heterogeneity within ethno-religious groupings (Wolff
2007). For those displaced from previously mixed neighbourhoods,
violence and intimidation consolidated a sense of groupness that recon-
figured meanings and understandings of intimidation. Increased violence

and individualised attacks were received and interpreted as attacks on the entire collective, and therefore functioned to solidify group identity and affiliations. Such perceptions of intimidation and insecurity resulted in a greater understanding and mobilisation of collective, ethno-religious identity, resulting in growing levels of inter-communal antagonisms and recriminations. In the Oldpark area of North Belfast in the early 1970s, Catholic families fled the mixed areas around the south-east between Manor Street and Rosapenna Street, and also towards the north in places like Heathfield Street, while similarly many Protestants fled the Ballynure streets in the mid-zone of Oldpark. Since August 1969, a steady flow of Protestants fled the mixed streets around the south of Duncairn Gardens, close to the Catholic areas of Lepper Street and the New Lodge Road, resettling a short distance away in Tiger's Bay. For those who consti-tuted a 'minority group' within a mixed residential setting, the pursuit of 'indirect' forms of forced displacement functioned by fear, suspicion, and vulnerability, which tended to cascade through a population via selective, individual attacks – a type of 'collective targeting by proxy'. Isaac Andrews and his family fled their New Barnsley home in the face of both a growing hostile environment of increasing violence coupled with rising levels of attacks on individuals and homes.

> But there were things happening in the days and weeks and even months leading up to that [forced movement]. You know, you had the odd brick put through your window, and stuff was being shouted at you. And so looking back now, you can see that things were already starting and this was part of it but we were already out by late '69; certainly a lot of families were gone before the [New Barnsley] parade in 1970. My uncle was actually big in the civil rights movement at that time and was running a civil rights branch from New Barnsley and worked with nationalists, and tragically he was shot coming out of his work in Mackies. But he was like a figurehead of the family, so [when] he said, 'Youse have to go', that was it; I'm not sure what he was hearing but he was adamant that 'youse have to get out' and I remember all the lorries coming up, flatbed lorries, and shouting all around, 'Go on get out youse bastards' and all that. But there were also neighbours there who were crying, saying, 'This is terrible, don't go, don't go' but there was a general feeling that we had to go, we had to go. And as we were heading with other families and kids were getting grabbed and bump, just like that, everyone was gone.

'Anna' and her family resettled in a house in Ballysillan after they were forced from their Hooker Street home in August 1969. Although a predom-inantly Protestant part of North Belfast, 'Anna' and her family felt relatively safe and secure in their new home. After the introduction of Internment on 9 August 1971, she noticed a distinct shift in atmosphere:

We were facing like an alleyway and there were people going up and down the street in lorries with union jacks on them telling the fenians to get out. So we had all these lorries going by our house shouting warnings to all Catholics and I was petrified. We phoned the police and they said there was nothing they could do for us and for us to leave for our own safety. We waited but someone across the alleyway was shouting for the fenians to get out and because I was pregnant I was terrified. So, we went out the backway over to my mummy and stayed there that night and my husband went up the next morning and our house was wrecked, totally wrecked, and they had painted on the walls 'no taigs here' 'fenians out'; smashed the bath, everything was smashed, all the furniture was completely wrecked. But we got a few things out and we stored them in a picture house where The Star is now...

While the targeting and violent attacks on other members of the collective is identified as the proximate cause of movement, other important factors such as attacks on cultural and political symbols, places of worship, cultural institutions, and activities such as sports and language all compounded existing levels of fear and insecurity. The targeting of businesses was also consistently singled out as a source of intimidation. For example, the intense violence of August 1969 in Belfast saw hundreds of businesses targeted, 85 per cent of which were public houses, mainly owned or managed by Catholics. In Londonderry, Newry, and along the border, the targeting of Protestant-owned businesses and farms was also interpreted as sectarian intimidation and a form of 'ethnic cleansing'. Throughout the conflict and up to the present day, sites of cultural and social importance, such as Orange Halls, GAA clubs, statues, and memorials, have been targeted, exacerbating levels of mistrust and anxiety, thus shredding and eroding feelings of belonging and safety.

Many respondents' experiences constituted what could be termed 'anticipatory' forms of displacement, because of either direct or indirect intimidation. Some relocated very short distances away to reside in perceived safer residential communities, while others travelled longer distances both within the state, but also to places such as Dundalk, Monaghan, Shannon, Cork in the Republic, and as far away as England, Australia, and the United States. While human rights violations, intimidation, fear, and the violence of armed conflict are the primary determinants of forced movement, recent studies have endeavoured to shed light on what has been termed the 'economic incentives' that lead to flight and exile (Czaika and Kis-Katos 2009). An emerging tendency has been to map models of conventional migration determinants ('rational choice' approaches) onto conflict-related displacement to re-frame displaced persons as agentic rather than simply reactive. Essentially these 'rational choice' approaches suggest multi-causal determinants, including 'push' factors like violence, conflict, and war, while also emphasising 'pull' factors such as housing, employment, and social and familial networks to places of resettlement, among others (Steele 2011). Within these forms of analysis, it is assumed that people weigh the benefits of fleeing their homes against the costs of remaining and therefore make strategic choices about whether or not to stay or go during conflict (Adhikari 2013; Davenport, Moore, and Poe 2003; Moore and Shellman 2004, 2006, 2007). The rationale and logic of these analyses is predicated on the assumption that people have sufficient information to make these choices. Though disagreement exists about the level of realism in such assumptions, it is plausible to assume that civilians pay close enough attention to patterns and trends of violence during conflict to make informed decisions about whether to leave their homes. In the context of violence and threats against 'their group', households have strong incentives to leave, which increase if others begin to do so, because the odds they will suffer increases (Steele 2011). In short, one will leave one's home when the probability of being a victim of persecution becomes sufficiently high that the expected utility of leaving exceeds the expected utility of staying (Moore and Shellman 2004). Once the threat to civilians has passed the threshold, displacement occurs without much delay but is often mediated by several factors, including transportation costs, social networks, variation in how individuals assess risk, degree of attachment to home, and economic opportunity.

The dominance of 'push and pull' models in explaining forms of migrations have been the subject of recent critique primarily for its deterministic outputs and its occlusion of other salient factors such as social networks and familial contacts, as well as state policies, among others (Samers and Collyer 2017). Whether an individual can freely exercise agency to emigrate, or is forced to do so, is at the heart of the distinction between voluntary and forced migration – the former synonymous with seeking a 'better life', the latter concerned with saving their lives (Crawley and Skleparis 2018; Erdal and Oeppen 2018; Jeffrey 2010; Vullnetari 2012; Zetter 2007). However, the construction of binary categories homogenises and over-simplifies the experiences of the people they contain, their unique circumstances, and the factors that led to flight (Crawley and Skleparis 2018), thus failing to accurately reflect how migration processes (including forced displacement) function and occur in the 'real world' (Zetter 2007). Migration scholars increasingly call our attention to a complex variety of economic, political, and social factors, including unemployment and poor economic prospects, which often co-exist with weak governance, breaches of human rights, ethnic discrimination, political regimes of dubious legitimacy, and ultimately conflict. Furthermore, once the decision to move is made, overlapping occurs in relation to migration trajectories, which include shared routes, networks, familial ties, or means of transport.

As a heterogenous group, experiences and reasons for flight throughout the Troubles were varied and diverse. Adopting the idea of forced/voluntary movement as a continuum (van Hear 1998), clearly many episodes of displacement were located firmly towards the 'forced' end of the spectrum. However, agentic qualities were clearly present among others, such as in the cases where employment or housing were sought and secured before flight; choices regarding time of departure, destinations, and transportation also indicate conscious actors securing pathways of flight while simultaneously appraising levels of intimidation, threat, and insecurity in their environment. While many respondents who survived direct forms of intimidation and displacement were repelled by any suggestions regarding volition or 'choice', as most stated that they fled for their lives, in other instances, most notably with indirect intimidation, there were degrees of agency regarding exercising of choice, particularly with regards to when and where to move.

The complexity of human movement, whether in conflict or otherwise, ensures that many fieldwork observations indicate a blurring of lines between 'forced' and 'voluntary', and convince some of the impossibility of describing someone's decision to migrate as entirely voluntary or entirely forced (Erdal and Oeppen 2018). Crawley and Skleparis's (2018) extensive research found that even in instances of movement prompted by socio-economic reasons, those factors had to be considered within the wider framework of conflict and political violence. Conflict, they argue, particularly where it becomes protracted, undermines the ability to earn a livelihood and feed a family by killing primary breadwinners, destroying businesses, and making it impossible to travel to work (Crawley and Skleparis 2018). Many Catholic interviewees certainly spoke of discrimination in employment; many Protestants highlighted the deliberate targeting of Protestant businesses in urban centres and farms in rural settings. Added to this is the fact that the conflict had a detrimental impact on the overall economy, leading to vast levels of economic subvention by the British Government. The point we make here is that, even where there appear to be clearly instances of socio-economic factors shaping decisions to leave, we contend that socio-economic insecurity in the place of origin needs to be considered within the overall framework of armed violence. Processes appraising new destinations for flight are therefore relative to and wholly contingent on perceptions of threat and risk in the current location. Notwithstanding the validity of degrees of agency in forced flight, no matter how minimal, for most interviewees, the presence of intimidation, fear, and violence represented the most significant predictor of forced flight during the Troubles.

Our research certainly uncovered a range of what could be called socio-economic factors that influenced decisions by some respondents to flee homes and communities. While such 'pull factors' typically comprised of opportunities for employment and housing, factors such as quality of life and existence of familial networks to new places of settlement were also decisive. Moreover, there is clear evidence also of factors beyond the limited economic assumptions embedded in the 'push and pull' model. In the case of the thousands who fled the North and resettled in Shannon, County Clare, two key factors are overlooked: first, that this movement was an outcome of state economic policy in the Republic, seeking to attract 'industrialised' workers from Britain and Northern Ireland to the new Industrial Zone being developed at Shannon and, second, this instigated a pathway of movement that created social and familial networks leading to further movements from the North throughout the 1970s and 1980s.[24] Many described a whole series of threatening incidents, sometimes stretching across months and even years – a slow grind. For most, there was no single causal event but a tipping point where the risks associated with staying were eventually outweighed by the benefits of finding security elsewhere. 'Shane's' family were receiving threats, including phone calls, letters, and sectarian graffiti on their home, for at least six months before they finally left their Whiteabbey home in 1972. They first went to relations in Strabane, and then Omagh before permanently relocating to Shannon in County Clare. Though initially the overriding determinant for their movement was fear and intimidation, their decision to settle in Shannon was also shaped by socio-economic reasons.

> My father had found work in the South and he was spending two days out of every eight days with us and the rest of the time he was away working. But when I heard we were moving south, I was devastated, the most traumatic period of my life. But there were jobs down south; houses down south; there were grants to get people down south; and when I heard Shannon I just thought of a very backward place. In fact, back then, I thought the entire South was a very backward place. And a lot of people from the North had and shared that impression. But I got a very rude awakening when I did get down here. But I hated it at first and immediately started planning my route back to the North within 24 hours. But my mum convinced me to go to the local karate club, which I did, and then I met a number of people who were also from the North and I didn't know there were any other Northerners here and I met this guy, was in the same class as me in Whiteabbey, and then more and more Northerners came and wow, all of a sudden there were Northern accents everywhere and so I didn't need to go back to the North because the North had come to me. And people came for different reasons; some people came because they were wanted by the authorities; some people just wanted to get away from the Troubles; some people came because there was jobs and housing here so a real mixture of reasons why.

After years of regularly visiting Shannon, Peter Flannigan left his Belfast home and resettled there in the mid-1970s. Peter's decision to relocate had as much to do with social networks forged through friendships and sporting connections as it had to do with the conflict. While the initial movement of persons from Belfast to Shannon was provoked by displacement, the reciprocal social networks back to family and friends in the North provided important pathways for others to consider relocation. For instance, Peter Flannigan fondly recalled his early trips to Shannon in the early to mid-1970s to participate in Easter and summer sporting tournaments, where St Agnes GAC from Andersonstown were hosted by Shannon's Wolfe Tones GAC. Such regular events led to strong, close ties socially, politically, and in many instances romantically. The existence of such networks invariably increased the likelihood of Shannon as a 'choice' of relocation for those in Belfast and throughout the North. Though evidence indicating socio-economic factors could be conceived as constituting the existence of 'choice', the salient issue of departing a home and community was consistently framed by most respondents as a 'forced choice'. The tendency to suggest conventional migration models of 'push and pull factors' as co-equal determinants within a logical, rational choice or cost–benefit process should therefore be treated with caution when applied to conflict-related displacement in the case of Northern Ireland's Troubles. The critical issue here is the primacy of fear and insecurity, which consistently precipitates and provokes considerations of socio-economic factors, which are constituted solely as attempts to address the overarching and most pressing issue, that being the safety and well-being of family members.

Clearly the development or presence of a clear path out of insecurity to a new life elsewhere is a significant factor in determining movement for some. Beyond key issues such as housing and employment, and issues of state economic policies and actions, social networks and familial connections to a new, 'safe' location were also deemed significant prior to departure. Those who comprised the 'anticipatory' group of displaced were also influenced by what is termed the 'social incentives', typically social networks that influence movement towards close proximity to family and friends. The social capital of making contact with family and co-ethnics in new, safer locations shape patterns of movement and choices of location (De Vroome and van Tubergan 2014). For some respondents who left the jurisdiction of the Northern Ireland state and re-settled in the Republic of Ireland, there is discernible evidence of 'network theory' – as other members of the family or community made that journey, information about their experiences and opportunities in their new settled location invariably filtered back to those who had not yet departed, thus increasing the appeal of departing the North for a new life in the Republic. Such vital networks and information are cited as lowering the costs and risks associated with making the decision to leave, thus making it more likely that should the cues in the environment continue to suggest a threat to the integrity of the person, the people left behind will be more likely to decide to abandon their homes (Davenport, Moore, and Poe 2003). Though the presence of 'forced movement' is understood by many as depicting individuals as solely reactionary to external events and therefore devoid of agency, the testimonies in the remaining chapters of this book document numerous instances of agency with regards to evacuations, relocation, networking, politicisation, and activism. The reason individuals, their families, and at times, entire communities left their homes was due to fear, vulnerability, and intimidation. Recognising that fear and displacement are consistently premised on perceptions of violence as a communicative practise broadens our understandings of violence associated with the Troubles and demonstrates the plurality of ways that violence, fear, and intimidation were utilised and dispersed at various times and locations throughout the duration of the conflict.

Mutual Arbitration

There was some evidence in our research interviews and elsewhere of people entering into informal (non-state sanctioned) forms of 'house swaps' as well as the widespread practice of squatting. This type of movement was prevalent in parts of Belfast where the (re)drawing of sectarian boundaries via physical barriers between communities in the early years of the conflict often meant the partitioning of streets, roads, and housing developments. By August 1969, the increasing inter-communal tensions initiated a wave of movement of people seeking to 'retreat to their own side' via 'mutual agreement' (McKee 2020). Even prior to the eruption of violence over 14 and 15 August there was evidence of semi-formal arrangements between voluntary bodies on either side of the communal divide to 'swap' houses (Prince and Warner 2019). According to first-hand accounts, the Woodvale Defence Association had been ordering local Catholic families to leave the Woodvale area. Seeking refuge in Ardoyne, Protestant families who had lived in Ardoyne for generations also felt vulnerable and insecure to threats of intimidation and left the area and sought refuge in the homes vacated by Catholics in Woodvale (McKee 2020: 7). Mickey Liggett stated:

> You had people swapping houses; like people saying, 'Fuck this; this is too dodgy; will you swap houses with me?' So voluntarily … so while some were done forcibly others were voluntary. Now it was something like, 'Right you've 48 hours to do the swap' and now those swaps and methods was also used in the 20s and 30s.

Some of the data gathered in the early 1970s certainly corroborates the existence of house swaps and squatting. Of the 2,069 forced moves in Belfast during the month of August 1971, 12 per cent of these moved to houses in close proximity to the homes they fled. In many instances, according to the Community Relations Commission report, families moved to houses that were 'up the street or in the next street' (Community Relations Commission 1971: np). During periods of mass evacuations, families and individuals would squat in empty houses, pending the outcome of decisions by the

Housing Executive. During the Troubles, squatting practices were used by individuals displaced from their homes to move into a more community-aligned estate at short notice, or by local paramilitaries to distribute housing to selected families. In the mid-1970s squatting had a pattern of a displaced community or estate being replaced by families from the other community at short notice, given the limited housing supply in areas such as West Belfast (Moffett et al. 2020). From August 1969 onwards, forced movement became both a symptom and cause of intercommunal conflict and tensions. Faced with thousands who had lost their homes and possessions in the violence of August 1969, the Housing Trust allowed displaced Catholic families to occupy completed or near completed houses in the Lenadoon estate, consequently altering the demographic composition of the area, which was intended to be mixed with a Protestant majority. Catholic evacuees from Rathcoole and other parts of Belfast also arrived into the newly built Twinbrook estate and squatted in houses there. The increased ratio of Catholics to Protestants engendered high levels of reluctance among Protestants to live there, effectively ending any hopes for Twinbrook as a mixed housing development. By February 1973, squatting had reached epidemic levels with 3,300 families squatting in Housing Executive property (Darby and Morris 1974: 57).

There is a cruel irony in that the coarse forms of demographic engineering inherent within the large-scale processes of forced displacement in the early years of the conflict created relatively homogenised communities, 'removed' ethno-religious minorities from contentious residential settings, and, in doing so, effectively mollified one of the primary determinants and causes for forced exile. While the 'spectacular' mass burnings and displacements were never repeated after 1970, and forced displacement appeared to fade from the political and public consciousness, certainly as a matter of national importance and urgency, nevertheless high levels of displacement remained a recurring characteristic of the Troubles, and rather dolefully, continue to the present day, despite the 1998 peace accord. Hundreds were forcibly moved during the Drumcree standoff from 1996 to 1998 while the loyalist internecine feud in the summer of 2000 also witnessed the forced expulsion of thousands from the lower Shankill. While levels of displacement generally declined and plateaued from 1975 to 1980, the hunger strikes of 1981 were the catalyst for much violence that led to the displacement of hundreds in Belfast, the largest forced movement since the mid-1970s.

Conclusion

Though our research extrapolates a plurality of forms of displacement and a range of factors that explain decisions to flee, nevertheless, the driving force is fear and the desire to seek safety. While there are clearly instances of socio-economic factors, state policy, existence of social and familial networks, in all cases our respondents expressed reluctance and sorrow to uproot themselves and their families and therefore the factors of fear, intimidation and vulnerability consistently preceded the factors of employment, housing, and familial networks. Though links between what could be called political and social causes of exile are clearly evident, invariably it is the former that is consistently identified as the foremost and overarching cause of flight. While the messy and complex reality of armed conflict often means that many of these competing factors overlap and blur one another, the overriding priority for those who fled their homes in Northern Ireland is safety not social mobility. The absence of 'direct attacks' and the increased tendency to highlight 'choice' and socio-economic determinants of conflict-related movement may lead to some accusations of myth-making, thus casting doubt on the validity of claims regarding intimidation. However, the central ingredients of fear, uncertainty, and vulnerability were clearly evident throughout our research. Feelings and perceptions of fear and insecurity may not be directly related to violence, however, they are invariably shaped by attitudes towards the 'other community' via the history and reproduction of collective memories (Shirlow and Murtagh 2006) and, as a result, played a significant role in impacting upon families' decisions to leave their homes.

The Flight Report of 1971 pithily summarises that 'to give up a home where one has lived for years, and which is itself a symbol of security, for the insecurity of squatting, which many did, is an act of desperation: to damage one's home on leaving, or allow others to do so, is an act of despair'. Regardless of the new opportunities of obtaining employment or housing, overwhelmingly the motivations for movement to a new destination resided solely in the absence of the source of 'distress' present in the place of origin. Perceptions of fear and insecurity are of course subjective and interpretive, nevertheless, fear remains a constant variable across all participants' decisions to leave their homes and communities (Darby and Morris 1974). While the likelihood of experiencing and suffering displacement was of course determined and shaped by ethno-re-ligious identity, our analysis also demonstrated the multi-layered causes and dynamics including one's geographical location, social class, and whether or not there existed the presence or establishment of a pathway of mobility out of a precarious and unsafe residential setting. Moreover, our research indicates clear rural–urban disparities regarding experiences and meanings associated with forced flight. While movement from the source of fear and intimidation undoubtedly brought relief for many, there is the obvious nexus between displacement and refuge. The tens of thousands forcibly exiled from their homes were now uprooted and homeless, desperately seeking shelter, food, clothing, bedding, and other vital services. For most, they faced journeys to unknown destinations and uncertain futures.

Notes

1   Additionally, it is important to note that people were also 'displaced' or intimidated out of workplaces. Furthermore, many persons were 'ordered' into exile by paramilitaries for alleged transgressions such as 'fraternising with the enemy' or 'anti-social behaviour'. Also, many buildings were also the target for violence, particularly public houses, which were deliberately targeted in 1969, as well as buildings linked to religious and cultural identities and practice.

2   The Central Citizens' Defence Committee (CCDC) in Belfast was the largest coordinated Citizens Defence grouping and was based primarily on the Falls Road with leading IRA man Jim Sullivan as its leader. He was subsequently replaced by Tom Conaty, a local businessman. Persons leading the committee included politicians such as Paddy Kennedy and Paddy Devlin as well as local trade unionists and clergy.

3   An important point here is to note that spates of inter-communal violence had been a recurring feature of life in the North both before and after the creation of the state in 1921, as outlined in the introductory chapter.

4   In addition to the extraordinary levels of displacement, the disturbances of August 1969 left 745 people injured, 154 of them with gunshot wounds. Some 179 homes and other buildings were demolished. Of the business premises that were damaged, 83 per cent were Catholic-owned and comprised public houses mostly.

5   While west and north Belfast was undoubtedly the epicentre of violence, it is important to point out that other outbreaks of violence occurred in east Belfast but also outside the city in Dungannon, Strabane, Coalisland, Armagh, and Newry. Though most of these incidents were relatively minor, shots were fired by the RUC in Armagh City on 14 August killing Catholic civilian John Gallagher.

6   The IRA spilt in December 1969, ostensibly over a proposal by some members to recognise the legitimacy of the Parliament in Dublin, a move regarded by others as ideological heresy. The reality, however, is that the violence of August 1969, the mass displacement of Catholics in Belfast, and the accusations levelled at the IRA for 'failing to protect Catholic communities from attack' exacerbated historical political and personal tensions within the movement. Though at the time of the split most members remained with the then republican leadership, labelled as the 'Official IRA' and 'Official Sinn Féin', a small but formidable group broke away and formed the 'Provisionals'. While the Officials called a ceasefire in 1972, the Provisional IRA and Sinn Féin, generally referred to as the Republican Movement, became the most prominent embodiment of republicanism throughout the Troubles. While there have been many republican groupings throughout the recent armed conflict, the group known as the Provisional IRA (PIRA), became the main militant republican protagonist in terms of its size, capabilities, and support and is responsible for more than 1,700 killings during the Troubles. Therefore, when using the terms IRA or Sinn Féin throughout the book, we are referring to this movement.

7   During one of our interviews, Sean Murray recalled the widespread fear in the Clonard area of West Belfast in August 1969 and noted that, as a result,

people began to build barricades across Bombay Street and Kashmir Road. The local priest, Father Egan told the people building the barricade to take it down because nothing was going to happen as he'd been given assurances of robust protection by the RUC. Sean stated: 'What he said was that he would ring the chapel bells if anything happened so people could protect the area. Fr Egan, the same priest who convinced us to take down the barricade actually went down to the police station on the Friday after the rioting had started and he found the police there sitting drinking tea and they said, "Oh we're not allowed to leave the barracks because we're expecting an attack from the IRA" and [laughs] sure everyone knew there was no IRA … sure half the Falls Road was lying burnt out, in ruins'.

8   While it is impossible to accurately pinpoint responsibility for these actions, some suggest that the escalation of violence and the side effects of civil disorder included the lessening of social controls over local teenagers and others (Ó Dochartaigh 2021), and so it is reasonable to suggest that the social and political flux that imbibed the North at this time engendered the ideal environment to engage in protracted and boorish though no less forceful forms of intimidation.

9   Orange or 'Orangie' is a derogatory and sectarian slur against Protestants.

10 Lenadoon estate in West Belfast was completed in 1970 and initially housed a Protestant majority of residents. It is at this point that Lenadoon became the focal point of a political power struggle between the UDA and IRA. The former was determined to keep lower Lenadoon Protestant, the latter determined to extend Catholic territory further down the estate. The final confrontation, at Mizen Gardens in July 1972, resulted in the resumption of hostilities after the IRA truce. It also resulted in a clear demarcation of the lines between Catholics and Protestants.

11 Formed in September 1971 out of a coalition of loosely organised vigilante groups, the Ulster Defence Association (UDA) is the largest loyalist paramilitary organisation. Incredibly, it was a legal organisation for most of the conflict, despite its widely known involvement in hundreds of killings. To avoid proscription, it formed the Ulster Freedom Fighters (UFF) as a purely military vanguard within the UDA. The British Government outlawed the UFF in November 1973, but the UDA itself was not proscribed as a terrorist group until August 1992. The UDA/UFF was responsible for more than 400 deaths. The Ulster Volunteer Force (UVF) (re-)emerged in 1966 and is named after the original UVF of the early twentieth century. The group undertook an armed campaign of almost 30 years during the Troubles with a declared intent of defending the state from Irish republicanism. Most of its victims, however, were uninvolved Catholics. It declared a ceasefire in 1994 and officially ended its campaign in 2007, although some of its members have continued to engage in violence and criminal activities.

12 'Taig' is a derogatory and sectarian slur used to describe Catholics.

13 According to reports, the UFF gunmen casually called to the family's home at teatime on 9 July 1976, duping Rosaleen McDonald into believing they were friends of her husband.

14 Demographically, New Barnsley was 96 per cent Protestant in 1964; by 1969 it had declined to 60 per cent (Darby and Morris 1974). While issues such as

minor dissatisfaction about the estate over matters like poor heating and the high transport costs into the city centre are cited as reasons for leaving the area, nevertheless, New Barnsley was a Protestant enclave and undoubtedly much of the decline was due to increasing tensions with the neighbouring Catholic Ballymurphy estate.

15 According to the Community Relation Commission's 1971 FLIGHT report, Protestant families fled Farringdon Gardens, Velsheda Park, and Cranbrook Gardens in Ardoyne, estimating some 240 houses destroyed by fleeing occupants, with 80 families going to the Ballysillan estates in north Belfast, including Silverstream, Benview, and Tyndale, and a further 56 families moving to Glencairn in the west of the city. Most interviewees in our research were taken to flats in Glencairn and Ballysillan.

16 Many respondents were sure that the local Catholic Church was buying up vacant houses and giving them to parishioners, thus exacerbating the sense of encroachment among the minority Protestant population.

17 Tragically, Sarah Worthington, a mother of nine children, was shot dead by a British soldier as she evacuated with the last of her personal belongings from her Velsheda Park home. Believing the house to be empty, a soldier entered the house and in the situation of intense rioting and gun battles going on in the area at the time, saw a figure in the kitchen and opened fire.

18 Twenty-nine prison officers were killed during the conflict and many more were forced to leave their homes as a result of intimidation. An estimated 50 prison guards took their own lives (Ryder 2000: 192).

19 One survey reports that the Protestant population along the border declined from 19 per cent to 1 per cent from 1971 to 1991, the period of the most intense violence and threat (Murtagh 1996).

20 Indicative of continuing levels of fear, all Protestant interviewees from Newry and the Mourne district requested that their participation be anonymous, not for any fears for their own safety as such, but derived from a fear that their identity would have consequences and possible detrimental outcomes for the safety of their adult children who live in the South Down area.

21 Despite the alarming decline of the Protestant population in Newry and their widespread isolation, nevertheless, they were highly active in campaigning for city status for Newry, along with Lisburn, as part of the Queen's Golden Jubilee celebrations in 2002.

22 Official figures from the Department of Defence in the Republic states that on 18 August 1971 there were a total of 1,550 'refugees' in army camps comprising 82 adult males, 356 adult females, and 1,112 children. Figures for refugee movements for the summer of 1971 state that some 2,695 were catered for by the Irish army directly with another 2,714 being accommodated by families and civil society groups, among others, bringing the total to 5,409. The same report states that all left their homes and communities 'largely through fear for personal safety, left in the spur of the moment, in great haste and bringing with them only what they wore' (National Archives of Ireland 1973).

23 Local Protestant school children attending the Everton Girls' School in Ardoyne were escorted to school daily by members of the British Army, including the Parachute Regiment, due to intensity of attacks.

24 Although the Republic of Ireland began experiencing industrial growth in the 1930s, by the 1960s and early 1970s it was still primarily an agricultural-based economy. In 1958, the first Programme for Economic Development instigated seismic policy shifts away from agriculture and a protectionist economy to one based on growing indigenous industries and attracting foreign investment. A key part of this strategy was the dispersal of new industry to rural areas via the creation of industrial estates, one of the first of which was developed in Shannon. The creation of a 'Free Trade Zone' in Shannon in 1959 where businesses availed of tax incentives, attracted many employers. However, workers in the region were not accustomed to industrial work or the long hours of shiftwork. To address the shortage of workers, the Irish state actively sought Irish emigrants working in Britain through newspaper advertisements. As a region of the UK, the same newspapers were in circulation in the North, which led to the initial batch of Catholics seeking to flee the intimidation and violence in favour of a new life in Shannon. Furthermore, the fact that Northern Ireland, particularly Belfast, had a thriving industrial economy and history also augmented the flow of industrialised workers from the North down to places such as Shannon.

Chapter Three

Evacuation, Exile, and Resettlement

Introduction

There is no clear pattern of flight or destination for those displaced during the Troubles; some moved within not only the state but, in some instances, resettled in housing a short distance from their original home, as detailed in the previous chapter. Others sought refuge in mass makeshift accommodation halls, while others travelled hundreds of miles to other parts of Ireland and Britain, and beyond. Nevertheless, one constant thread of commonality was the centrality of civil society, community groups, and families to the evacuation and refuge of tens of thousands across Northern Ireland, the Republic, and cities in Britain. Within the early years of the Troubles, civil society and its role in mass evacuations functioned as a parallel universe to the Northern Ireland state, whereby thousands of citizens crossed borders and seas seeking refuge – mass mobilisation and movement of persons with little or no input from the state. While formal 'settlement programmes' are often an integral part of what are deemed successful resettlement and integration processes, the story of Northern Ireland's displacement is more akin to informal, and sometimes ad hoc forms of organised movement. While the Irish Government was instrumental in addressing the mass refugee movement south from 1969 to the mid-1970s, a formal, state-led settlement programme is conspicuously absent throughout much of the conflict. Moreover, from 1971 onwards, the Irish Government decided to transfer the relief of refugees away from the Irish State solely into the hands of civil society groups and families.

Instances of large-scale displacement amid intense violence perfectly embody C. Wright Mills's (1999 [1959]) contention regarding the intersection between private Troubles and public issues; the collisions between personal biography and historical processes and structures. Though the painful experiences of displacement are of course personal and individual, nevertheless, all 'disasters' and significant moments of rupture are not only individual but invariably communal and sometimes national (Gilligan 2008). Social capital is consistently identified as the principal resource for disaster preparedness, with social connections and access to multiple forms of social capital deemed a critical component in recovery processes (Aldrich 2012). Moments of crisis and disaster undoubtedly present significant challenges and often harm, yet they also offer opportunities for persons to recognise their common predicaments, identities, needs, and interests, engendering a collective sense of 'us' that fuels the engine of collective action (Gilligan 2008). This chapter examines the extraordinary stories of how thousands of active citizens and groups forged sustained levels of collective action to coordinate and manage the evacuation and shelter of the thousands forced from their homes and communities in the absence of an apathetic, anarchic, or impotent state.

Evacuation

Civil society is often defined and characterised as the space in between individuals and the state that is populated by a range of groups, associations, and communities, and is typically allied with stronger levels of democracy via the empowerment of sub-state actors and institutions (Little 2004). In situations where a benign relationship between state and society exists, civil society is framed as a site of recognising and mediating a plurality of competing needs and interests, therefore constituting an essential component to a modern, health democracy. While much of Northern Ireland's civil society was (and remains) deeply polarised, adhering broadly to the dominant two ethno-religious cleavages, they were instrumental in coordinating the Herculean task of evacuating and resettling tens of thousands of displaced citizens, particularly in the early years of the Troubles. Despite the inherently fragmented nature of civil society in the North, the prevalence of ethno-religious identities furnished the 'social glue' that united many disparate persons and voluntary groups together to find common cause in the face of an inept, and in many instances (as we argue throughout this book), an unprotective state. While the idea of an autonomous civil society that seeks to counter the centralised power of a state is not exceptional or unique to Northern Ireland, the unprecedented outbreak of forced displacement gave rise to a new form of communal power and sense of self-reliance, thus establishing a strong, enduring, and vibrant civic society that saw itself, and frequently acted as, a salient counterweight to the state.

The people, families, and communities directly impacted by forced displacement and intimidation came to a not so unreasonable conclusion: that the state was either unwilling to, or in fact incapable of, defending and assisting vulnerable populations and communities. The absence of faith in the ability and capacity of the state to fulfil the needs and interests of those at the coalface of displacement engendered a strong sense of self-reliance, most prominently manifested in the many episodes of mass evacuations, refuge centres, and resettlement, particularly in Belfast and Derry. It was therefore civil society, incorporating existing institutions such as the Orange Order, the Catholic Church, trade unions, and tenants' associations, as well as the creation of new ones such as the myriad citizens' defence committees established in Catholic and nationalist areas and the emergence of local vigilante and defence organisations in Protestant areas that assembled to coordinate and manage the evacuation and resettlement of thousands of citizens forcibly uprooted. Being attentive to the actions undertaken underscores the agentic qualities of those displaced; in lieu of little or no formal state or international humanitarian assistance, it was those displaced, their families and communities that collectively pooled a variety of resources that managed and coordinated the movement of tens of thousands over the course of the conflict.

In the international arena, the case of refugees from the former Yugoslavia is worth mentioning as a useful comparator. The absence of institutional or developed systems of services forced those displaced during the war in the Balkans to establish and rely upon their own networks for survival (Korac 2001). Social capital theory has been widely used to examine how particular individuals and groups are able to mobilise resources within intra and inter-community relationships, with many contending that social capital is the principal resource for disaster preparedness and response (Aldrich 2012). Although the idea of social capital has a relatively long history, it was Robert Putnam (2000) who demonstrated the saliency of social capital as a form of reciprocity and trust, arising from a range of social networks seeking to exercise control over political, social, and economic issues. Putnam's three typologies of social capital – bonding, bridging, and linking – are of particular interest when we consider the context of flight and forced displacement in the context of Northern Ireland's Troubles. In consideration of the first two, Putnam notes, 'Bonding capital is good for under-girding specific reciprocity and mobilizing solidarity … Bridging networks, by contrast, are better for linkage to external assets and for information diffusion …' Bonding social capital constitutes a kind of 'sociological superglue', whereas bridging social capital provides a 'sociological WD-40' that lubricates connections between people from different groups, backgrounds, and networks (Putnam 2000). Bonding capital refers to instances when people who are similar to one another work together to facilitate strong and supportive community relationships (Marlowe 2017). Given the deep-seated divisions in Northern Ireland, many civil society groups and associations have historically embodied high levels of bonding capital insofar as communities and traditions have coalesced around shared historical, cultural, and political events, with distinctly less evidence of any widespread appetite for bridging social capital whereby different traditions engaged in relations of reciprocity with one another (Little 2004). The advancement of a healthy and empowered civil society is therefore premised on the principle of reciprocity embedded in social relations and networks that generate and sustain civic engagement, mutual obligation, and responsibility for social action (Putnam 2000).

It is important to stress that civil society is heterogenous and amorphous, populated by a diverse range of groups and associations with varying degrees of power, membership, and influence. The diversity and divisions among civil society actors is even more pronounced in deeply divided societies such as Northern Ireland. While Putnam's contention assumes that greater engagement by people with civil society and activism is necessary for greater community cohesion, in Northern Ireland, high levels of activism and associational life have tended to align to ethno-religious identities thus the potential to exacerbate instability and division (Cochrane and Dunn 2002). Even in what could be described as stable, liberal democracies, it is important to frame civic society as a space of contestation and competing needs and interests, as opposed to a coherent or unified terrain of associational life. For theorists such as Putnam, the value of social capital generated in relationship to associational life is because they become a significant source of democratic control over the state's resources and capacities. The pluralist underpinnings of such standpoints pivot on assumptions regarding the relatively stable and mutually reinforcing relationship between a vibrant civil society comprising of competing needs and interests on the one hand, and the role of the responsive state as key arbitrator on the other. Predominant social capital theories, therefore, pay insufficient attention to the dynamic nature of the relationship between civil society and democracy (Acheson and Milofsky 2008). While social capital sometimes plays an important role in involving citizens in the processes of government policy making and passage of legislation, at other times civil society organisations may be excluded from these processes and, in fact, work as a competitor to the institutions of government represented by elected politicians (Acheson and Milofsky 2008: 64).

In sum, Putnam's theory suggests that strong associational networks generate valuable bridging social capital that binds people together into communal action and participation, which serves to strengthen levels of trust in government and law and order. Putnam's work has been widely criticised for either ignoring or misunderstanding structural inequalities and the contested role of the state (Acheson and Milofsky 2008; Little 2004; Portes 2014) – this is particularly the case with the Catholic community but also pertinent to working-class Protestant communities who suffered economic hardships equal to their counterparts in the Catholic community. Acheson and Milofsky (2008) contend that social movement theories regarding resource mobilisation and political opportunity structures offer a more nuanced understanding of the fluctuating patterns of mobilisation among civil society. Unlike pluralist approaches that neglect the role of the state, they suggest that collective action in any situation is varied and contextual, and therefore, it is the structures and cultures of a given state that shape collective grievances, and thus influences the likelihood of mobilisation and its various manifestations. For instance, Leonard (2004) contends that trust at the local level in many Catholic districts may in fact be derived from a profound distrust of wider institutions. In West Belfast, ways of getting by were perceived as political options and not just survival strategies, where lack of economic and human capital were a direct consequence of years of sectarian government policies and webs of support based on family, kinship, friendship, and neighbourhood and community networks fed on distrust of political institutions. Extensive research with working-class Catholic and Protestant communities reveals the importance of shared politics and shared spatial dimensions in explaining the prevalence of community networks and organisations (Cassidy 2005, 2008; Cochrane and Dunn 2002). Undoubtedly, the instability brought about in the early years of the Troubles provided an impetus within working-class Catholic communities for grassroots collective action, thus giving expression to a community 'in revolt' and reflecting a historically strong communal, self-help tradition (Bean 2011: 165). Within working-class republican communities, the participatory ethos and political activist culture derives from a collective sense of historical powerlessness at the hands of the state and deprived of rights going back centuries (Cassidy 2005). The relatively lower levels of social capital (though by no means insignificant) within the Protestant working class in Northern Ireland perhaps stemmed from a view of the government as the official agent of its interests, and therefore to see the defence of that government as fundamental to its identity and material well-being (Cassidy 2008). Although professing a profound loyalty to the Northern Ireland state, nevertheless, Protestant interviewees expressed similar sentiments regarding the failure, inability, or ineptness of the state to protect against intimidation or assist in the harrowing and sometimes perilous process of flight of Protestants from hostile areas and territories. Even those who at the time of their forced movement were serving members of state forces, including former B-Specials, RUC, and UDR, were unreserved in expressing their frustration at what they perceived as state failures.

Given the long history and existence of altruism and reciprocity, the originality of Putnam's concept of social capital has also been questioned. Moreover, there is a tendency to make an equivalence between social capital and economic and cultural forms of capital. Economically privileged individuals have the financial resources to fund the development of cultural capital and their privileged position can be utilised to create social capital. However, according to pluralists, social capital is given an equal place alongside economic and cultural capital. Madeleine Leonard (2004) contends there is a misplaced optimism that somehow social capital can compensate for the other two or in some cases pave the way for the acquisition of other forms of capital. Furthermore, implicit within social capital theory is the assumption of equality within reciprocal relationships and networks, which are often far more complicated and heterogenous than those presented or assumed. Networks and relationships are of course based on trust and reciprocity, but Putnam and other pluralists assume that 'trustworthiness' is an objective, unproblematic, and self-evident notion shared and accessed equally by all members of a community. But what about those individuals who may be defined as untrustworthy simply through their inability to repay favours, such as the elderly or those with a disability (Leonard 2004)? Reciprocal relationships may therefore be highly unequal and induce the neglect and isolation of those unable to participate because of their inability to reciprocate. Communities with an abundance of bonding social capital, therefore, can often mask internal inequalities, where certain persons may be marginalised or excluded. Despite these criticisms, many have latched onto Putnam's idea that an abundance of social capital offers a panacea for long-term structural disadvantage, without acknowledging the pre-existing inequalities existing within such communities (Leonard 2004: 935). The issue here is that the reality of social life and civic society is more complicated than what is assumed within liberal and pluralist theoretical works. This becomes apparent when applied to deeply divided societies and where the legitimacy and authority of the state is challenged.

According to Putnam (2000: 318), in regions where people have little economic capital and face enormous barriers in accumulating human capital, social capital becomes absolutely central to their welfare. The effects of poverty, ill health, and adult unemployment, according to Putnam, can be mitigated through the accumulation of social capital. However, he suggests that areas exhibiting these elements of disadvantage are precisely those that are lacking in social capital. While Putnam and others frame their work within what could be termed a liberal democratic state that commands legitimacy, the assumptions underpinning ideas of social capital are flawed when applied to societies of ethno-religious division or where the legit-imacy of the state is questioned by a significant portion of the population. Madeleine Leonard's research of social capital in Belfast indicates that the areas demonstrating high levels of informal networks and associational life were located in working-class Catholic communities, where they suffered not only economic hardship and high levels of poverty but also political and cultural marginalisation. Blame for the apathy, deprivation, and destruction that existed in these areas could be transferred from the shoulders of the residents to the Protestant-controlled Stormont Government and then later to the British State. Trust, community, reciprocity, and social support networks emerged as ways of challenging the state's inability to provide employment for its citizens. As part of this, bonding social capital came to be seen as a political strategy rather than simply a solution to individual or community disadvantage (Leonard 2004: 932–93). Similarly, our research indicates that the mammoth task of organising evacuations and refuge centres within Catholic communities had less to do with Putnam's pluralist concept of social capital and was instead rooted in a profound and prevalent sense of alienation, fear, and mistrust of the state. In the case of displacement, the state was consistently interpreted not as some neutral arbiter or benign bureaucracy, but as the actual root cause of their political, economic, and social ills. Moreover, the unwillingness or inability to prevent displacement or assist in addressing its multiple consequences during and afterwards, meant that many Catholics viewed the state as either participants in their displacement or completely indifferent to it. While much of the criticism levelled at pluralist exaltation of tight co-ethnic bonds of trust and reciprocity rests on economic inequalities and market outcomes within defined communities (Portes 2014), nevertheless, the overabundance of communal networks and associational life in the case of the Troubles have less to do with communitarianism as a public good and more to do with a self-reliance derived from a fractured and often antagonistic relationship between many Catholic communities and the Northern Ireland state. This distrust in the role of the state has, we suggest, played a role in maintaining the high levels of residential segregation that remain a present-day feature in 'post-conflict' Northern Ireland. Many of those who were displaced chose not to return to areas in which they were brought up. In fact, when it was put to a former senior member of the IRA that one of our participants who had been burned out of their home as a child in East Belfast, moving to Andersonstown, had subsequently decided to return to East Belfast to get married and start a family, there was a palpable sense of confusion and concern surrounding the rationale for making such a decision. The logic for doing so, in his eyes, did not exist given the high level of support and protection afforded by the 'state within the state' and the likelihood in his eyes of a future threat to his and his family's well-being. Therefore, the high levels of reciprocity and trust in many Catholic (and Protestant communities) derived from their profound mistrust of the state, its institutions, and apparatus.

Prior to the outbreak of political violence in August 1969, community and civil society activism was vibrant and widespread, embodied in tenants' associations, the Belfast Voluntary Welfare Society, trade unions, and various forms of local Co-Ops. While the principles of civil society are often premised on models of stable and coherent liberal democracies, the febrile and polarised context of violent conflicts, such as Northern Ireland, begets a form of social capital that adheres to, and is often a direct product and reproducer of, ethno-sectarian identities and division. Though many advocates of strong civil society see it as a powerful antidote to war and political violence (Kaldor 2012), the predominance of communalism and political division can manifest in 'bad' or uncivil society (Brewer 2010; Little 2004). Northern Ireland, like most regions enmeshed in political violence and division, was, and remains, characterised by a thriving civil society sector but one that is scarred by tensions and divisions along traditional communal lines (Little 2004). While organisations such as the Orange Order and GAA were, and remain, prominent institutions of Northern Irish civil society, Chris Farrington (2004) correctly suggests it more pertinent and accurate to think of these as associational organisations rather than strictly civil society groups.

The early 1970s saw the emergence of powerful community action groups, such as the Bogside Community Association, and talk of participatory democracy at the time was rife. By 1975, Griffiths (1975) identified 500 community action groups, which he saw as a measure of the dislocation of the fabric of society in Northern Ireland, due to the conflict and its consequences. The rapid growth of community action in this period was a direct response to the urgency of need and a partial breakdown in the statutory provision of health, education, and housing services (McCarron 2006). Undoubtedly the 'bonding social capital' augmented pre-existing ethno-national identities and ties, thus engendering a stronger sense of 'community', providing the necessary capacity and resources for an effective response to the immediacy of the crises as they emerged. Many of these organisations involved in the evacuations of the displaced, and the subsequent management of refuge centres, were ad hoc bodies that had only been recently developed, often in relation to a specific local concern. They generally had no written constitution or other formal rules and they often had only a loosely defined structure, a dramatically fluctuating membership, and an institutional culture that might be best summed up as 'getting on with it'. All these features did not help to facilitate long-term planning, but they were well suited to dealing with a complex and rapidly evolving situation concerning the early episodes of mass displacement (Gilligan 2008). Unlike the state ministries and agencies that were of course centralised organisations completely 'detached' from the lived experience and conditions in which displacement and violence were occurring, community groups were based in the locality where the disaster was being experienced and so were on hand to deal with the immediacy of the problems as they arose. Furthermore, the personnel of these organisations often had intimate knowledge of local issues and of where resources could be accessed and distributed (Gilligan 2008).

While the (il)legitimacy of the state is unquestionably a feature within working-class Catholic communities, the locus of power and authority with regards to evacuation and resettlement in both communities resided overwhelmingly in civil society, individuals, and families, thus offering a form of relative stability and safety against the febrile background of fear and violence.[1] The high status bestowed on many persons and institutions directly involved in refuge, flight, and evacuations stemmed from a sense that civil society was rising to the demands, needs, and interests of those caught in such dire and immediate circumstances. Regardless of whether persons were displaced within the state or crossed into the Republic or

Britain, refugees from both communities relied upon the collective response and support, largely built upon ethno-cultural ties and identities.

The initial mobilisation and coordination of civil society had less to do with a deliberate rejection or challenge to the state and instead was motivated and sustained by an altruistic spirit and sense of collective purpose concerned with the safety and well-being of clearly demarcated communities. John McKeague of the Shankill Defence Association testified to the Scarman Tribunal that he assisted the movement of Protestants from parts of Hooker Street in Ardoyne, while 'encouraging' Catholic families to move out of Protestant streets in southern parts of Ardoyne. Ciaran Groan stated that in the aftermath of the attacks on Ardoyne in August 1969, he spent several hours using his work van to bring those who had lost their homes to relatives living in the west of the city (cited in McKee 2020: 99). Many Catholics displaced by the mass burnings of 1969 fled with only the clothes they were wearing, losing most and in many instances all furniture and possessions. Many of these were ferried by cars, lorries, and vans either to school halls and church halls in the Falls area of West Belfast or to relatives in other parts of the city. Some interviewees had memories of members of the Traveller community in Ardoyne assisting with moving people and furniture. Hugh Ferrin lived in the Bone area of North Belfast and witnessed and experienced displacement on several occasions and stated that all evacuations were frenetic and chaotic:

> In August '69, there was like a mass evacuation, so a few local lads hijacked a van on the Cliftonville Road and drove it up to the Bone and the bus was filled with women and children and they were taken up to St Gerard's up on the Antrim Road,[2] which had about 150 rooms; we were all piled up there as things got worse. Now there were some who completely upped sticks and left and were gone, completely gone and never came back again. Houses were all damaged and, of course, the Bone area was a little enclave surrounded by loyalist areas, so it was always under siege, always a battle. There was actually more movement in 1972 to be honest when a lot of Protestant families moved out of the Ballybone, I remember the vans coming up and filling up the vans, and then the houses. The empty houses were set on fire as they left. I think it was the UDA that did that.

Patricia McGuigan and her family were forced out of their Oldpark home on several occasions:

> July or August 1972 … I just remember the buses arriving and being told we were all going, Ardoyne and the Bone people, all of us, all packed onto these buses, mothers, fathers, kids … and brought to the train station and sure we had a great time singing and that's what I remember, I don't remember anything bad. For most of us it was our

first time on a train, so it was like a big adventure. So, onto Carlow, well Dublin first then onto more buses and then onto Carlow and then into this big hall with mattresses and food and drinks and that there, that's where we slept that first night and then onto a convent. So, all our family were there ... but there was Relief Committees set up and when things got to boiling points, women and children was taken out because Ardoyne and the Bone were very vulnerable because they are surrounded by loyalist communities, where now they're not. The Relief Committees were helping, instigating things, you know advising people to get the women and children out, if things were kicking off. Anybody that was willing to do a bit of work was on the committee – republicans, nationalists, ex-servicemen – you name it.

On the night of 11–12 August 1971, as the post-Internment violence increased, approximately 5,000 people left their homes and were being cared for in makeshift halls and centres. In many districts of Belfast, the streets were piled high with possessions as residents tried to flee to other areas or away from the North. The Community Relations Committee started co-ordinating the Belfast dispersal of those whom they described as 'displaced persons'. In the Markets area of South Belfast, the Central Citizens' Defence Committee moved 185 people to the train station to enable them to flee south. Others used private transport to reach Dundalk where the county medical officer had assured the army commanding officer in charge of relief that the county hospital facilities were available (Conroy, McKearney, and Oliver 2005).

The movement of Protestants from New Barnsley and Moyard over to Highfield and Glencairn in 1969 and 1970 typically involved the borrowing of milk floats, vans, and flatbed lorries. Protestants forced from Ardoyne in August 1971 were evacuated by coal lorries, milk floats, and flatbed lorries that came from the Shankill and Woodvale roads (Mulvenna 2016); recollections depict an often chaotic and frightening exodus.[3] Ken Hefferon recalled the ad hoc and chaotic scenes as hundreds of Protestants fled their Ardoyne home in August 1971:

There was no police but there was some army there but some of the lads that were helping us move ... so people, or someone knew that there were empty flats in Ballysillan and the boy in the lorry took me up there and said to this guy, 'Is there any flats left?' and he brought me round the corner and showed me this maisonette in Ballysillan Avenue and he kicked the door in, now it was empty, but he kicked the door in and said, 'Move your furniture in there.' Now it wasn't the greatest of places to be in but you couldn't pick and choose, that's for sure.

Reta McAlister had lived all her life in the Bone area of North Belfast but was growing increasingly tense and frightened for the safety of herself and family. With the introduction of Internment in August 1971, Reta evacuated her children over to her sister in Finaghy. By the time she returned a few hours later, the Protestant population of her street were gone.

> I came back to the house and a soldier was guarding my house; he was at my door and he says to me, 'Oh, do you live here?' and I says, 'Yes' and he says, 'Well you've got about ten minutes because I'm being brought back then' and he says, 'I'll stand here but you'll have to be quick about it' and so there was a lorry and a fella and he says, 'I'll help you take your stuff out' and everything was just thrown onto the lorry. A lot of lorries came up from the Shankill to help people get out of the Oldpark. Lorries arrived with Union flags on them and they were just throwing what furniture they could onto a lorry and that was then just dumped wherever; ours was left in a garage.

Testimonies from Protestants in Londonderry recalled groups' evacuations in Gordon Place in the Bogside by way of a caravan of milk floats and lorries, depicting a menacing feeling and febrile mood as furniture and belongings were hastily loaded. As noted above, the facilitation of communal Protestant exodus right across Belfast and beyond stemmed from the collective action of citizens with hijacked lorries and vans from the Shankill used to transport furniture and family belongings (Mulvenna 2016: 110). According to Mulvenna, it was the nascent networks of loyalist paramilitaries that were instrumental in the movement of Protestant families during this period, with many working-class loyalists directing, coordinating, or assisting the movement of Protestant families across Belfast. Many of these were either members of paramilitaries at the time or would go on to join them at later dates. Loyalist Bobby Rodgers recalled 'moving families out of the Grosvenor Road, Ardoyne ... there used to be a dairy on Tate's Avenue (south Belfast) ... we would've went in and asked for a lend of a flat-back truck ... people were contacting you ... I remember a woman in the village and she says, "My son lives in Ardoyne, can youse move him?"' (quoted in Mulvenna 2016: 111). Rural forms of evacuation were equally arduous and as chaotic. After several threats and direct bomb attacks on their family farm in Garrison, County Fermanagh, the McClure family evacuated their home and farm. John McClure's son, Richard, like so many interviewees across this research, was scathing in his appraisal of the inactions of the state:

> [T]he government done absolutely nothing for us; the people father worked with in the UDR collected enough money for the price of a washing machine, through like a benevolent fund and that was it. There was no help at all from the government. And I remember when we were leaving, it was fellas that you [father] worked with in the UDR that arrived with trucks and that to help move furniture. So absolutely

no recognition from the government to say that you've been put out of your home; nothing like a rented house or suitable house here for you.

John added: 'Nobody has the right to put anybody out of their house and the British Government had a duty to protect us and they didn't.' Despite a lifetime of service to the state and the constant risks that entailed to the McClure family, they felt abandoned by the state and like so many others forced from their homes, were assisted solely by those in their local social networks.

Refuge Centres

The primacy of the state and sovereignty within prevailing categorisations of forced movement invariably foregrounds 'refugees', those who have crossed an internationally recognised border (as opposed to those who remained within the state and became nominally known as internally displaced persons – an issue we noted in the introductory chapter). Consequently, much of the public attention with regards to displacement during the conflict has tended to focus on those who crossed into the Republic's various state-run centres, typically army camps. While the refugee camps in the Republic were resourced by both the state and citizen-led programmes, the fate of those 'internally displaced' rested overwhelmingly upon the altruism and collectivism of civil society, primarily within working-class communities across the North. The unprecedented numbers and movements of those forcibly expelled in the early years of the Troubles meant that the immediate demands of secure accommodation, food, and shelter were the sole and most pressing priority. All over Northern Ireland, makeshift refuge centres were hastily established, often with few resources. Forced displacement, particularly acute forms of mass displacement, presented a host of needs and demands, both short-term and long-term, but the immediate target for resources and energies was the provision of shelter and food, in the form of large church and school halls, transformed into makeshift accommodation and holding centres, established as interim and pragmatic solutions to the urgency of the crisis. The breakdown of the state, and the rise in sectarian violence that accompanied this, threw people onto their own resources, and forced them in many cases to run their own areas and relief programmes. The emergence of vigilante groups and defence committees and the organisation of relief centres and evacuation transportation was a form of community action that developed in response to political crisis, and not merely out of economic necessity (Cochrane and Dunn 2002).

A range of local groups and organisations, many of them ad hoc, spontaneously formed to provide accommodation, food, and if possible, money to intimidated families, without which the 'repercussions of intimidation would have been much more severe' (Darby and Morris 1974: 97). Some housing committees charged with organising refuge centres, such as that in Ballymurphy, formed women's corps who organised the collection of food, clothing, bedding, medicines, communications, and transport for the relief operation at various school and church halls (De Baroid 2000). Although not involved directly in evacuation and refuge, several other voluntary organisations emerged during the early years of the Troubles, for instance, the Belfast Housing Aid Society, a voluntary organisation providing information, advice, and action on housing. Many interviewees confirmed that some local corporations in the North provided bedding and blankets but not food or any monetary type of welfare payment to those who were now effectively homeless. The disorganised and uneven state response can be seen in the divergent ways that state welfare agencies and services responded. The social services departments in the counties bordering Belfast (Antrim and Down) 'responded in whole-hearted and flexible manner, and their staffs worked virtually around the clock to relieve distress' (Darby and Williamson 1978: 81). This contrasted significantly with the response of the Belfast Welfare Authority, the main state body responsible for welfare in Belfast city, who 'maintained normal routine and refused to accept that social upheavals generated by political turmoil were part of its remit until it was compelled by government' (ibid.)

Given the relative lack of state or international humanitarian support, the establishment of temporary shelters, typically within large school and church halls, clearly required significant levels of coordination, leadership, and resources. Within the Catholic community, many refuge centres were organised and coordinated by the Catholic Church, assisted by those in the newly established Citizens Defence Committee and Relief Committees. In 1969 the Catholic Church in Ardoyne spearheaded the relief effort with a two-column appeal in *The Irish News* making an 'urgent appeal for funds to aid the hundreds of homeless families in our district, and those in need of food and shelter', requesting that all donations be sent to the rector of Holy Cross Retreat (McKee 2020: 23). Fergal McGuigan stated that 'my mammy was doing the Relief Committee, she was chairperson, this was for anybody being displaced, in Holy Cross School and assembly halls and making food for them all in the school assembly hall, so she was chairperson and doing all that organising'. Marie McNally (née Keenan) remembers:

A place on Balkans Street was set up for those displaced and a priest was there, and it was the first time I heard a priest curse. But the next morning at 7am I was brought up to St Theresa's on the Glen Road and all I had was a blanket. I didn't sleep during the night, because during the night they were bringing people in who were displaced and that and I was helping with them and so I slept during the day. After six weeks we were moved into a house on the Glen Road, 81 Ramoan Gardens, and it was a bungalow, no doors, no windows, no water, no toilets, or anything at all so we fixed blankets on the windows to try and keep the cold out. So we survived that.

Agnes Moran and her family were burnt out from their Ardoyne home and never returned: she recalled:

So we went to the school [refuge centre] ... stayed there; now this is the first time we were burnt out. So then we went to live in a caravan in Beechmount off the Falls Road and we were there for three to six months and again my dad took another break down ... and it was all down to fear ... My mummy and daddy never got over the loss of their home, never. Especially when you are left with nothing but what you are standing in. And my parents were not forceful people ... They weren't ones to go looking for things. All they wanted was to get back and get a home again; they were hard times, really hard times. And I suppose the stigma of being a refugee too ... was like you were poorer than the poorest people living near you if that was possible.

Interviewees evacuated to refuge centres, such as Maureen Collins (née Dugan), described the centres as being both places of safety and chaos, with many centres brimming with wardrobes, chairs, tables, sofas, and other belongings, often with family names scribed onto the sides or underneath. In some makeshift refuge centres, the Welfare Authority provided food as well as 'health personnel', who alongside Red Cross volunteers, checked the safety and hygiene of the centres and the well-being of evacuees. The running of refuge centres was based entirely on the voluntary participation and contributions of citizens. The relative inaction of the RUC, and subsequently the British Army, either through lack of resources or willingness, was compounded by the lack of a coordinated evacuation and resettlement response from the Northern Ireland Government and local city corporations.[4]

Experiences within Protestant communities on the other hand tended to reflect a hybrid form of mobilisation with regard to evacuation and refuge, with clear instances of state interjection, typically in the form of police assistance and the provision of clothing and bedding at makeshift refuge centres. Although Protestants had to primarily rely on their own civil society organisations to evacuate, there were certainly instances where the RUC were central to moving Protestant families safely out of hostile neighbourhoods. Accounts from those coordinating a refuge centre for Protestants in the Grosvenor Hall in June 1970 reported that the 'RUC were most helpful', providing excellent security for the Hall. Protestant families from the Springmartin estate were evacuated during the introduction of Internment in August 1971 and took refuge in Blackmountain School, which was also home to various regiments of the British Army who billeted there alongside the refugees. Betty Morrison (née Smyth), whose family were displaced from their home off the Grosvenor Road in West Belfast, recalled 'the police were at the side door and were there saying, "C'mon we have to get ye out." So they loaded us all up into this police van and we were taken up the Shankill and we were spread out among friends, aunts, and uncles.' After leaving the increasingly febrile and tense New Lodge area of North Belfast, 'Robert' and his father only returned to collect family furniture and belongings after their uncle, who was a B-Special, gathered together some other B-Specials and accompanied them back to the family home for one last time. 'Robert' recalled that his uncle and colleagues parked the cars as a type of sentry post at the top of the street and vividly recalled visible weapons pointing from the car as they gathered what furniture and belongings they could.

In the escalating violence of late June 1970, hundreds of Protestants, mainly from New Barnsley and Moyard, took refuge at a designated centre in the Grosvenor Hall, coordinated and overseen by Methodist minister R. D. Eric Gallagher, who drafted meticulous notes on the centre's operations. Associations such as the Scouts, the Girls' Brigade, and the Boys' Brigade provided camp beds and bedding material. Unlike refuge centres in Catholic communities, archival documents reveal that Protestant refuge centres recorded a degree of coordination between 'statutory authorities, voluntary organisations and church units'. Daily visits by Belfast's Welfare officials as well as various Stormont government ministers and the Lord Mayor were also recorded, and particularly valued for boosting the morale of volunteers and refugees.

During the introduction of Internment in August 1971, Butler Street School in Ardoyne was used as a temporary refuge centre, acting as a 'displacement camp' (McKee 2020: 106), and essentially a holding centre prior to evacuation to the Irish Republic, which was invariably once again, Gormanston Army Camp. 'Anna' and her family were displaced on three occasions during the early years of the Troubles. Her recollection is that the Red Cross were instrumental in helping her and her family temporarily settle in the South in 1969. In 1971, it is clear from her recollections, and from others, that strong, coordinated citizens' defence committees were now actively involved in evacuation and resettlement programmes.

Well there was a committee here at the time, mostly men but some women too, Citizens Defence; now it wasn't political just ordinary men and women. So, they organised all that; how they did it, I don't know. They were handing out bread and milk at the school ... and there were medical people on the bus too, nurses and that. I remember one nurse, Fidelma, and I knew her well and she was looking after me because I was pregnant and she was with others, like kids who had no parents with them. But she was assigned to that bus and she had kids of her own too and her daddy was involved in the Committee and very active in other residents' groups.

Sean Murray recalled:

Very quickly after this [August 1969 burnings], there was the Central Defence Committee and they had a headquarters below the Falls Library. Now there were a few old republicans involved such as Jim Sullivan but mainly just ordinary people, Catholic Church; the Catholic Church played a huge role because St Paul's Hall was Catholic and all the schools in Andersonstown were all Catholic so it was a coming together that we have to do something about this here, all these homeless people because many were left with what they were standing in; they literally ran for their lives and lost everything in their homes. We went to Beechmount and stayed with relatives there in Cavendish Street, my aunt, and we stayed there. There were people in St Paul's Hall, a large hall on Hawthorn Street, and they put on food, mattresses covering the whole floor and then they opened up the schools in Andytown and then they built temporary dwellings, chalets on the Whiterock [Road] and so many people from Bombay street stayed there until the houses were rebuilt.

In the violence of August 1969, Paddy Devlin (1983) recalled that hundreds of weary 'refugee families' arrived into the Falls Road area and were housed in schools and halls where bedding and food were provided by charities and social services. Mary McAleese recalled that in the burnings of August 1969, people were constantly coming to her house looking for clothes and blankets for people who had just lost their homes. Given that many refugee crises occurred during the summer, large school halls (otherwise unavailable) and religious halls and centres were frequently transformed into makeshift refuge centres. While some left these centres after relatively short stays, relocating to the Republic, Britain, or to relatives in 'safer' parts of the city, others had to endure harsh conditions for months while waiting on the rebuilding of destroyed homes or the allocation of new homes by the state. Hundreds of families who were initially housed in schools were later transferred to prefabricated buildings, many of them in a sub-standard condition, thus adding to the anxieties of those who lost their homes. Agnes Moran recalled:

So we ended up in caravans with a good lot of our neighbours, prefabs in Beechmount Avenue; old war-time prefabs. We still had gas lights which just broke all the time, we had a gas iron pumped in with a tube ... madness. Mobile toilets, mobile showers ... most caravans had their own keys. But we ended up getting scabies. We got nits. You name it, we caught it. So anyhow, that was the first time we were made refugees; the second time was in 1971. So we got the chance to go to Australia; refugee families were offered the chance to go to Australia by the government ... the £10 boat ... and my daddy had a brother there.

And I really wanted to go to Australia ... the thoughts about ... the
chance to go to Australia, the sun, kangaroos but no, my daddy said,
'No, we're going back to Ardoyne.'

Interviewees and archival accounts of the refuge centres depict a place
that was welcoming and relatively safe, staffed by many hard-working
volunteers handing out bedding and blankets, providing food and clothing,
as well as donations of toys, shoes, and other such items. Some recalled
the presence of medical personnel there providing first-aid and comfort
to those in need. The refuge centres were, of course, ad hoc, informal,
and a wholly irregular form of accommodation and living. Due to the
volume of people in makeshift dormitories in large halls, interviewees also
recalled much sleeplessness, noise, trauma, anxiety, and waiting. While
some were among extended family, neighbours, and friends, often the
centres contained disparate groups of persons unknown to one another but
who had a shared bond of experiencing violent upheaval. The initial refuge
centres provided an essential place of safety and security for those violently
exiled, yet they were also a place characterised by precariousness and
liminality. Although all interviewees expressed their relief upon arriving
at these makeshift sites of refuge, nevertheless, all were cognisant that
this was a purely interim space that addressed their immediate needs but
simultaneously augmented their sense of uncertainty. Essentially, like those
housed in Irish army camps (detailed in the next section), this accommodation was a staging post to an unknown destination. In the context of
the violent upheaval experienced, temporary shelter was a place of relative
safety, yet this security was tempered by the inherent precarity associated
within these tentative arrangements. For many research participants, there
was a tension between the security it offered and its role in reaffirming the
devastating loss they had incurred.

Given the deeply held divisions that imbibe Northern Irish society, an
abundance of 'bonding capital' is unsurprisingly evident and ultimately
central to the mobilisation and actions of civil society in providing care
and assistance to those displaced. Notwithstanding, there were also clear
instances of 'bridging capital' across traditional cleavages that sought
to prevent and mitigate instances of intimidation and displacement.
Several districts and estates with mixed populations established 'Peace
Committees' in places like Upper Ardoyne, New Barnsley, and Rathcoole,
mounting 'vigilante' patrols to prevent intimidation and any outbreak of
sectarian violence. In Cregagh in East Belfast, a mixed religion vigilante
group supported by the Cregagh Tenants Association patrolled the area
to prevent intimidation. Despite their endeavours, the increase in general
violence from August 1971 onwards meant that by the summer of 1972, 45
per cent of all Catholics living in the estate had abandoned their homes
and settled in Twinbrook. The Springfield Joint Committee comprised of
up to 1,000 men from both communities who patrolled the New Barnsley,

Moyard, and Ballymurphy estates, effectively suppressing violence and movement from 1969 to April 1970. While the actual cause of Protestant movement out of New Barnsley is disputed, Darby and Morris contend that on Easter Tuesday 1970, a highly organised evacuation of Protestant families from the estate to Glencairn and the Shankill was provoked by known political leaders from outside the area (1974: 41). Regardless, the Protestant population of New Barnsley was in significant decline up to that point, indicating that many were already fleeing the estate due to fear and intimidation.

The accounts of early forms of displacement reveal the chaotic contexts of mass evacuations and often claustrophobic conditions of makeshift refuge centres, many of which were ad hoc and hastily organised. On 9 July 1970 Minister Eric Gallagher began making detailed notes reflecting on the experiences of the refuge centre he and other volunteers established at Grosvenor Hall on 26 June. He ended his notes with a prescient but foreboding conclusion, entitled 'additions that can help future operations'. Like many people living in the areas at the coalface of forced movement, it was clear to him and many others that the violent uprooting of citizens, families, and communities was not an aberrational feature that would quickly diminish. On the contrary, many were certain it would be an endemic feature for the foreseeable future and so began to plan and organise accordingly.

Buses, Boats, and Trains: Seeking Refuge Outside Northern Ireland

While numerous interviewees described scenarios whereby the Northern Ireland state offered financial incentives for families to permanently relocate to Britain and Australia in the early 1970s,[5] the state is otherwise conspicuously absent in the processes of movement and resettlement. As will be detailed in this section, while the mass evacuation of Protestant refugees to Liverpool and Glasgow was devised and conducted almost exclusively by members of the Loyal Orders, civil society and the state in the Republic of Ireland coalesced in a show of unprecedented solidarity with northern nationalists from 1969 to the mid-1970s, providing temporary refuge and shelter, monetary contributions, and successful repatriation to the North.

Hands across the Border

In the immediate aftermath of the violence and displacement of August 1969, leaders from various citizens defence groups as well as local political figures travelled to Dublin in search of urgent aid and assistance. Their analysis was that the large-scale violence was not an anomaly, and that defence of Catholic ghettoes was the primary, short-term objective. In his recollections, Paddy Devlin stated that he and fellow MP Paddy Kennedy phoned various government agencies in the Republic in August 1969, whereafter relief centres were hastily assembled with staff and other resources. Paddy Devlin, Paddy O'Hanlon, and Paddy Kennedy then travelled to Dublin on Saturday 16 August 1969 to obtain 'financial help for the many families who had lost their homes, but also temporary accommodation for them, even if it was only in a school or military camp' (Devlin 1993: 108). There they met Eamonn Gallagher, senior civil servant for Northern Ireland affairs, who listened to the demands of the Northern MPs and promised help of some sort. A direct outcome was the movement of refugee families from Belfast to Gormanston Camp as well as funds designated for distribution via the Irish Red Cross. In addition, a television appeal for help by Paddy Devlin on Irish state television, RTÉ, resulted in a prompt and positive response where aid committees were established and 'private money was sent north in large amounts' (Devlin 1993). On 16 August 1969, the Irish cabinet included a source of central funding, most likely the Irish exchequer, to 'provide aid for the victims of the current unrest' (Craig 2010: 51). A National Relief Fund Coordinating Committee was established after August 1969, chaired by Fine Gael's Declan Costello. Republicans formed the National Solidarity Committee, which facilitated support and donations from left-wing organisations, cultural activists, and trade unions. Civil society responded with thousands of citizens offering their homes as refuge for the 'stricken brethren' of the North while a host of civil society organisations, such as the Irish Countrywomen's Association, National Farmers' Association, and branches of the Gaelic Athletic Association (GAA) collected money, food, and clothes right across the state (Hanley 2018). While the intensity of the August violence subsided significantly by the winter of 1969, the Irish Government pursued with its plan to distribute £100,000 as a 'Relief for Distress' fund.[6] While almost £30,000 went to the Irish Red Cross, and £4,500 went to a newspaper called *The Voice of the North*,[7] the remaining funds were 'spent on attempts to purchase and distribute illegal weapons to the Provisional IRA' (Craig 2010: 67).

In the early years of the conflict, temporary shelter and accommodation was provided by the Irish Army across a variety of locations, including most prominently Gormanston Camp in County Meath, but also Finner Camp in Donegal, Kilworth in County Cork, Coolmoney in County Wicklow, and camps located in Kildare, Kilkenny, Waterford, and Tralee. Support and back-up to the army was provided by the Civil Defence, the Irish Red Cross, and later the local authorities, health authorities, and voluntary organisations and individuals (Conroy, McKearney, and Oliver. 2005) in the second week of August 1971, some 2,825 northern refugees were received into Gormanston Army Camp in County Meath. A further 2,714 were accommodated elsewhere, including Finner Camp in Donegal (50),

Kilworth in County Cork (222), Coolmoney in County Wicklow (107), and camps in Kildare (308), Kilkenny (377), Waterford (228), and Tralee (220), among others (Mulroe 2017). According to Department of Defence records housed in the National Archives, the Irish Army 'accommodated and fed' 720 refugees in 1969, and 1,558 in 1970. Approximately 9,800 refugees were 'handled' by the Irish state agencies in July and August 1972 (National Archives of Ireland 1973: 1).

From 1971 onwards however, government records convey their growing concern at the increasing numbers of refugees arriving into the South, so much so that Irish army camps alone were considered to be unable to accommodate the unprecedented numbers. In the summer of 1971, the government called upon local authorities to assist them in addressing the refugee crisis whereby a host of 'religious leaders and communities, in addition to various other organisations and individuals, very generously placed their facilities and services at the disposal of the refugee' (National Archives of Ireland 1971). As the flow of refugees across the border developed into something of an annual event that could be anticipated and planned for, state and civil society in the Republic coalesced to engineer a more suitable and long-term solution via the dispersal and distribution of refugees across myriad sites, including private homes, hospitals, community halls, religious homes and institutions, with a much-diminished role for the Irish military. In early 1972 the Irish Government decided that, 'for military reasons', the Irish Army would not be asked to accommodate or undertake any care for refugees in 'any future Northern refugee situation' (National Archives of Ireland 1973: 2). Instead, all local authorities would be asked to make contingency plans for the 'reception and care' for any future refugee situations. Every local authority was expected to take 'a quota' of refugees and additionally, overall coordination and control would reside in the Department of Defence (Civil Defence Branch). Despite the high levels of aid, accommodation, and support, the Irish Government did consider using powers of compulsory acquisition of accommodation such as halls and boarding schools if numbers swelled.

Refugee accommodation is of course supposed to be a temporal arrangement – a spontaneous outcome and a symptom and consequence of exceptional circumstances. The arrival of thousands of displaced persons into the South demanded a mass form of 'hospitality', involving high levels of organising, coordination, and resources. The initial refugees of August 1969 were met by an assortment of organisations and institutions including the Irish Army, the Order of Malta, An Garda Siochanna, and the Irish Red Cross, among others. Though many of these initial refugee centres were housed within Irish army camps, the Irish Red Cross was the primary conduit of providing all aspects of care and assistance, including food, clothing, and footwear, medicine, first-aid, bedding, baby foods, disinfectants, washing machines, and personal toilet requisites, as well as small allowances for adults and pocket money for children. Despite the passage of more than 50 years in some instances, many interviewees vividly recalled their journeys to the camps and their experiences within them. Hugh Ferrin was evacuated from his home in the Bone area of Belfast on two occasions; he recalled his experience of the army camp before his transfer to a hospital or institution for those with mental illness:

> To be honest, it was all very exciting … the army camp and the tents but it was also terrifying with people all gathered around wee radios and listening to hear news and you'd hear people shouting, 'They're burning the place to the ground' so that was tense … but kids being kids, we got on with it. So there were dormitories and tents and that was the set up. In the hospital, I didn't like it because it was freezing; there was no heating and a lot of nuns around, and nuns out in the gardens. There was a few disturbed people walking around, so you could see these people who were sick walking about the place; some people would be shouting to themselves, and I just wanted to get back home at that stage.

For some, their memories of evacuation are drenched in acute sadness and loss. Like many residents of districts such as Ballymurphy and Ardoyne, Carmel Quinn (née Laverty) was evacuated on multiple occasions in the early years of the conflict. Many interviewees described the conflicting emotions and memories of evacuation – relief at the idea of safety and sanctuary on the one hand but also the heartache, fear, and concern for the safety of loved ones left behind on the other. As her 20-year-old brother John scooped her up and carried her to the bus to take her and many others on a journey south in search of refuge and safety, Carmel's departure from Ballymurphy on 9 August 1971, then aged eight, was the last time she saw her brother, who was shot dead by the British Army the following day.[8] John Laverty was one of eleven unarmed civilians shot by the British Army over three days following the introduction of internment, in what is often more commonly referred to as The Ballymurphy Massacre. Carmel:

> August 1971 … it was really tense in the lead up to Internment. But on the day, the 9 August, the British Army came in and shot dead Noel Philips, who lived straight across the street from us and was John's friend; Mrs. Connolly, Mr Taggert, Mr Murphy who was wounded, and wee Eddie Butler who was only nine years of age was wounded as well. So, it was decided on a mass evacuation of the area because people knew the army would be coming in again and so women and children were to be evacuated. But my mum was refusing to leave and didn't want to leave her husband and sons behind, so my older sister Sue, who was 23, said she'd take us. And our John was lifting me because I was crying because I didn't want to leave my mommy, and he said, 'You'll be fine;

it will be great and it will be all back to normal when you get back'
and that was the last time I ever saw him.

Carmel's memories and emotions surrounding the mass evacuations
are replete with a profound sadness and loss that has not diminished,
despite the passage of 50 years. Tragically, the children of other victims of
the massacre, such as Joan Connolly, were also evacuated as refugees to
the South at the time their mother was shot dead. Feelings of relief and
relative safety brought about by mass evacuations were therefore always
tempered by anxiety regarding family back in Belfast and other places.
Many interviewees stressed the lack of reliable information and news,
recalling memories of large groups gathering around a single phone located
in an army camp or convent, listening for scraps of news about what was
going on back home.

   While many recounted feelings of relief, excitement, adventure, and, of
course, safety, others were less enamoured by both the conditions and the
daily grind of sustaining their subsistence in exile. Although many refugee
camps and centres in the Republic provided essential services, such as
meals, medical aid, and bedding, some interviewees recalled instances of
'self-sufficiency'. Paddy Davidson lived with his family in what was known
locally as the 'bullring' in the centre of Ballymurphy and was evacuated
several times in the early 1970s. On one occasion Paddy recalled his time
in a refuge centre, a convent in County Donegal, where evacuees, mainly
women and children, had to cook and clean for themselves, much to the
chagrin of some. Others recalled the coldness and damp of the tin-huts
in the army camps and the daily grind of digging up turf for the fire.
By mid-1970, official figures state that 1,558 persons were being cared for
by the Southern state. The introduction of Internment on 9 August 1971,
however, was the catalyst for one of the largest movements of refugees and
evacuees, where official figures recorded that 5,409 persons had fled the
North, housed again in camps at Gormanston, Finner, Kilworth, Kilkenny,
Mullingar, Waterford, and even as far as Tralee. By 14 August 1971, 6,000
people were recorded as being housed in army camps, schools, convents,
and hospitals. In New Barnsley, Ballymurphy, and Ardoyne, thousands of
Catholic residents, primarily children and women, were evacuated from
their homes and communities. Paddy Davidson, then aged ten, once again
found himself, his family, and neighbours evacuated and transported to
refugee camps in the South:

   It was a wholesale clear-out of the estate. We were moved out in the
   middle of the night, into a mini-bus and eventually made the journey
   to Gormanston; conditions were bad. We were sleeping four or five to a
   single bed, army issue single beds, you know soldiers' beds. It was very
   cramped, a lot of people in a small place. In terms of the food, it was like
   rations you were given rather than the opportunity to cook or make your

own food. We were there for a good few nights until they started firing [transferring] people around the country. I remember people saying they were off to Cork or off to the Curragh. A lot of people did come back from other army camps almost straight away because conditions were so bad they couldn't stick it. But we then went to the Curragh [in Kildare] and these were much better conditions, and we were in Nissen huts that soldiers would have used, and we were all given new clothes and the people there were dedicated and caring and befriended the kids and we were really made to feel really welcome. Some soldiers and locals brought us in board games and stuff because in the evenings there wasn't much to do. But we could walk around the camp and walk into the town and so our family and all the other families were very happy there, very happy once we got out of Gormanston. We were treated very, very well and I'm sure my mum and aunt were given cash as we were leaving, and we were given clothes and sweets and the families were very grateful for that.

Certainly, the more coordinated programmes of evacuation tended to display high levels of organisation and coordination between nationalist civil society in the North and state agencies in the Republic. In Catholic areas, particularly from 1969 to 1972, the Catholic Church is frequently identified as a central coordinating body in the evacuation of citizens. Paddy Davidson is sure that the mass evacuations of civilians from Ballymurphy to the South was organised by the Tenants Association, particularly the endeavours of local man Frank Cahill who was chairman of the Tenants Association and local parish priest Fr Des Wilson along with the local Citizens' Defence Committee. Michael Liggett recalled one of his first experiences of displacement from Ardoyne:

Well my understanding is that the Church had something to do with it, Catholic Church networked people ... all I know is that my ma said, 'Right we're leaving the area' and my Dad was left behind to defend the area with all the other men but all the kids, boys and girls and women had to leave; everyone had to leave. So we went to Gormanston but Gormanston was only like a clearing centre. And then we were brought to a convent I think, in Carlow, a place called Tullow and from there we went to Cork and stayed with a family there in Cork and I think the parents were in the Officials ... but also the Free Staters must have had something to do with coordinating all of this because you couldn't just turn up at Gormanston Army Camp.

Agnes Moran shared her experiences of being evacuated to the South:

I think the church was involved in it ... back then the church was big, and they had the numbers, and in them days they'd be still calling round your house regularly. And then maybe the like of St. Johns ambulance brigade but as kids we were put on trucks or vans and to tell you the truth I don't remember even getting there; don't remember the journey. We were there for a few weeks and then we were shipped off, split off to so many families to Dublin and other places; whoever would take you in. We actually ended up in the North Circular Road in Dublin. A big gorgeous place; it had a hand ball alley, big fields, big dormitories but we found out later it was a refuge for alcoholics.

While food provisions and bedding were provided in all refugee centres, there was nevertheless little or no opportunity for active participation by refugees in terms of preparing food or having any input into how their needs and interests were being addressed. The lack of adequate and appropriate accommodation was consistently highlighted by those interviewees housed at various army camps and religious and health-care institutions. While they were and remain incredibly grateful for the support and sanctuary, it is clear from their vivid descriptions that facilities and host sites were wholly inappropriate for those fleeing the Troubles. Rita McAuley and her three children were evacuated from Ardoyne during internment and sent to the train station in Belfast. Like other interviewees, Rita also recalled loyalist crowds throwing bricks and bottles at the families as they waited to board the trains to Dublin, recalling the terror of children who were 'squealing with fright' and having to abandon one train and run to another for safety.

The train brought us to Gormanston, which was a terrible place … but you were glad of it at the same time, given the situation and they tried to do their best but the huts had been lying [empty] for years and years, and nobody had bothered cleaning them and so it was terrible really but when you walked in, there was like a big fire in the middle, like a big fire pit, if that's what you could call it … but people did their best for us but there were hundreds there. And this place was like a prefab, like a tin hut and so there were all these families crammed in. But we met people from Ballymurphy and met a family from Ballymurphy and we stuck together with them. And then food and meals, it was just horrible and as I said, they did their best for us but if you can imagine all hundreds of families all lying about in camp beds, and kids running about, and some of them throwing food about … oh God … and no privacy at all; you were sleeping alongside all other families.

Geraldine Nelson and her brother Joe lived in Strathroy Park in Ardoyne and were evacuated as the violence in the district intensified, particularly around Internment in August 1971. Joe Nelson recounted:

We were taken on a train to Gormanston and we arrived there at night and were met with officials and they were looking after us that night.

Then the next day we were moved on to Cork, into an army camp there. It was a big compound where they put a huge pile of turf right in the middle of it; across from that was a huge dinner hall and round the back of that, there were soldiers there peeling all the potatoes by hand and so we were in there with people from Ardoyne, the Bone, the Whiterock. So, we were all put into these huts, army huts with all these different families and it was just all full of beds ... bunk beds and single beds. And in the middle was a hot stove, like a boiler and so you had to go and get the turf from the compound and bring it in buckets and my granny used to light the stove because it got cold at night. But in the dinner halls, you met with kids from other districts and you formed your own wee gangs and we were let run wild, because we were in a compound, you could run wild ... but the food, like breakfast, was boiled eggs, toast, and your Rice Krispies and you could eat as much as you like, they just fed us. And the Irish Army were staying in the camp with us and you could have went and spoke to the soldiers and they were very, very welcoming.

Although many arrived in the summer and returned before the end of August, Geraldine and Joe Nelson recalled being sent to a local school near the Irish Army compound in Cork, where the teacher spoke in Irish only. Geraldine described:

We were put on these benches right at the back of the classroom because there was no room and the teacher was also dealing with three different levels [students of different age groups], and then there was us [refugees] added in and we were sitting on the floor and using the benches as a desk to lean on and I remember her trying to teach us Irish and we didn't really have any Irish and it was really hard.

Geraldine recalled fondly how the soldiers used to make them packed lunches and then take them to the school in the large army vehicles. Agnes Moran recalled:

Internment happened and we were shipped out again to Gormanston Army Camp. Again we picked up all sorts there too. I can't remember how long we were there for but I do remember queuing up for food. All our family and neighbours were there; all herded into these army dormitories ... so army blankets and that, and they were itchy. It was a hard time too because you got the feeling that they did not want you there, you got that feeling; you were a nuisance. You just felt you were in the way a wee bit, but you knew people did not want us there.

The response of the Irish Government adhered to a strategy of segregated spatial sites whereby, for the most part, the working assumption was that those displaced from the North would return to their original homes and communities. Commandant Maurice Brennan of the Irish Army said the policy at the time was 'to move the refugees out as fast as possible. Nearly all of last night's group were sent to schools, convents and a psychiatric hospital in Dublin and a military camp in Cork' (Lewis 1971). Like the refuge centres in the North established by civil society groups, the refugee camps run by the Irish Army were effectively 'holding centres' before transferring thousands to an eclectic range of hosts, including boarding schools, convents, individual families, monasteries, 'hospitals', and other various health institutions. At this point public and private authorities across the country announced their contributions: ranging from hospital blocks in Cork, the Killarney County Home, Glenstal Abbey in Limerick, the Elphin Diocesan College in County Sligo, schools in Navan, and other refuge places in County Longford. On 14 August 1969 *The Irish Times* reported that the GAA and the Irish Countrywomen's Association had called on every member to support the Irish Red Cross as volunteers or by giving clothing and bedding for northern refugees. On 14 August 1971, 700 refugees were fed at two hours' notice thanks to 'Dundalk housewives and daughters' (Mulroe 2017: 103). The telephone Branch of the Post Office Officials Association asked the Department of Posts and Telegraphs for extra phone lines to be installed at 'refugee centres' enabling the Central Citizens' Defence Association in Belfast together with Civil Defence in the Republic to establish a system to put wives and children in touch with their husbands and fathers still in the North. An Irish army spokesman described the refugee situation as having reached saturation point for the army but that many refugees were now being transferred to accommodation provided privately or by other bodies (Conroy, McKearney, and Oliver 2005). Though similar to the makeshift shelters in the North, state-run refugee camps in the Republic were of course more organised, formal, with a distinctly regimented feel to them. Needless to say, like the makeshift centre in the North, the Irish army camps were not suited to the long-term accommodation of families. Therefore, it was essential to transfer and disperse refugees out to more suitable forms of accommodation. Patricia McGuigan's family who were displaced from their North Belfast home on several occasions from 1971 onwards recalled her evacuation to Carlow:

> So I remember getting there and it was like a countryside town, that's what it seemed like, and there were people all there taking us off the buses, take us into this, I would say it was a community centre or church hall, so lemonade and biscuits and then a mattress to lie on and then we were up the next morning early, onto the convent. The first one was like cubical holes, small ones and the nuns were very strict. You had to be asleep at a certain time every night; that was not a holiday part of it. But you had your own wee space and that. In the smaller place

there was five or six beds to a room and so they could put families into a room. I can just remember being in lovely places, good people. The first night that we were in Carlow a businessman owned a shoe shop and took all us kids and bought us new sandals for the summer – brand new shoes. People were brilliant; I can remember as a young girl, teenage girls would have taken us out for a walk, into the countryside and along the river, a good reception from the people, well from what I remember, nothing negative.

Joe Nelson and his sister Geraldine were staying at an Irish army camp in Cork in 1971, where one day they were taken into the local village for haircuts. When the barber realised they were refugees from Belfast, he cut everyone's hair for free. As outlined by Agnes, Patricia, and others, despite the kindness, refuge, aid, and shelter, there is of course an inherently hierarchical relationship between 'host' and 'refugee'. Categories of 'hosts' and 'guests' are imbued with hierarchies of power and social relations and have individual and social implications for those assigned to them (Brun 2003). Many recalled a tension between feelings of relief on the one hand but also a sense that those displaced were solely contingent on the kindness and empathy of others and, moreover, felt that they signified something of an anomalous, even 'exotic' figure in terms of their experiences, treatment, and representation. After 1971, certainly there is much evidence indicating an increasingly less-welcome environment in some parts of the Republic, characterised by reductive stereotypes and negative attitudes towards those seeking refuge. While the generous and accommodating roles and processes afforded by the Irish Government in 1969, 1970, and 1971 are not in doubt, unquestionably by 1972, state documents reveal a discernible reconsideration of 'northern refugees' by the Irish State, recasting some of them as burdens, ingrates, and potential subversive threats rather than those deserving of aid and assistance. The changing response of the Irish state to the perennial and increasing refugee movements across the Irish Border in the early 1970s resonates with large-scale population movements internationally whereby refugee movements were not only a consequence of insecurity, but could also be a cause of instability for host states (Loescher and Milner 2005). For those who permanently relocated to the South, tensions and frictions tended to pivot on competition for resources, including employment, housing, education, and health care. Over longer periods, refugees can be scapegoated for a range of ills including economic woes and increased levels of crime and violence. Long before the rise of the 'securitisation of refugees and migrants' and the persistent and deliberate conflation of displaced persons with crime and terrorism by Western nation-states post-9/11, archival documents from the Irish State reveal concerns at high levels of governance at the possible security consequences and destabilising effects resulting from links between Northern refugees and a variety of forms of support for the IRA. While places such as Monaghan, Dundalk, and Drogheda were perhaps the obvious sites of relocation of refugees, clearly the authorities in the South sought to consistently fragment and disperse refugees across a range of counties, ranging from Dublin right down to places as far south as Cork, Limerick, and Waterford. The comments from the Irish Government memorandum and the testimonies of those in this research resonate with what Haddad (2008) has termed the 'refugee problem'; this concept of burden is often derived from medicalised and individualised discourses of trauma as expressed in unemployability, adverse mental health, lawlessness, and incompatibility in resettlement contexts (Marlowe 2017)

In short, while many have noted the costs of refugee absorption, the potential benefits that refugees provide states have not been fully explored or empirically tested, especially in the context of international politics. Moorthy and Brathwaite (2019) contend that given the precarious human-itarian situation, refugees can be exploited for political purposes to fight proxy battles between interstate rivals in the international system; therefore, refugees from rivalling states are of strategic benefit to host states as an opportunity to weaken their adversary. A state finds it advantageous to accept refugees into their territory as both they and the refugees, have in common a fractious relationship with the refugees' home state. The forced exile of citizens provides a framework for the host state to question both the domestic powers and legitimacy – after all, these countries either repressed parts of their population and forced them to flee, or were not capable enough to ensure their security (Moorthy and Brathwaite 2019). The acceptance and humanitarian assistance afforded to refugees and displaced persons cannot be divorced from wider questions of ethical and political failures in the inter-state system, and so automatically makes a political statement about the country of origin (Haddad 2008). Although relations between both states on the island of Ireland had improved significantly in the years preceding the outbreak of the Troubles, undoubtedly, the eruption of violence in August 1969 signified a major crisis and the plight of refugees and the increasing instability in the North was an issue of concern to the Irish Government. It is important to also foreground the fact that the Republic of Ireland's constitution still laid sovereign claim over the six counties of the Northern state, accompanied by strong irredentism within the ruling Fianna Fáil Party. For many in the Republic, partition was an inept and enforced 'solution' and the thousands who perennially streamed across the border into the Republic served as a potent embodiment of Northern Ireland as a 'failed state'. Beyond the important ethical and humanitarian considerations, the continuing acceptance of thousands of Catholic refugees by the Irish Government signified the physical territory of the Republic as a 'safe' space for Catholics, solidifying their identities and politics of belonging to the 'imagined community' (Anderson 1983) while simultaneously casting Northern Ireland as a place of danger, persecution, and insecurity.

Documents examined at the National Archives in Dublin further convey a sense of frustration that the Northern Ireland state had no specific body that could exercise control or coordination in relation to refugees and displacement, no more so than with regard to processes of repatriation to the North. National Archive records of meeting minutes recorded on 19 August 1971 by the Department of the Taoiseach reveal high levels of diplomatic friction between the Republic and Northern Ireland on the subject of refugees (National Archives of Ireland 1971). These documents outline the Republic's willingness to pay both children's allowances and pensions to refugees but expressed frustration regarding the reticence and lack of cooperation with the corresponding Northern Ireland ministry. According to the minutes, the 'Northern Ireland Ministry were not disposed' to the Republic paying out pensions but 'reluctantly agreed' once they were informed that pensions were already payable in the Republic. With regard to Children's Allowance, in 1969 the Republic and the Northern Ireland Ministry of Health and Social Security agreed for the allowances to be paid in the Republic's post office, which were subsequently refunded by the Northern Ireland Ministry. However, this arrangement proved to be a one-off, with Northern Ireland Ministries 'refusing to agree' to any arrangement allowing the payment of any future social security entitlements. Consequently, many family members in refugee camps travelled to the North to collect social security payments and returned to the camps on the same day.

The axiomatic and durable solution to the Northern refugee crisis from the perspective of the Irish Government was based on the interim nature of displacement, with almost all refugees returning to the North after relatively short periods of shelter and accommodation. (Those who decided to remain in the south were later offered the opportunity to return North, should they so wish, in the post-conflict period with assistance provided by the Irish Government, as is discussed later in the book.) The temporal characteristics of displacement, much of which occurred during the Troublesome summer months, meant that permanent resettlement in the Republic was never a stated objective, either by those exiled from the North or the authorities in the Republic. While the 'extraordinary' mass movements of refugees to the South consistently concluded with the repatriation of almost all to their original place of residence, many more thousands continued to cross over the border to escape violence, fear, and intimidation, but did so in very 'everyday ways', endeavouring to establish new lives in what were then unfamiliar and sometimes hostile places. Furthermore, many thousands internally displaced within the state of Northern Ireland found themselves in equally unfamiliar and often under-developed places of residence.

Hands across the Water

Though much of the focus and attention on refugee movements during this period has tended to focus on the plight of Catholics fleeing south of the border in their thousands, one of the most remarkable, but little-known parts of the displacement story concerns the evacuation and transfer of hundreds of Protestant refugees from various parts of Belfast to Liverpool and Glasgow in 1971. The Belfast Protestant Relief Committee arranged for women and children refugees to be shipped from East Belfast to Glasgow and Liverpool. More than 1,000 Protestant women and children, primarily from East Belfast, were taken by specially commissioned boats to Scotland where they were offered refuge by members of the Orange Order. Women and children were also hosted by private families in the Liverpool area under the auspices of the Liverpool Loyal Institutions. While the eventual mass evacuation to Liverpool and Glasgow in 1971 was a spontaneous reaction to the intensity of violence in the aftermath of the introduction of Internment, nevertheless, mass evacuation plans for Protestants were already devised and in place for some time preceding this. By the summer of 1971 the Orange Order in Liverpool and Glasgow had devised detailed plans for the mass evacuation of Protestants from vulnerable parts of Belfast, with many local lodges raising funds and securing local accommodation for the anticipated mass exile. During the course of research for the book, the authors secured access to previously undisclosed minutes from meetings of several local Orange Lodges in Liverpool and surrounding districts, and records indicate that an 'Ulster Distress Fund' or 'Ulster Relief Fund' was in existence with the specific purpose of providing monetary assistance and, if needs be, emergency refuge and accommodation for Protestants.[9] A meeting in February 1970 by the No. 3 North District Lodge makes specific mention of the 'Ulster Distress Fund' while also referencing the possibility of 'evacuees from Ulster if position there worsened'. In February 1971 the Loyal Orange Lodge (LOL) 5 Pride of West Derby discussed a plethora of letters from brethren in Northern Ireland seeking donations towards a 'target of £1000 to help our brethren in Ulster' via what was now officially termed the 'Ulster Fund'. On 18 August 1971 the same lodge again notes the continuing donations to the 'Ulster Relief Fund' and the availability of a large hall for 'Ulster Evacuees'.

On 10 August 1971, in the aftermath of the introduction of Internment the previous day, Protestant families were evacuated from Malt Street in the Grosvenor Road area of West Belfast and housed in a large hall in Linfield Street, in Sandy Row. Additionally, most Protestant residents in Springfield Park left their homes, while many residents of the Springmartin estate were evacuated and took refuge at the nearby Black Mountain Primary School, where British soldiers were also billeted. By 12 August, approximately 200 Protestant children from the Springmartin estate were being housed in the Blackmountain Primary School, while a number of Protestant families left the Suffolk area of West Belfast, which borders Andersonstown and occupied houses on the Old Warren estate in nearby Lisburn. Rev Frederick Baillie's St Columba Church also became a makeshift refuge centre for Protestants from Springmartin and surrounding areas with steady supplies of food and other essentials coming from Edinburgh and Glasgow, while traders in Bangor, County Down sent carloads of meat, vegetables, and fruit (East Belfast Historical and Cultural Society 2000). The Welfare Department of Belfast Corporation reported that they had 19 relief centres operating in the city, catering for more than 1,200 people (East Belfast Historical and Cultural Society 2000). Given the deteriorating security situation and the fact that many Protestant refuge centres were now at full capacity, a decision was made to activate the plans devised by the Loyal Orders and evacuate hundreds of Protestants across the Irish Sea to pre-arranged refuge centres and families in Glasgow and Liverpool.

'Robert' was involved in some of the tentative efforts to arrange the transfer to Scotland and recalled that the 'Orange Order had lined up boats, fishing boats mainly, to bring people over, and at the time, there was this idea that this could develop into a major civil war and they were arranging boats over to Scotland from Larne'. Elsie Doyle, a member of the Lily of the North Ladies LOL79 and her husband Billy, also a member of several Loyal Orders, were regular visitors to Belfast prior to the Troubles. Watching the news footage of Protestant families fleeing their homes during the intro-duction of internment in 1971, Elsie, her husband, and father-in-law Joe set sail for Belfast the following night with the full backing of the Orange Order in Liverpool.[10] The purpose of the trip was to transfer by boat as many Protestant families from Belfast across the Irish Sea to Liverpool to provide safety and refuge. After arriving in Belfast, they met Shankill Road fruit shop owner George Quinn who put them in touch with two brothers, Kenny and Billy Hagan, who suggested they direct their energies towards Protestant evacuees in Springmartin. Arrangements were then made with the Belfast Steamship Company and within 12 hours of their arrival, Elsie and her husband departed Belfast Dock with the first boat of Protestant evacuees, including the Hagan brothers, and set sail for Liverpool where the local lodges had organised halls packed with food, blankets, and prams as well as ensuring the presence of medical people and social services. The first 120 evacuees, overwhelmingly children and women, were taken to the Orange Hall in South Hill Road, Toxteth and to the Southern Area Memorial Social Club where they were fed and distributed to houses and accommodation from local Orange Order members.

Elsie recalled:

On 12th August 1971, the Rev. Bailey took us round Springmartin and what we found was horrifying. All the children in the estate were holed up in a school because the front of the estate faced down onto Ballymurphy and all the trouble was emanating from Ballymurphy, shooting up to the Springmartin; the fronts of the houses were all bullet marked. And the army was trying to help them out as best they could, bringing them down food and rations and that. Anyway, we intended to bring 25 to 30 children back with us to Liverpool, but we ended up with 120 that night. But we got the Belfast ship company, told them what was happening, and they laid on toast and cups of cocoa and the same the next day for breakfast. So anyway, the word went round that you could go to Liverpool, and we ended up with over 800 children and women going to Liverpool. So we brought children back on the boat that night, 120 children. But I phoned the Grand master at the time, a fella called Richard Roberts and he said, 'We have everything here, so Elsie, don't worry, bring as many as you can.' So, there were buses taking the children from the Springmartin down to the docks to the boat and then from there up to the Orange Halls in the south-end of the City [Liverpool]. And there were people there waiting and ready to take them ... and then the next time we went back, it was north-end people who gathered to take the children and they were all well looked after, no complaints. But it was all just people coming together, but I suppose we're like a clique, all for one and one for all and we all came together. So 120 was the first and then I went back the same night ... I didn't get changed for three days [laughs] ... so you'd leave here at 11 o'clock at night and then arrive in Belfast at 7am the next morning, then gather them all together, on the boat by 8 or 9, get them bedded down, get them to Liverpool and then back to Belfast again.

Elsie and her husband continued their repeated boat trips across the Irish Sea for the next three days and nights bringing back hundreds more evacuees, from the Oldpark area, Ardoyne, as well as Cupar Street and other parts of West Belfast. Thoroughly exhausted after three days and nights of sailing, other members of the local Orange institutions continued with the sea crossings bringing back more and more evacuees. Some of those who crossed the Irish Sea to Liverpool stayed a number of weeks; others stayed on for months.[11] Davy Round recalled: 'We were like refugees. We went to an Orange Hall in Liverpool and there were tables with clothes and toys and whatever we wanted.' Joan Acheson and her younger brother Colin lived with their aunt on 81 Alliance Avenue, directly facing into Ardoyne's Jamaica Street. Like many Protestant residents of Ardoyne, the deteriorating and precarious situation reached the tipping point of internment in August 1971. Joan and her family were evacuated from their home in a matter of minutes but rather than being taken to a nearby refuge centre or new dwelling, Joan and Colin were taken by army landrover and dropped off at Belfast Dock where they boarded a boat for Liverpool with hundreds of others.

I don't know who organised this but Ivy [their aunt and guardian] was elderly and all the other houses were burning and I suppose someone just decided that it was safer for me and Colin to get out of Belfast and go to Liverpool for a week and I remember being put in the back of a big army truck and we were taken away and brought us down to the Docks where we were all put onto this boat and next thing you know, here we were in Liverpool. The only place I'd ever been was Bangor or Millisle. We stayed with a family in an estate that I cannot recall the exact location. But you see a lot of people don't know about all this, the trips to Liverpool. But we were there for a couple of weeks but I wanted home after a few weeks.

Thelma Worthington was one of several people actively involved with the Loyal Orders resettlement of Protestant evacuees who came to Liverpool from Belfast. She described a flurry of activity by scores of volunteers who worked tirelessly prior to and during the hosting of Protestant evacuees.

I know there were a core of people who did the fundraising. I was part of the fundraising and worked in the old Provincial Hall where we did all the fundraising; all the unsung heroes, the quiet ones that didn't stand out … that did all the work and raised the funds … through bring-and-buy sales, raffles, chase the bottle … and I used to do a lot of fundraising … there were no organising committees as such and you're here on this and there on that. If I give you one name … Rita Gallagher … and she was older than me but not much older but my god, when she said jump, you jumped, you know, how high? So, she was organising and knew what she was doing, so her, Gladys Cromwell, and Elsie Allan, and you just knew the look they gave when they needed something. And so we would sit around and knit things like babies' clothing and that's how the funds were raised. And so it was all really well organised without someone having to say, 'Right you do this and you do that…' I remember that the funds raised by the knitting and all that was also distributed to any families taking on some of the children. But as I said it was not spoken of, you just got on with it. We also had a nursing corps if you like so we all learned how to practice wrapping bandages and all that.

Louise Sewell's father and wider family were originally from the Shankill Road and moved to Liverpool in the 1950s but maintained strong connections with family and friends in Belfast. The family in Liverpool were dedicated and active members of the Loyal Order and like many members of the Lodge, were centrally involved in housing Protestant evacuees from Belfast. Louise recalled:

It was exciting … exciting. I do remember it being the thing like two or three of us kids to a single bed; we all slept head to toe in our house. My dad has a Morris Minor and there were not a whole lot of cars around in those days, so he folded all the seats with six kids in there and he gave them anything we could give them … brought them to Blackpool. Now we couldn't afford to go on the fair rides, but it was fish and chips, took them to beaches but we were excited to have them around. My dad took a lot of time out, off work too, and I remember every day we were taking them out somewhere, something different every day. I have to say the three kids we had were near the same age as us and I remember the sadness and the crying when they were leaving and the tears.

Ivan Thompson was ten years old and lived in the Springmartin estate. The months leading up to internment were described by Ivan as one of daily gun battles and riots between Springmartin, the nearby Springhill/ Westrock, and Ballymurphy. By 10 August 1971, with a worsening situation, Ivan and his family were taking refuge in the nearby Blackmountain Primary School before being transferred over to Liverpool.

Well that was the Orange Order that organised that, and it was women and children who were all [taking refuge] in Blackmountain Primary School and they were sleeping in the army beds. But a lot of double decker buses arrived on a Friday, and we got on the buses and left Belfast at 10 o'clock that night on the boat for Liverpool and we arrived in Liverpool the next morning and we were met there by people who I now know were members of the Orange Order. We were then bused to a large Orange Hall where it was like a party atmosphere; there was juice, sweets, biscuits, there were toys to play with. And then everyone was separated and allocated a family to go to and I went with a woman called Elsie Brough who lived in the Edinburgh Tower off the Netherfield Road. I'm not sure but I have it in my head that we stayed there about two, maybe three weeks, but Elsie and her family were very good to me and my mother. I was never in a high-rise building before and so it was all exciting to me. Elsie had a grandson John and he brought me to Everton games, went to the cinema, went to Liverpool training ground, went over to Birkenhead on the ferry a few times, went to the Lake District, went to Southport for an Orange Parade, taken to a beach in Wales again for an Orange Order parade or event and so we were really well looked after and these were all Orange Order; all the families were linked into the Orange Order. And then we returned to Belfast, where to be honest, things were still the same.

The remarkable voyages to Glasgow and Liverpool occurred only once but were indicative of the strong cultural and political bonds between the Orange institutions on both sides of the Irish Sea. Although undoubtedly a collective effort, clearly women from the Loyal Institutions were central to the transfer and accommodation of Protestant refugees in Liverpool (Busteed 2022). While this was undoubtedly the largest single project undertaken by the Liverpool Province and indeed, the English Grand Lodge, in support of their brethren in Northern Ireland, interest in the welfare of Ulster Protestants persisted and informal contacts endured throughout the period of the Troubles (Busteed 2022).

While most displaced and evacuated Protestants moved within the state, the ability for masses of Catholics to annually cross the border into the Republic effectively functioned as a pressure relief valve, bringing much-needed respite for evacuees and undoubtedly their communities. Despite the 'success' of the evacuation of Protestants to Liverpool, the exodus of Protestants across the Irish Sea in August 1971 proved to be a one-off. Unlike those in the Catholic community, the displacement and evacuation of Protestants overwhelmingly occurred within the six counties of Northern Ireland. Official figures and our own research presented here indicate that, for Catholics, the perennial pathways into the Republic provided a welcome place of refuge and sanctuary, undoubtedly augmented by a prevalent mistrust of and alienation from the Northern Ireland state and of course assisted by the willingness of the state and civil society in the South to extend empathy, support, and solidarity. Although Protestants too were largely left to evacuate and resettle themselves, nonetheless, many had both an affinity and allegiance to the Northern Ireland state and many saw the RUC, and ruling government in general, as legitimate. Moreover, unlike their Catholic counterparts, departing the Northern Ireland State in search of refuge, such as in the case of Liverpool and Glasgow, was much more arduous and therefore never really a pragmatic or realistic option for future episodes of Protestant displacement.

A strong theme within political theory approaches to the state contends that a strong civil society, comprising community organisations, associational networks, and active citizenship are both important checks and balances on state power and mechanisms for the delivery of public goods and services. In the case of Northern Ireland's displacement, however, civil society effectively filled the void left by a state incapable or unwilling to provide safety, refuge, and security for those at the coalface of intimidation and upheaval. In this instance, civil society was not providing an alternative or complimentary role to the state with respect to displacement; they were primarily providing the sole providers of mass evacuations and resettlement. While social theorists such as Putnam (2000) situate social capital and associations as essential not only for personal and community development, but also for maintenance of strong democracy, in Northern Ireland, the experiences of displacement led many to believe that the state had failed them, engendering widespread beliefs that communities needed to rely on themselves for the purpose of defence and survival. Civil society in Northern Ireland therefore provided a conduit for mobilising collective action within very defined communities that shared a broad common identity and purpose. The high status bestowed on many persons and organisations directly involved in refuge, flight, and evacuations stemmed from a sense that civil society was rising to the demands, needs, and interests of those caught in such dire and immediate circumstances. Regardless of whether persons were displaced within the state or crossed into the Republic or Britain, refugees from both communities relied upon the collective response and support of civic society, largely built upon ethno-cultural ties and identities and undoubtedly sustained by a spectrum of perceptions of a state, perceptions ranging from incapable at one end and outright complicit at the other.

Conclusion

This chapter endeavoured to highlight not only the scale of organising and managing mass movements amid intense conflict, but also sought to shed light on the narratives and experiences of evacuation, exile, and the daunting journeys to unknown destinations and places. While many assume that escape from the immediate dangers of intimidation and threats signify the axiomatic endpoint of harm and peril, the immense loss of home and community is exacerbated by the sometimes ambiguous and challenging processes of 'refuge and resettlement'. The unwillingness or inability of the Northern Ireland state to either prevent displacement or assist in the mass evacuations bequeathed a vacuum that was fulfilled by a vast range of civil society groups. The lack of resources from the state was amply counter-balanced by an abundance of community resources, including funding, food, and clothing donations, transport, recreation, and accommodation. While there was an abundance of civil society groups in existence prior to August 1969, particularly within the Catholic community, the groups that emerged in the wake of displacement in the early years of the Troubles and their actions were clearly rooted in a spontaneous reaction to the consequences of political instability and immediacy of providing humanitarian assistance to those forced from their homes.

While trauma and communal experiences of loss and harm can silence individuals and destabilise collective groupings, it is also important to consider the ways in which such experiences can create a sense of solidarity and collective consciousness against the face of oppression (Marlowe 2017: 66). As this chapter demonstrates, conflict and political violence engender the social bonds that promote collective action, a shared discourse, group loyalty, and, importantly, a sense of voluntary action tied to pledging allegiance to the nation, state, or community (Shirlow 2014: 737). Furthermore, the validity of claims regarding the unwillingness or inability of the state to prevent displacement or assist with its deleterious outcomes augmented a belief in the need to build self-sufficient and resourceful communities sustained through the perennial, existential threat from the 'other' community. Displacement invariably involved the physical uprooting and movement from a place, often involving the loss or destruction of homes. However, forced exile also entailed a form of social displacement via a loss of belonging and rootedness, furnishing a perennial sense of liminality despite the passage of time and regardless of the new lives rebuilt, a theme that weaves its way through this book. Therefore, we now shift our attention to the afterlives of those displaced, examining the short- and long-term impact on their lives, communities, and the wider conflict.

Notes

1   Feargal Cochrane and Seamus Dunn's in-depth analysis of the voluntary and community sector in Northern Ireland suggests that since partition in 1921, civil society organising was more prevalent within the Catholic community, owing to issues regarding legitimacy and allegiance to the new Northern Ireland state. On the other hand, they suggest that working-class Protestants looked overwhelmingly to the state as the primary provider for service delivery.

2   St Gerard's is a Catholic parish in North Belfast but is officially part of Newtownabbey. Founded in 1961, St Gerard's consisted of a church and a large retreat hall, which housed hundreds of displaced Catholics in the early years of the Troubles.

3   A now world-famous picture taken during this particular time was later used by the English band Dexys Midnight Runners; the front cover for their album *Searching for the Young Soul Rebels* shows a group of young Catholic brothers preparing to leave Cranbrook Gardens amid the chaos of August 1971. The arresting image of the young boy holding onto a bag and suitcase is Tony O'Shaughnessy, then aged 13. Also in the picture are loyalists Robert 'Basher' Bates and Roy Stewart who are assisting with the evacuation. Sadly, Tony O'Shaughnessy died in October 2021.

4   Despite the unprecedented numbers involved in displacement, particularly from 1969 to 1974, the Northern Ireland state did not establish any state-led body or agency to coordinate, assist, or monitor the forced movement of thousands of citizens. State documents reveal frustration and concern by the Irish Government at the time regarding the absence of a state-led body for refugees in the North to liaise with.

5   Following the outbreak of increased violence in 1971, the Northern Ireland Government established the Emergency Relief Scheme where those intim-idated from their homes could apply for assistance in being permanently relocated to Britain. Successful applicants needed to prove they had secured both employment and accommodation in Britain (Darby and Morris 1974).

6   In October 1969, a bank account titled 'The Belfast Fund for the Relief of Distress' was set up at a Bank of Ireland branch in Clones, County Monaghan. Then government minister, Charles Haughey, transferred £5,000 and £10,000 to the Irish Red Cross for the explicit purpose and understanding that these funds would be transferred directly into the relief fund. From 12 November 1969 to 9 April 1970, £59,000 of Irish Government funds were transferred to the relief account, of which £20,000 was transferred to the Belfast Refugee

Re-establishment Committee. The remainder of the money was spent on paying those manning the barricades in Belfast and Derry and, most controversially, the procurement of arms (Hennessey 2005: 353).

7   *The Voice of the North* was edited by Seamus Brady, a former speech writer for Fianna *Fáil* Donegal TD, Neil Blaney, who had been tried and acquitted in the Arms Trial of 1970. Also on its editorial board were republicans John Kelly and Sean Keenan. The paper's outlook and standpoint were overtly anti-communist and traditionally Catholic and nationalist (Patterson 1989).

8   Carmel's older brother, Terry, was 18 at the time and was detained by the British Army the same morning as his brother John was shot dead. Terry was held for 36 hours, and physically assaulted, leaving him with horrific injuries.

9   The authors wish to express our sincere gratitude to Mervyn Busteed for securing access to these records and for his constant support for the research from its inception.

10 While the Orange Order is understandably synonymous with Ireland, the Orange Order have lodges in Britain, Canada, the United States, Australia, and Ghana. Liverpool is the headquarters of the Orange Institution in England and was, and remains a key home to Orangeism outside Northern Ireland. Outside Liverpool, there are lodges in Manchester, Derby, Bootle, Corby, Sheffield, and Cheshire. Although the first Orange Order lodges in England were located in Manchester, the influx of Catholic Irish diaspora into Liverpool in search of work increased sectarian tensions in the city, engendering the need among Liverpool Protestants to counter the perceived political, social, and economic threat from the growing Catholic population. The first Orange Lodge in the city dates to the early 1800s with its first 12 July parade occurring in 1819. It has been estimated that as late as the 1940s the membership of the Orange Institution on Merseyside was approximately 50,000 while throughout most of the twentieth century its annual 12 July parades could consistently attract upwards of 10,000 participants and spectators. In recent times however, like most religious institutions, its membership and influence has steadily declined in the Merseyside area.

11 The Orange Order hosted a 'Grand Lodge' event in Belfast in August 2011 to mark the 40th anniversary of the evacuation of Protestant refugees over to Liverpool. The event brought together some of those involved in the planning and coordination of the evacuation and some of those who were evacuated.

Chapter Four

Ruptured Lives: Harms, Loss, and Grievances

Introduction

While there are numerous examples of conflicts internationally that sought to avoid 'dealing with the past' via policies and practices of forgetting, denial, restrictions on accessing archives, victim-blaming, or the segregation of communities, acknowledging and addressing past wrongdoings through some form of transitional justice has become the global norm (Hourmat 2016). Whereas the 1998 Belfast or Good Friday Agreement (hereinafter GFA) had up until recent times drawn plaudits home and abroad as a prudent model of conflict resolution, a position that is subject to critique, the fact remains that unlike many other regions emerging from the aftermath of protracted armed conflict, Northern Ireland has proven to be something of an exception with regards to the legacy of its violent past. The unprecedented political partnership between unionism and nationalism at an institutional level – particularly in the period of a relatively stable devolved government from 2007 to 2016 – deflected from the reality that approaches to legacy and reconciliation have been at best fragmented, staggered, and inept, leaving thousands of citizens without truth, acknowledgement, and accountability (Coulter, Gilmartin, Hayward, and Shirlow 2021).[1] Despite the cursory commitments to addressing the issue of victims in the 1998 peace accord, no state-led, formal structure or process was stipulated or established. If anything, in the intervening years the state has been zealous in removing itself from direct involvement in devising comprehensive approaches to legacy. The absence of a formal state-led approach to legacy, insufficient levels of social reconciliation, combined with a lack of victims' support and services ensures that, for many, the 'post-conflict' landscape represents a continuum of violence, hurt, and trauma, despite prevailing declarations regarding 'peace and prosperity'. The chasm created by the lack of an overarching, comprehensive 'truth and justice' mechanism has led to what Christine Bell (2003) has called a 'piecemeal approach' to dealing with the past in Northern Ireland, including public legal enquiries, the formation of a Historical Enquiries Team (HET), the establishment of a Police Ombudsman, community and grassroots initiatives, legal challenges such as private prosecutions and civil actions, policing initiatives, and victim-centred state-led initiatives.

Though there is a growing recognition that refugees and internally displaced persons (IDPs) have a major stake in the success of transitional justice (TJ) processes that can shape the stability of post-conflict communities (Parry 2020), in many cases, displaced persons have not been recognised as critical stakeholders when it comes to managing the issues of a conflictual past. Furthermore, mechanisms such as truth commissions have often failed to substantively address forced movement as a human rights violation. Despite growing calls for a more adequate and nuanced understanding of displacement and its impact on peacebuilding, it is one that has simply not figured prominently in either the literature or the practice of transitional justice (Browne and Asprooth-Jackson 2019; Duthie 2011). As argued by Megan Bradley (2012), Northern Ireland's peacebuilding process represents yet another case whereby displaced persons have not been recognised as an important category of victims and survivors, nor have their experiences been acknowledged. There remains an all-pervasive assumption that once re-settled, the sense of injustice, loss, and vulnerability among displaced persons has been largely addressed and therefore warrants no further action or consideration. By exploring the marginalised narratives of those displaced, this chapter sheds light on the multi-layered short- and long-term harms and consequences of displacement for individuals, families, and community relations. By doing so, the chapter seeks to map issues of legacy, harm, and victimhood onto the experiences of forced displacement during the conflict. In considering the narratives of those displaced, we suggest a strong need to broaden understandings of conflict-related violence in Northern Ireland to include displacement and its long-term impact on individuals and communities as part of our ongoing peacebuilding endeavours.

Loss, Grievance, and Injustice: The Consequences of Displacement

Prevailing and popular understandings of victimhood and loss caused by the Troubles has typically (and understandably) focused on harms caused by shootings, bombings, and related physical violence. The construction of meaning with regards to the conventional understandings of violence and harm not only solidifies its privileged status as an exceptional, and therefore paramount, existential source of harm; in doing so, it diminishes the meaning associated with other forms of violence, such as displacement. It is important to re-state that there was no archetypal form or experience of displacement, as detailed in Chapter Two. Some literally fled their homes as they were torched; others left quietly in the dead of night after years of incremental intimidation. While acknowledging the heterogenous experiences among participants, nevertheless, there were discernible patterns of commonality. With regards to their individual experiences of displacement, all research participants spoke of the pain, loss, distress, and 'heart-break' of losing their family home, their communities, social networks, their places of employment, worship, and education. Despite the propensity of conventions depicting war and peace as two distinct temporal forms of social and political action, the emotional impact of violent uprooting is clearly deep-seated and, importantly, ever present. Jeanette Warke and her family were directly intimidated from their home close to Londonderry city centre in 1972:

> I have to tell you it was heart-breaking leaving our wee house, that you had paid for, that you had furnished and done up, built on a bathroom and kitchen – heart-breaking. But it was very, very hard to walk away and go live in another house and another area. This was your life: where you were brought up, schooled, churched, brought up three kids.

When asked about the actual event of losing their home, many responded that while it was painful, there was an element of 'making the best of the situation' but also an acute realisation that they had no choice; they were *forced* to move for their own safety. Despite the sentiments expressing the pragmatism of 'not dwelling too much on it at the time', it was clear that many still felt a visceral sense of pain and loss when recalling these events. Marian Kane was married with three children living in Ardoyne when, in the summer of 1971 she, along with hundreds of others were evacuated to refugee centres in the Republic of Ireland. To this day, she is still shaken by the memories of leaving that day:

> Later that day the big corporation buses arrived, and they were parked around the school and everyone in the school was evacuated and because I was pregnant my husband was saying, 'You have to go; you have to go' but I didn't want to go; it was breaking my heart. When I was younger, there was a [television] programme on about Warsaw and the Jews and the Nazis and the series was about a wee girl who was evacuated and she had lost touch with everybody and it was all a big sad thing, awful, and I just thought, 'That's what is going to happen to me here' and I had this terrible feeling that you'd never be back again, you'd never see your family again and that the entire place was going to be burnt to the ground – the most horrible feeling ever.

Up until 13 August 1969, Joe Doyle had lived all his life in Conway Street in the Lower Falls and, as was typical of the time, had a large family circle who lived nearby in the close-knit streets of West Belfast. Conway Street adjoins the Protestant Shankill and Catholic Falls Road and was completely destroyed in a single night on 13 August 1969 by loyalists. After losing his home, Joe was taken to a school in Turf Lodge and eventually rehoused in Andersonstown. Now aged in his late 70s, Joe still finds it difficult to comprehend the ways in which a single night of violence destroyed an entire neighbourhood forever:

> All the houses were to be rebuilt. In Bombay Street, they all got together, the people got together, and they re-built them. But you see that didn't happen in Conway Street and then they cut the street in half with the big permanent [peace] wall. I lost a lot of friends – they were scattered everywhere – and it was sad to see. All good people that lived there and they were all scattered over the bloody world; some went to England, America, other parts of Belfast because I had no intention of ever leaving Conway Street until that night. But that street was never, ever the same again.

Despite rebuilding their lives after their relocation or return, nevertheless, the act of displacement(s) (some respondents were displaced on more than one occasion) continues to instil negative emotions regarding the significance of loss. Agnes Moran and her family were displaced twice from their Ardoyne home in Belfast in the early 1970s. On the first occasion in 1969, they left their family home as rioting and violence intensified but they had no idea that their home and street were eventually burned later that night:

> We ended up in my aunt's home in Andersonstown so we were able to stay there overnight but we just left with what we were standing in; we thought we were only going for the night. But I remember the next day, we turned on the news and I can still remember my mommy and daddy standing watching the news in my aunt's living room and they pointed out our house on the news and there was only two walls left; that's all that was left. Nothing else [emotional pause] and a plate of Our Lady of Lourdes hanging on the wall; that's how we knew it was our house. Everything was taken from us – everything. We had nowhere to go so [we] ended up in the local school, sleeping there for the next few weeks.

All of those displaced through mass house burnings and attacks vividly described the loss of treasured family possessions and heirlooms, such as photographs and jewellery, as well as clothing and furniture; many stated, 'All that was left was the clothes we fled in.' The disruption and debilitating impact of displacement also went beyond these immense losses; many of those who were children at the time recalled the sadness of leaving friends, of never having the opportunity to say goodbye to neighbours and friends; others spoke about the upheaval in changing schools, particularly those who re-settled in other jurisdictions. Christina Bennett's family were forced from their home in Whiteabbey on the outskirts of North Belfast in 1975. The family re-settled in Shannon in County Clare. She described the final moments before her family left their home:

> [My parents] said they didn't want any of the neighbours to know that we were moving because they were afraid of being attacked in the lead up to it so none of my friends knew that I was leaving; you never really got to say goodbye. But everywhere was deserted and we were all in the car and nobody was speaking. I think everyone was just in shock or just worn out and my dad, God love him, he was closing up the house and he came out with a pint of water and he said, 'Who wants the last drink from the house?' and I was the only one who took the drink. But I turned around and I watched the house as we drove away down the road and watched it until we turned and until it disappeared out of view.

Christina's description of her dad bringing out the glass of water is a powerful and moving vignette. Because of the clandestine nature of her family's departure from Whiteabbey, Christina interpreted her dad's actions as a gesture to signify the enormity of the moment but doing so in a very quiet and everyday way. The moment of departure for Christina is as significant for her as it is for those who fled burning homes and streets. Moreover, the passage of more than 45 years has not diminished the memory and the meaning of her family's departure. When thinking about displacement during the Troubles, the images most immediately conjured are those of burning streets and rows of gutted houses. While this was clearly the case for many, Christina's experience like many others was more akin to a silent movement, the consequence of a slow grind consisting of years of subtle forms of sectarianism and intimidation. Notwithstanding the plurality of displacement experiences among respondents, the common thread linking each testimony are memories and stories drenched in sadness and loss, which, for many, remains unresolved and unrecognised.

A 2010 study by the Northern Ireland Statistics and Research Agency concluded that about 500,000 (out of a population of 1.75 million) have been 'affected by the Troubles', while other studies suggest that there are approximately 34,000 people in Northern Ireland with post-traumatic stress disorder (PTSD) (Ferry et al. 2011, 2017). Aggregating these studies has led David Bolton to concur that more than 200,000 people have been 'bereaved' by the Troubles in some way, concluding that an estimated 8.8 per cent of the Northern Ireland adult population met the criteria for PTSD at some point in their life. Trauma typically refers to the psychological impact of some violent or otherwise shocking event, producing deep-rooted effects that overwhelm the individual, making it difficult to process and come to terms with (Dawson 2007, 2017). Post-traumatic stress disorder (PTSD) can manifest in multiple forms of physical and psychological distress; while the 'event' may have occurred in the past, its effects may be long-term, and manifest in multiple and contrasting ways. Trauma recurs in conflict-ridden societies in various ways, but always involves concerns over loss, grievance, culpability, and complicity in the hurts and injustices caused by terror and political violence in the past (McGrattan 2016). Victims may deal with the enormity of the event by experiencing partial or full amnesia, or in other words, developing a fragmented memory. Trauma is typically defined and interpreted as a response to an event out of the range of ordinary human experience, generating feelings of helplessness and fear (Dawson 2017), and therefore does not manifest in the actual event, but in the ways the mind processes and memorises these events in later times. Dawson's (2007) development of the concept 'traumatized community' draws upon three key proposals regarding past violence: first, a sense of profound suffering has been inflicted on and endured by a community; second, the persistence into the present of a harmful social past with disturbing legacies; and third, a relation of memory whereby the suffering of the past is remembered, often incompletely, by a community or alternatively forgotten or rendered invisible. Notwithstanding the shockingly high levels of persons affected by the conflict, Mary O'Rawe (2003) suggests that the 'true extent and impact of victimhood is not currently apparent. We are only touching the surface in many ways.' The testimonies of those forcibly displaced certainly resonate with O'Rawe's contention and demonstrate the need for a broader conceptualisation of victimhood, trauma, and harm.

Despite the passage of time and physical changes to the landscape, there remains deep-seated feelings of loss and grievance. While the meanings and understandings associated with displacement memories can and do change across time, nevertheless, testimonies here indicate that experiences of displacement have taken on increased significance in the years since the ending of the Troubles. As Marian Kane stated, 'at the time you can't really fathom it and you just get on and forget about things'. Avoidance and distraction are considered short-term protective devices during the initial stages of trauma exposure to enable people to get on with basic survival tasks such as fleeing (Puvimanasinghe et al. 2015). Moreover, much of the larger incidents of displacement occurred in the early to mid-1970s, a time when the conflict in Northern Ireland was at its most intense. Many of the communities affected by displacement were also those that disproportionately suffered the worst incidents of violence throughout the Troubles. Several research participants stated that the intensity of the conflict precluded any space for reflection. As many respondents recalled, there were daily bombings, shootings, arrests, and funeral after funeral, and so there was no time or space for reflection. And yet most respondents stated that the memories of their displacement have become more persistent and have taken on more importance in the years of the peace process. Patricia McGuigans's family were displaced from their home in the Oldpark area of Belfast on three separate occasions. She contends that there was little reflection on the impact of these and other subsequent violent incidents. It is only in the last few years that the trauma of what she and her family experienced has begun to manifest:

> I don't like watching anything about the Troubles or really talk about it. I ended up with health problems from it all … to think of us as kids going through all of that and it was supposed to just wash over your head and a thing like, 'well that's the way it is' … part of everyday life. But then when you get older, it starts to have a real effect. So, I am now going through counselling because it is all only starting to hit me now. So, like you might 'move on' on the outside, but inside there's still … [pause] … like my counsellor told me that I have retained all of this in my nervous system and it only eases by talking about it. And it's an ongoing battle.

Although Christina Bennett stated that she has been affected by her family's displacement all her life, it was only in adulthood and when she had children of her own that she began to really confront the trauma of her experiences a young child:

> I had a great fear of going back to Whiteabbey later on in adult life; I would have bad dreams. I remember when my first child was born, I would bring her on the back of my bike and one night I dreamt I was back on the Doagh Road close to Rathfern and I was on my bicycle and I was worried that I would sound Southern up there, and then I didn't know how to get my way out of there, so in my dream, I cycled towards the Doagh Road and make my way to Belfast and find the Falls Road where my husband is from. We took the kids up in the early 2000s to Belfast and they asked, 'When are we going to see your house, Mum?' and this is where it all started to come back for me, and I said, 'No we can't go there' and they said, 'Why not?' and I really didn't know what to say to them but I just said, 'We can't' and then my [artistic] work after that was trying to deal with that and then I found my house on Google street view and that was a bit of closure for me because I was able to walk, virtually, around that whole block.

The experiences and memories outlined here are embedded in a wider literature that challenges the notion that trauma and harm is something that improves over time. Increasingly there is an understanding that memories of conflict-related violence do not have a pre-determined endpoint; in fact, what we are talking about is human loss, hurt, broken relationships, and these emotions and experiences will undoubtedly shift across time and space but the emotions and experiences do not come to an end, irrespective of the process or mechanism. All too often, glib phrases such as 'closure', 'dealing with the past', and 'moving on' assume a self-evident and measurable endpoint.

Many people in this research were displaced more than 50 years ago and have long since resettled in various parts of Northern Ireland, the Republic of Ireland, and beyond. For many though, there is a lasting and durable sense of loss for home, neighbours, and community that has not mitigated in the intervening decades. Regardless of the spatial and temporal barriers, there seems a collective psyche among many respondents who still feel 'dislocated' in their contemporary social worlds and remain oriented towards their original home and place. For instance, many of those who re-settled in the Republic of Ireland still refer to Belfast, Whiteabbey, or Omagh as their *true* home, despite being resident in towns such as Dundalk and Shannon for well over 45 years. Peter Flannagan describes the contradictions of 'living' in Shannon but not really belonging:

> [T]here was a lot of suspicion of people from the North, especially with Special Branch and the like, but generally the populace was very suspicious and treating you as if you're not really Irish. I've been here close to 40 years and I still maintain my links with Belfast and … I love Ireland and I would not move anywhere else, but I love Belfast and I love Shannon but to be honest I'm not sure I'd call it [Shannon] home.

Our research with Protestants forced from their homes in Londonderry also indicate that although they have rebuilt their lives in places like Newbuildings and other parts of the city and further afield, all spoke of their original home in Londonderry as their true home. For some, that sense of loss is exacerbated by the collective sense of 'retreat', a phrase that is ubiquitous across the interviews in that city. For many Protestants, the city of Derry is of significant historical and symbolic value in unionist culture. For Jonathan, 'nobody talked about it because there is a good deal of shame attached to it, that they had run away; people felt that they ran away and there was a deal of shame attached that. And then people were told that it never happened.' 'Phyllis' also stated that although her husband died recently

> his death was listed as 'formerly of' and he lived in Newbuildings for 40 years but even then, you still had formerly of Creggan Hill. If you look at the Protestant deaths listed you'll see 'formerly of' as their address and you just think those people never really got over losing their house.

The loss of a community and a home was particularly felt by parents who interpreted it as the loss of dignity, self-worth, a sense of shame, and as an abject failure by them to 'protect' the family home and the safety of their children. For some respondents, the effect on their parents was immediate and lasted until their final days; for others the impact and effects only began to manifest in the subsequent years. After leaving the family home in Londonderry city, which had been in the family for generations, Victor Wray recalled the effect it had on his parents:

> At the end of the day my mother and father did not want to move but for their own safety they had to and then the house was up for sale and it was up for sale for I don't know how long but nobody put a bid on the house. And the house was worth £15,000 and I think she got £5,000. But my mother only lasted six years after that; she died six years after that and certainly part of it was that she missed the area; she missed the area she grew up in.

Victor's father died a short time after his wife and Victor is adamant that the loss of the family home, which had been in the family for genera-tions, was a significant factor in the untimely deaths of his parents. Many participants in other parts of Northern Ireland and beyond also recounted how the loss of the family home damaged their parents emotionally and psychologically. Maureen Collins (née Dugan) and her parents were forced from their Manor Street home in North Belfast in 1971, leading to a sequence of temporary forms of accommodation, including staying with relatives and living in provisional refuge shelter while her father searched for a new home. Maureen's father died suddenly of a heart attack six months after securing a new home on the Glen Road in West Belfast. With no history of ill-health, Maureen's family are sure that the stress of the previous two years of intermittent displacement and, ultimately, the loss of the family was the cause of his untimely death, aged just 50 years old. Martin McAleese and his family were displaced by loyalists in August 1971 from their Ballymacarrett home in East Belfast. The loss of their home exerted significant strain on his parents' health and well-being:

> They never talked about it but I do know that the things that most affected my mother was the pictures of us when we were kids, and she also had this tea set thing, like a China tea set, maybe a wedding present, that were never used and just kept in a cabinet and they were taken and she never ever got over that. She was never the same ever again and she died very young, in her early 60s.

Kate Rankin (née Hefferon) and her family were forced from their Ardoyne home on 10 August 1971, and hastily rehoused in a disused flat in the Glencairn estate. Although a relatively short distance from their exiled home in Ardoyne, Kate's parents never got over the loss not only of their family home but also their social networks and affinity and attachment to that part of the city. Kate and her family endeavoured for years with the Northern Ireland Housing Executive to rehouse their parents closer to their original home. Although Kate's father sadly passed away before they could fulfil their wishes, Kate's mum was allocated a new home in the Ballysillan area in 1985, which is in proximity to their original home, which according to Kate and her husband Raymond, brought immense joy and relief to her mum, despite the passage of almost 14 years. However, Kate's mum heartbreakingly died just a month after moving to her new home in North Belfast.

'Robert's' family were part of a small group of Protestants living close to the mainly Catholic New Lodge area of North Belfast. In the immediate aftermath of the inter-communal violence over the course of 12 to 15 August 1969, 'Robert's' family and all other Protestant families left after their homes came under attack. They initially went to stay with Robert's grandparents, assuming the violence would end quickly, and the family would return to their home shortly. When it became apparent that a return by the family was not feasible due to the increasing violence and intimidation by local nationalists and republicans, Robert accompanied his dad and some uncles to retrieve as much furniture and personal belongings as possible.

> We lost our home, [and] my father was never the same again. After that, he was not the same man that he was beforehand, and until the day he died, I never saw that man, that same man ever again. And until the day my father died, he lived until he was 72, and until the day my father died, he never spoke about it, ever.

Charlie Toner described the impact that the loss of the family home and business in Ardoyne in August 1969 had on his parents: 'that nearly broke my mother's heart because she had built up a lovely home. We lost things that could never be replaced, like family photographs and wee things that makes a house a home ... we found out on the news the next morning that our house has been burnt out. My father was just broken after that. It was the first time I ever saw him cry. My mother took it very badly too and we had to get a doctor for her. I don't think she ever really got over it. Everything they had built up was wiped out in a couple of days of madness' (Ardoyne Commemoration Project 2002: 21). Sharon O'Connor recalled the devastation felt by her father in the aftermath of losing their Ardoyne home. According to Sharon, 'he lost everything he had worked for', having a massive impact on all their lives, so much so that her father considered moving to South Africa. Sharon's father died when he was 56 years of age, and she contends that 'he is a victim of the Troubles. I have no doubt about that. He is dead because of all the pressure and tension, losing everything. That is what killed him, without a shadow of doubt' (McKee 2020: 122). There is a general but discernible gender pattern throughout the narratives recounted in this book. In many instances it was women and children who were evacuated while 'the men' were expected to stay behind to defend and protect their respective areas. Feminist scholars have long drawn attention to the ways in which gendered role distinctions function through the use of the gendered dichotomy of 'male protector/ female protected' (Enloe 2014; Tickner 1992) and many respondents spoke of the differential impact the loss of the family home had on their parents. For many male parents, the loss of home was interpreted as a failure of their primary role and duty to protect family and home, thus engendering feelings of emasculation, inefficacy, resentment, and loss of status. While not seeking to diminish the importance of home and place in the urban setting, for those in rural settings, displacement or mutual arbitration had greater significance and consequence where historical ties between ethnic identity, kinship, and place were strong, particularly among Protestants close to the border (Donnan 2005). Among rural farmers, displacement had three major implications: first, the loss of a home (often a multi-generation household); second, the loss of livelihood and income; and finally, the loss of lineage to a homestead going back generations. Leslie Long lived with his family on their farm in Garrison, County Fermanagh. After the IRA killing of Johnny Fletcher in 1972 and after receiving warnings from the police that their farm was being actively targeted by the IRA, the family were forced from their home and farm. Leslie described the anguish and tears of his parents as they watched the last of their cattle being loaded onto the trucks, sold on shortly before the family fled the farm to relocate in Enniskillen. Leslie stated that the loss of the home, the farm, and their livelihood had a devastating impact on his parents' health and well-being. According to Leslie, they never got over it. Furthermore, the grievance of forced movement was bound up in a collective consciousness regarding the increasing patterns of communal exodus and the loss of territory. For some interviewees, it was the implications of the latter that caused much anguish and often resistance to flee. The forced abandonment of farms among Protestants represented a 'personal' tragedy for all involved but was also interpreted as a wider socio-political issue, with a distinct fear of being 'bought out' or 'bred out' (Donnan 2005).

According to Priscilla Hayner (2001), many survivors of political violence suffer psychological and emotional trauma for years. Some are remarkably resilient; forced by the necessity of daily survival, they effectively suppress their memories and continue to function day to day. Many others, however, are not so lucky and suffer from the memory of violence and loss. Darby and Morris's research with displaced families found that many family doctors were prescribing various tranquillisers and anti-depressants to those forced from their homes. Their research indicates high levels of 'reactive depression' from displacement experiences with symptoms including insomnia, less interest in everyday activities, loss of appetite, energy, and weight, and decreased libido (1974: 80). While recognising the diversity of displacement experiences, most testimonies were replete with accounts regarding the immense adverse impact displacement and the loss of a home had on their parents. The many instances of 'scorched earth' destruction of houses by those departing can be interpreted as an attempt by those forced to flee to exercise agency or some control in this situation while clearly providing an expressive outlet for the anger, loss, and resentment.

In addition to the immense loss of homes, neighbours, and communities, forced movement also brought other forms of dislocation via ruptured access to resources, education, work, social and familial networks, status, and of course their sense of identity and belonging. The concept of ontological security draws upon the idea of continuity and levels of certainty and predictability in the lives, identities, and social knowledge of individuals and collectives, based on a taken-for-granted knowledge of what to expect and how to 'be' in the world (Giddens 1991).[2] While Giddens's original concept did not have displacement in mind, the idea has been adopted and refashioned by scholars of refugees and conflict into the more pertinent 'ontological insecurity', asking critical questions regarding peace, security, and humanitarian assistance. According to Healey (2006), forced movement disturbs an individual's ontological security, that being a person's understanding of their place within their worldview and with which they feel comfortable, through the loss of relative stability in their known world. Many respondents were urban dwellers and always had been; in the aftermath of displacement they now found themselves relocated to villages and areas that were essentially rural and, in many instances, vastly underdeveloped. While exile was essentially a necessity to escape insecurity and vulnerability, resettlement brought new forms of isolation and vulnerability. Phyllis and her young family were forced from their homes in the Rosemount area of Londonderry and were re-housed in a small village called Newbuildings, some seven miles outside the city.

> It was my husband's home, he was born and reared there. Prior to 1968 it was a good place to live because you're not in the city centre but you are in walking distance; your school was local, your church, your butchers, buses, everything on hand and there were no problems in the area. Then we were heading [displaced] for Newbuildings and while the houses were ready for occupation, there was no roads, there's no infrastructure, no streetlights. You're out in the country area so no shops. I think there was one post office but you had to go wherever you are sent, and I never got over it; people took that to the graves with them.

For those who were parents and adults at the time of displacement such as Phyllis, the relocation and rehousing experience was a mixture of relief tempered by the precarious nature of post-displacement life. The impact therefore went beyond the immediate loss of home and possessions; in all cases, it led to the disruption of social networks and structures that form the foundations of ontological security. These experiences reveal a dissonance between the idea that resettlement brings safety and security and the reality that, for many, the years of post-displacement were marked by new forms of insecurity and precariousness as many found themselves and their families living in unfamiliar housing developments and communities. Many spoke of losing jobs or being forced to terminate employment due to their movement. At a time when means of communication were rudimentary, many lost contacts with friends and neighbours permanently. Other issues such as the practicalities of grocery shopping, education, and attending church also presented many new challenges. This was particularly evident among those who moved from urban to rural settings and of course for those who resettled in a different jurisdiction. Christina recalled that after settling in Shannon, her mother 'hated it; didn't like the shops, hated what was on television, could not get used to the money'. As detailed in Chapter Three, many re-settled people were treated as outsiders or with suspicion, with many respondents still contending that the home they were forced from remained their true home, despite the passage of more than 50 years in some instances. These accounts detail the rupture in predictability and reflects the challenges they faced in new environments, which undoubtedly brought immediate safety and refuge but, in many instances, also presented new forms of isolation, anxiety, and uncertainty.

Processes of 'home-making' by those who voluntarily or involuntarily left their homes, involves much more than the materiality of a new house or dwelling; invariably, it invokes important processes of belonging, attachment, and security, which eluded and vexed many interviewees despite that passage of time and resettlement in new homes and communities. Giddens's and Laing's idea of ontological security pivots on the notion that individuals and groups negotiate and address social risks, anxieties, and insecurities by seeking stable anchors such as daily practices, routines, and familiarity that essentially constitute our biographies. These practices, when successful, reify our identity and bracket out existential questions. Routines – the repetition of behaviours, physical, and social practices – are necessarily spatially situated within our familiar environments and frequently associated with the notion of 'home'. Forced movement therefore entails more than the material loss of home and possessions; the acute obliteration of an established way of 'being' in the social world furnished a visceral sense of liminality, where 'one finds oneself cut off from the past, unsettled in the present, and unsure of the future' (Ghorashi 2005). 'Jenny' and her family were displaced on many occasions in the 1970s and 1980s due to IRA threats and attacks against her father and the family home. The constant movement impacted their lives greatly on each occasion, but it also left a legacy of dislocation and 'uprootedness':

When people say to me and my husband, 'Oh where are youse from?' and my husband is from [named place] and then I always have to stop and think, 'Well I'm not really sure where I'm from' ... it's quite sad, you know [Jenny is upset; pause in interview]. I just think it is quite sad and I don't know why because I have lived in [named town] almost all my life but I don't feel I am from there. And I was just thinking about it this morning, there's something displaced there; what is it that makes me feel that I don't belong to any of these places? I have lived in [named place] for over 15 years and yet why do I not feel I'm from there and that's part of this displacement because you need to be from somewhere, so I don't really understand it and it is just part of being displaced that you don't attach yourself to particular places but I just can't get a handle on this.

While the idea of an automatic or 'natural' link between people and place has been questioned, the process of persons being forced to leave the geographical location they have called home may actually solidify the idea of home as a tangible physical place. While an individual or group may believe that their relationship to the physical space that surrounds them is singular, places are more accurately seen as cultural processes, acquiring and changing meaning over time as a result of the social activity that occurs within them (Taylor 2015). The contribution of the idea of 'spatial homes' broadens understandings of loss beyond the materiality of cherished homes, furniture, and other possessions, and signifies an expansive sense of dislocation invoked by an uprootedness from a lost place and community. Memories, descriptions, and meanings of 'home' consistently extended far beyond the physical house; the most striking aspect of interviewees' accounts was, respectfully, their banality and simplicity. Most described 'home' via the daily routines and practices revolving around social life. Invariably, this entailed narrating memories of going to shops, work, schools, dances, sports and recreation, religious and cultural events, running errands, visiting relatives – in addition, for rural participants, their narratives outlined daily tasks related to farming. The meaning and attachment to 'home' is therefore not a given but ascribed through the repetition of daily practices (Taylor 2015). In any migration process, forced or voluntary, making sense of 'home' invariably involves a range of ways of remembering and even tentatively reproducing 'home' no matter how physically remote they are (Boccagni 2014). Among interviewees, feelings of dislocation and biographical uncertainty in the months and years after displacement undoubtedly shaped memories of place and meanings of home and belonging. For many interviewees, the notion of 'home' was constituted via memories and attachments to physical places and particular geographical locations such as streets or defined communities. The emotional attachment to home and sense of loss and dislocation is undoubtedly shaped by the context of departure, which for most interviewees was one of necessity rather than volition. The primacy of being forced from their home continues to engender a profound sense of injustice. The thoughts and perspectives of Mary McAleese regarding the post-displacement dislocation are a powerful expression of the enduring sadness, loss, and injustice:

> But the downstream consequences for us now was all sorts of disloca-tions for us. The tight community that we had, the aunts, the uncles, the cousins, that was all gone. The businesses that I mentioned, all gone, all closed. Family all scattered, friends all scattered, friends that I never set eyes on again because we never knew where each other went to. I don't feel that way [emotional or personal attachment] about Belfast; I still feel dislocated; I still feel like I still don't have a home. We made a home here [current home] and we made a home in Dublin, but I still feel that we have been robbed of something. Many people have a great love of the place they were born and a great affection for it and can't wait to go back to it and that they feel a real sense of belonging and a sense of peace and a sense of return. I don't feel that. When I go up the Crumlin Road, I feel nervous, I feel frightened; it all comes back. I feel uncomfortable and I feel that the life that we had was disrupted so quickly. I just feel a great sense of loss. It's a place I can't trust and I don't trust, and I just feel a great sense of loss. It's a place that betrayed us, took away our childhood, took away our right to a childhood, took away our home, never said sorry, never acknowledged the awfulness and the reality of it but in fact did the opposite in 'just move on', so it's a place for me of great mistrust and I think that is a real loss there, a real loss.

While the narratives and accounts of respondents are enmeshed with feelings and memories of 'powerlessness' and a lack of control over what had happened to them and their families, there is also evidence of anger and resentment that this was something that had been forced upon them. Unlike other displacement situations such as those in Chile or Palestine, in the case of Northern Ireland there is no prospect and no great demands for a return of those displaced and exiled to their original homes. The geopolitics of segregation in large parts of Northern Ireland remains as significant today as it did 50 years ago and so the same concerns regarding safety, fear, and vulnerability are omnipresent despite the last 25 years of the peace process. Many respondents expressed fear and unease about even visiting their old homes and communities. Nevertheless, there are many instances of symbolic and virtual forms of return among research partici-pants, indicating the strong levels of attachments and bonds to their original homes and communities. Our research indicates a visceral and emotional dissonance between memories and/or desire to revisit their original homes and a pragmatic and often doleful acceptance that they will never return to those places. As already described above by Christina, all research partic-ipants have re-visited their original homes, either physically, if possible, or through the medium of Google Street View or Google Satellite. Jeanette

who still travels to the West Bank in Londonderry every day for work states
that 'to this day, I still wander back to those streets'. Even after the passage
of 45 years, Jeanette says she cannot 'get that house out of my head'. Most
respondents stated that the memories of their displacement have become
more persistent and have taken on more importance in the years since the
signing of the peace process, describing an array of psychological harms
over the intervening decades, including anger, resentment, nightmares,
isolation, vulnerability, and, in some instances, feelings of shame and guilt
for leaving.

All of this, we suggest, shows that, for many, the experiences of losing
their homes and forced exile caused significant and enduring suffering,
and therefore should be recognised as a form of conflict-related harm and
victimhood in the context of endeavours to deal with and address the
legacy of armed conflict in Northern Ireland. Though there were differences among participants as to whether they 'qualified' as victims, all were
united in their belief that their suffering and loss has not been recognised
by the state and wider society. The violence of the Troubles has typically
been measured using standardised assessments (for example, number of
deaths, injuries, economic impact) with much of the transitional focus,
understandably, centring on the needs and interests of those who lost loved
ones or those physically and psychologically harmed through shootings and
bombings. Imposing a reductive framework that 'measures' violence solely
by limited and crude forms such as body counts, injuries, and other forms
of physical harms is of course wholly contingent upon the trivialisation and
concealment of multiple forms of violence and insecurity situated outside
the boundaries of seemingly orthodox understandings of violence and
harm. If we accept that conflict-related displacement constitutes a form of
harm and loss, it therefore begs the question: should those forcibly displaced
during the Troubles be considered victims?

The Contested Politics of Victimhood

A central feature of the problem in dealing with legacy of conflict in
Northern Ireland concerns victims and victimhood. The designation of
'innocent victimhood' serves a two-fold purpose; it not only denotes
certain forms of harm as being illegitimate and unjust, but is also a means
of apportioning blame for past violence (McEvoy and McConnachie 2012).
In terms of depictions and symbolism, the idea of 'victim' has historically acted as a powerful totemic symbol of the destruction, misery,
and suffering of war. For some, victims become the 'moral beacons'
(Brewer and Hayes 2011), displaying resilience and strength, providing
models of restraint for the rest of society to aspire to. This reified victim,
or what Bouris (2007) termed as 'ideal victims', are assumed to hold
essentialist qualities and often unidimensional characteristics such as

blamelessness, non-involvement in acts of violence, a lack of agency, apolitical standpoints, and being persons who are in need of assistance. Such reductive assumptions fit neatly within orthodox conventions and typically find expression in the over-simplistic dichotomy of 'victim–perpetrator' (Bouris 2007; Brewer 2018; Jankowitz 2018). In conceptual terms, the construction of victims and victimhood are embedded within a moral and political framework, where conventional tropes of 'innocence' and 'guilt' are central to constituting the ideal victim identity. Placed at the apex of a hierarchy of victims (McEvoy and McConnachie 2012), the reification of the 'innocent victim' therefore becomes the benchmark or reference point in which all other persons affected by political violence are measured and stratified.

A fundamental problem with the notion of a truly 'innocent victim' is that it overlooks the fluidity of social identities and, moreover, assumes that identities and experiences of armed conflict are linear, fixed, self-evident, and unproblematic. There is now a relatively sizable volume of literature considering the idea that persons can be both victims and perpetrators (Borer 2003). While those of a nationalist and republican background in Northern Ireland advocate for a broad definition, unionist parties and victims groups with unionist links have endeavoured to promote a strict definition using terms such as 'real' or 'innocent' victims as a way of distinguishing those killed by terrorist organisations (Hayes and McAllister 2013). In their comprehensive study with a range of actors, Ferguson et al. (2010) found that some people felt victimised enough to become involved in a violent armed campaign. In the same research, others argued that such persons who chose to engage in armed violence were not 'real victims' in the same moral and political sense as those who were completely uninvolved in any part of the conflict. Reflecting this hierarchy of victimhood are ideas of 'deserving' and 'undeserving' victims. In other words, there is an acknowledgement among some that members of paramilitaries and the security forces may be deemed a type or a 'class of victims' (Ferguson, Burgess, and Hollywood 2010). In the context of Northern Ireland, many interpret paramilitary claims for victimhood status as attempts to justify and legitimise their violent actions. While such rejections operate within a particular ethical and moral framework, research with former combatants, however, reveals that their exposure to incidents of violence, such as violent attacks, house searches, loss of family members and/friends, and state brutality shaped their decisions to join armed organisations (Ferguson, Burgess, and Hollywood 2010; McEvoy and McConnachie 2012; Gilmartin 2019; Shirlow and McEvoy 2008; White 2017). While population surveys indicate degrees of empathy and (at the very least) a partial acceptance among the general population that perpetrators of violence were products of an abnormal society, many insist on a hierarchy of victims, with perpetrators perceived as 'lesser victims', if victims at all (Ferguson, Burgess, and Hollywood 2010). While academic explorations of victimhood may seem abstract, even tangential, ultimately, defining victims and victimhood has material consequences in terms of recognition, funding, consultation, and of course, compensation. Moreover, in Northern Ireland, the post-Troubles battle over victimhood is embedded in a wider, adversarial framework whereby definitions of victim identity are ultimately vehicles for advancing particular narrative constructions for apportioning culpability for the 30 years of violence.

As a conflict with no clear victor, there are multiple and competing perspectives regarding blame and liability for the violence, with all sides claiming some degree of victimhood as justification for their role in the conflict. The 1998 GFA contained no provisions for victims' rights or definitive mechanisms for truth recovery, with victims mentioned in only two paragraphs. Furthermore, not only did the GFA not put in place any mechanisms for victims, it also failed to define the term 'victim'. The consequences of this omittance (deliberate or not) have reverberated over the last 20 years with real-world consequences and impacts for those who continue to live with the harms of the Troubles – a distinct 'constructive ambiguity' that was the driving force behind the peace accord, thus deliberately eschewing the potentially destabilising and virulent topic of victims and legacy. As one of the first state-led engagements with legacy, Kenneth Bloomfield's 1998 report *We Will Remember Them* furnished a dominant interpretation of victims in Northern Ireland as 'the surviving injured and those who care for them, together with those close relatives who mourn their dead' (14), with a notable balance tipped well in favour of those killed by non-state groups. Perhaps aware of the political and moral maze he now found himself immersed in, Bloomfield subsequently suggested in the report that perhaps all citizens of Northern Ireland could be considered victims. Such a claim, however, needs to be significantly refined given that the violence of the Troubles was dispersed unevenly across the Six Counties. Even in a city like Belfast with an overall high concentration of violence, conflict-related deaths mapped almost identically onto patterns of affluence and socio-economic disadvantage. While the average conflict-related death in Northern Ireland was 2.2 per 1,000, in Ardoyne it was five times that figure (Smyth 2007).

In light of Bloomfield's generalised label, and in absence of a clear definition within the GFA, The Victims and Survivors (Northern Ireland) Order 2006 sought to provide a comprehensive and workable definition of a victim. It defined a victim and survivor of the Troubles as an individual appearing to be any of the following:

(a) someone who is or has been physically or psychologically injured as a result of or in consequence of a conflict-related incident;
(b) someone who provides a substantial amount of care on a regular basis for an individual mentioned in paragraph (a); or

(c) someone who has been bereaved as a result of or in consequence of a conflict-related incident.

(2) Without prejudice to the generality of paragraph (1), an individual may be psychologically injured as a result of or in consequence of –

(a) witnessing a conflict-related incident or the consequences of such an incident; or

(b) providing medical or other emergency assistance to an individual in connection with a conflict-related incident.

While republicans and many nationalists favour such a broad definition, unionists have understandably criticised it as leaving the door ajar for 'former terrorists' to be classified as 'victims', and there have been several attempts to introduce legislation that disqualifies anyone convicted of criminal conflict-related violence from the definition outlined in the 2006 Order. The 2006 broad definition has engendered anxiety among some who believe such an expansion undermines victim identity by tarnishing it with the inclusion (or potential inclusion) of those deemed as perpetrators (Graham 2016). Essentially, the argument against such a wide-ranging definition is that protagonists, loyalist or republican, had a choice to commit violent actions or not; 'innocent' victims did not.

The category of victim and the wider contested politics of victimhood are constituted by a series of competing post-Troubles narratives that seek validation by constructing a hierarchy of victims. The boundary construction around the 'innocent victim' is instrumental in delegitimising the violence enacted by the 'other'. Moreover, the designation of the 'perpetrator' solely as a 'terrorist' seeks to make a distinct classification between 'violence' and 'war'. The separating of 'war and violence' and that of state forces and non-state paramilitaries is to also designate the violence of the Troubles as illegal, illegitimate, unjustified, and, hence, criminality. As Shirlow argues, 'the extreme performances of selective truth claiming that subjugates other harms is at times founded upon an assertion that one form of violence was legitimate. Any such normalisation of violence aims for an essentialist form that purposefully subverts an inter-community logic of societal restoration' (2018: 424). To understand the complex issue of 'victim' is to unpack the competing narratives about the past and the contemporary relations of power between unionism and nationalism, which ultimately function as 'gate-keepers' to the identity of victims and the right to claim oneself as such. Moreover, the idea of a victim in Northern Ireland is a form of communicative practice, centrally constituted by relations of antagonisms vying to legitimise and delegitimise selective truths.

Mapping competing understandings of victimhood onto the diverse lives of those displaced demonstrates the complexity and emotiveness that underpin the contested politics of victimhood in Northern Ireland. As we saw in the last chapter, experiences and fears of displacement were central to the emergence and growth of many non-state military actors in the conflict. Moreover, some of those displaced went on to support and/or joined some of these groups, therefore complicating the idea of a mutually exclusive victim/perpetrator dichotomy. Though these tensions and antagonisms regarding victimhood were present in our research, there was, however, a broad consensus that those forcibly displaced should be considered victims of the Troubles. Significant sections of research respondents from both communities contended that as persons directly affected by a form of violence, intimidation, and fear, they certainly consti-tuted 'victims' or a form of victimhood. In some instances, victimhood was described as something shared by all those displaced, irrespective of their background. Unsurprisingly, however, the labelling and denial of victimhood was often embedded in narratives that sought to cast the 'other' community as the aggressor and perpetrator. Additionally, a common caveat among many was to qualify that their displacement victimhood is qualitatively and morally different to those killed in bombings or gun attacks, but their experiences qualified them as victims nonetheless. Michael from Ardoyne was evacuated and sent across the border on at least two occasions in the early 1970s and he expressed his view that 'people are scarred but I don't think our scars as people evacuated are the same as those who were killed, or injured; [but] it's on the same spectrum and it should be there on the spectrum'. Hugh Ferrin was displaced from the Bone district of North Belfast:

> In certain respects I could be considered a victim. I don't know if I'm comfortable with the term; it's a loaded term and it's become a loaded term here but certainly I suffered from the Troubles. I mean there are areas barely touched by the conflict; our daily experience was conflict; there was trauma most of the time, especially in our area. So undoubtedly refugees suffered trauma; undoubtedly they were victims and undoubtedly it pushed people in directions they would have never gone down, on both sides.

The malleable and changing memories, meanings, and understandings associated with experiences of displacement also exerted a discernible impact on interpretations of harm, loss, and victimhood. Patricia McGuigan outlines how her interpretations of victimhood have changed in the inter-vening decades:

> I wouldn't have considered my myself a victim a few years back but the more realisation of what you've been through, you are a victim, but I don't like to feel like that, I like to think, that's just what happened. Because I like to think of myself as a stronger person who wouldn't want those things to impact on my life and that could be a problem with my health, like a barrier, maybe denial about things that happened. I think if you lived in any of these areas ... there were areas in the North

that were not impacted in any way but if you lived in places like we lived [Oldpark, Belfast], everyone was a victim; people seeing people murdered, you were a victim when your house was wrecked or searched or stopped by the army ... everyone was a victim.

The conflation of victimhood with popular perceptions of 'weakness', 'helplessness', and 'passiveness' highlights levels of resistance for some who had previously refuted any suggestion that their lives and experiences constituted the status of victims. As stated earlier, there existed some differences in definitions and interpretations of victimhood from members of both communities. A common trend within existing research depicts discernible levels of reticence among the Protestant community to identify as victim or claim victimhood status, with Catholic respondents more willing to state their victim identity. The power and perceptions of victimhood and innocence among Protestants forms a central part in unionist narratives and understandings of the Troubles, which seek to cast the blame and responsibility for the violence squarely with paramilitary perpetrators. 'Robert' was a young man when his family were forced out of their home in the New Lodge area of Belfast. He maintains that the loss of their home changed his father but that said, when asked if he and his family were victims:

I think the answer to that would be no. It happened [but] we all came out of it in one piece; if any of us were injured or killed then yes would be the answer, but at the end of the day it was only a house. I look at it, like that. We all got out safe and we moved on. The only thing that really annoyed me was what happened to my father. But to say traumatised is a modern word; you wouldn't have used that back then, so we just got out of it and got on with it.

Paul Browne, whose family were forced from the Garnerville Road area in outer East Belfast, accepted that the term 'victims' was appropriate, however he qualified the statement by saying, 'But we were lucky victims ... there was hurt, and we suffered a lot, in particular my mother and father, they really suffered, but no-one was killed, so we were lucky victims in this sense.' Terry Wright was a prominent member of the Ulster Unionist Party in Londonderry in the late 1960s and throughout most of the Troubles. Although also offering some caveats, essentially Terry sees Derry's Protestant community on the city's West Bank as victims:

Well victim is a word that is played around with politically but yes I think they are, they are. I tend to believe as a community, on many levels, we are a traumatised community and so many of us are carrying around baggage. Obviously those who have died or experienced physical violence or lost a loved one to physical violence. But if you're living in a house on the Foyle Road and you come out and find 'IRA' scratched on your front door or you have people shouting threats in your letterbox, then they have to be seen as victims.

The outworkings of these visceral and important debates have real-world consequences. In the Pantheon of war and armed conflict, undoubtedly the displaced refugee is the embodiment of the ideal 'victim' of war. The boundary maintenance surrounding the reified refugee therefore precludes any suggestion at all that refugees or those displaced could be agents of conflict, either through support or active participation in armed violence. Acknowledgement of a perpetrator's victimhood not only poses ethical and moral dilemmas, politically it can be used to justify and legitimise acts of violence and terrorism. The messy reality of contemporary armed conflicts, particularly protracted conflicts such as Northern Ireland, rarely adheres to ascribed rules of identity and agency. As already alluded to, the role of displacement is central to the constitutive purposes of loyalist and republican armed groups and, moreover, some respondents in this research who suffered and were victimised by displacement, were ultimately politicised by their experiences and did join non-state armed groups. It is often assumed, however, that any deviation from the strict cultural and discursive constructions of the non-political, passive refugee, immediately abrogates all claims to both refugee and by extension victimhood identity.

As subjectively constructed and essentially contested, all definitions of victimhood are value-laden and reflect competing standpoints regarding the source and culpability for the conflict. Therefore, the orthodox idea of a singular victim identity or category is a biased construction, which invariably functions as a process of inclusion and exclusion. The boundary construction of victim and perpetrator are constituted by questions and understanding regarding the blame and culpability for the violent actions (Brewer and Hayes 2011). Constructions of victimhood in Northern Ireland are underpinned through multiple dualisms of approval and disapproval, allegation and counter-allegation, therefore bequeathing subjective and selective forms of truthseeking (Shirlow 2018). While the exact text of one of the most recent attempts to address legacy issues in post-conflict Northern Ireland, the Stormont House Agreement, talks of 'conflict-related violence', victims and victimhood have become vehicles for the advancement of a particular truth, which, by their very nature, are practices of inclusion *and* exclusion. The visceral debates and exchanges regarding 'real victims' remain proxies for broader cultural and discursive battles regarding the 'truth' of Northern Ireland's conflict (Shirlow 2018). Therefore, the very notion of a pluralised category of 'victim' challenges those definitions that place 'victims' outside of armed actions and beyond blame and culpability. The issue came to a head when as part of their recommendations, the Consultative Group on the Past, otherwise known as the Eames–Bradley Report, a civic society led attempt to garner as many insights into how best to manage legacy issues, suggested that a £12,000 payment be made to all victims of the conflict, including non-state combatants (CGPNI 2009). Unionists, among others, reacted with fury to any suggestions or processes that equate 'innocent victims' with terrorists. While the idea that those involved in perpetrating armed violence may also be considered as victims or a 'class of victims' is unfathomable and perhaps incongruent for many, the blanket generalisation that all non-state combatants are terrorists precludes alternative understandings or any explanatory mechanism for their actions during the Troubles. To be sure, we are not suggesting a moral equivalence between a person who has chosen to engage in political violence with someone wholly uninvolved in conflict. We do, however, contend that the idea of neat and mutually exclusive categories as expressed in a victim/perpetrator dichotomy is imprecise and wholly inept for encapsulating the complex reality of contemporary armed conflicts, which are often protracted, involve non-state fighters, and typically blur the lines of combatant and civilian. Analysing such factors complicates the orthodoxies and conventions regarding victim and perpetrators and undermines those who seek to create both categories as mutually exclusive. Additionally, the construction of narratives regarding victimhood are central to the constitutive purposes of those who say they waged war as a 'last option' in the face of oppression and injustice. In other words, a collective sense of victimhood provides the legitimation of those who engaged in political violence who state that their violent actions were simply defending or avenging an existing or historical injustice. The collective deployment of victimhood engenders sympathy and support for political violence and is therefore particularly important for the sustenance of collective grievances over time, such as forced exile.

Sarah Jankowitz (2018) suggests a broader understanding of the variations in hierarchies of victims, outlining a four-fold typology of: moral hierarchies (normative constructions of innocent victims and wicked perpetrators), hierarchies of attention (disproportionate political and media attention); pragmatic hierarchies (severity of physical and psychological injury); and inter-group hierarchies (perceptions of victimhood informed by group identification). In contemporary armed conflicts therefore, there are 'degrees of participation and victimhood' (Brewer and Hayes 2011). Given the passage of more than 25 years since the first republican and loyalist ceasefires, it is unlikely that Northern Ireland will come to a consensus over who and what constitutes a victim of the conflict. While this issue remains a major barrier to progress on legacy, it is perhaps more productive to think in terms of trauma and those who were traumatised by the 30 years of political violence as a method for overcoming the antagonisms at the heart of the 'victimhood' debate.

Notwithstanding the divergence regarding victim status in the voluminous literature generated by the issue, there is a tendency to universalise victims, their needs and experiences, and so it is also important not to reduce victims to homogenous groups or to situate them outside of the identities and allegiances at the heart of the conflict. All too often, conventional approaches tend to situate 'victims' on the sidelines, invariably depicted as voiceless, powerless, and bereft of agency. Though there is a growing appreciation internationally for the inclusion of refugees and those forcibly displaced to be incorporated as active participants in processes of peacebuilding and transitional justice, displacement in Northern Ireland has been virtually absent from academic research, policy endeavours, and the wider public conversation regarding legacy and reconciliation. If we accept that those who suffered forced displacement constitute a category of victims, it therefore invariably invokes the self-evident though no less important questions of how we address the loss and harm of displacement, and, moreover, how we position displaced persons as meaningful actors in the ongoing processes of 'dealing with the legacy of violence' in Northern Ireland.

Conclusion

The visceral sense of being silenced, ignored, or marginalised are the outcomes of reductive discourse and policy outputs that continue to frame loss, suffering, and victimhood solely as those acts associated with conventional forms of physical, armed violence, thus cultivating a hierarchy of harms and victims. Given the state's abject failure to prevent past displacement and, moreover, its continuing failure to address its legacy in the present, any future state-led endeavours to address the legacy of conflict needs to incorporate displacement as a source of harms and should consider some form of symbolic acknowledgement as an important means of recognising the high levels of displacement experienced by its citizens. Public acknowledgement of forced displacement is more than simply being mindful or knowing about past hurts; it is about conferring public recognition on an injustice that was committed in the name of a specific political unit or collective. In doing so, it validates the hurt and suffering of those forcibly uprooted and has the potential to establish new relations and understandings regarding conflict-related harms and their long-term impacts. The eclectic initiatives through which victims and survivors artic- ulate their memories, needs, and perspectives are, of course, anchored in practices and processes that are often confrontational and selective and serve to reinforce the antagonisms and divisions central to the conflict. Despite this, confronting the past, with all its pain and complexity, also holds the potential to create new forms of dialogue and understanding that can lead to re-evaluations and new comprehensions that are truth-seeking in genuinely non-adversarial ways characterised issue of how we recognise and address the impact of displacement in the Northern Ireland conflict that was migrants of violence in Great Britain, the Republic of Ireland,

Notes

and in some instances, mainland Europe throughout the conflict. Indeed, the worst day of the conflict in terms of death toll entailed events that took place south of the Irish border. On 17 May 1974, bombs planted by loyalists in Monaghan and Dublin claimed the lives of 33 civilians. Therefore, while much attention is understandably concentrated on victims in Northern Ireland, it is also important to bear in mind victims in the Republic, Great Britain, and further afield.

2   Ontological security was originally conceptualised in psychoanalytic theory by R. D. Laing (2010 [1960]), although it was further developed sociologically by Anthony Giddens.

Chapter Five

Addressing the Legacy
of Displacement

Introduction

While the right of return of refugees often represents one of the most
contentious aspects of peace settlements, such as the cases of the Dayton
accord dealing with Bosnia and Herzegovina and the much maligned
Palestine–Israel 'negotiations' in the 1990s (in the case of the latter, the
issue can completely derail a nascent peace process) consideration of
those forcibly displaced during the Troubles was completely absent from
the GFA – as noted above – and has not figured prominently in many of
the subsequent endeavours to deal with the legacy of the past (Browne
and Asprooth-Jackson 2019; Gilmartin 2021). As a result, we should
caution against the persistent exaltation of Northern Ireland as a 'model
of conflict resolution' while living in a society imbued with many forms
of unresolved and in this instance, unacknowledged harms. Despite the
tenacious framing of Northern Ireland as a 'post-conflict' society, broader
interpretations of violence and transitional justice paves the way for a
more critical consideration of dealing with the legacy of displacement in
a meaningful and holistic way. As the testimonies in the previous chapter
reveal, the long-term harm and trauma experienced by those who were
forced from their home during the Troubles suggests that those who were
impacted fall within the broader category of victim and/or survivor and
as such should have this recognised.

As a set of judicial and quasi-judicial measures designed to redress the
legacies of massive human rights abuses that occur during conflict, the
sub-discipline of transitional justice has emerged as a means of attempting
to reinstall human rights values and norms that were systematically
violated. Transitional justice aims to provide recognition for victims,
foster civic trust, and strengthen the rule of law through a range of

mechanisms including but not limited to criminal prosecutions, reparations programmes, restitution programmes, truth-telling initiatives, and justice-sensitive security sector reform (Bradley 2012). Throughout its development, the field has been continuously vexed by the pursuit of two seemingly irreconcilable elements – the idea of justice and the idea of change through time – thus posing challenging questions as to whether it is possible to define transitional justice as a form of special justice or if, instead, it has to be regarded as a form of normal justice (Corradetti, Eisikovits, and Rotondi 2015; Teitel 2003). Though initially concerned with the pursuit of individual accountability for human rights violations through criminal and legalistic trials, the aftermath of the Cold War witnessed a discernible shift towards alternative strategies, eschewing criminal trials in favour of a new institutional mechanism – the truth commission, essentially establishing a dichotomy between truth and justice. The departure from retributive forms of justice to the advocacy of issues such as healing, reconciliation, and peace, whereby accountability and justice were reframed as restorative rather that retributive, juxtaposed the pursuit of justice with the task of peacebuilding and reconciliation (Hamber and Lundy 2020). Thus, the pursuit of truth and justice became primarily a vehicle for victims to reconcile and recover from past harms, whereby transitional justice became a dialogue between victim and perpetrator (Teitel 2003).

While one of the principal goals of transitional justice is to avoid a reoccurrence of violence, many also contend that it is a necessary component of sustainable peacebuilding processes in post-conflict societies, particularly in those that remain deeply divided along entrenched lines of religious or ethnonational identity (Aiken 2010). Furthermore, transitional justice approaches are often cited as being 'victim centred' and the importance of victim participation is increasingly recognised as a significant departure in positioning victims as active rather than passive participants (Hamber and Lundy 2020; Kerr and Mobekk 2007). Northern Ireland has become somewhat of a transitional justice laboratory with significant scholarly and practitioner interventions contributing to its burgeoning growth and development. However, as noted before, the prevailing approaches to justice and accountability in Northern Ireland have tended to be embedded in a legalist and positivist understanding (McEvoy 2007; Lundy and McGovern 2008), with justice essentially equated to legal, individual accountability through the medium of juridical practices and processes. Constructions of 'victim–perpetrator' frameworks are premised on individualistic approaches to truth recovery and accountability, while overlooking the fluidity and plurality of social identities and experiences during armed conflict. Whether transitional justice approaches promote retributive forms of justice or reconciliation-based approaches that focus on truth, restoration, and forgiveness, invariably, the focus is often centred on individuals who committed crimes as opposed to widespread, structural harm (ibid.). As we have detailed above, Northern Ireland's peacebuilding processes represent yet another case whereby displaced persons have not been recognised as an important category of victims and survivors, nor have their experiences been acknowledged (Bradley 2012).

The case of displacement in Northern Ireland therefore represents unique challenges for those who are interested in transitional justice approaches to dealing with the past. As is argued in the previous chapter, we argue that first and foremost, those who suffered and survived displacement as a result of political violence constitute a category of victims consistently overlooked and therefore their conflict-related experiences warrant inclusion on the broad spectrum of victimhood and consideration within a reparatory justice framework. Our aim in this chapter is to begin by unpacking the rationale for reparations for those who were forcibly displaced during the Troubles in Northern Ireland, situating the discussion within an extensive body of international transitional justice literature. Next it is to critique the state's response (or lack thereof) in terms of offering compensation and restitution at the time for those who suffered forcible displacement due to actual violence or the threat of violence. In doing so we focus on the emergence of the Scheme for the Purchase of Evacuated Dwellings (SPED) and query the efficacy and suitability of such a scheme, noting how it was considered by some to be bureaucratic, complex, and exclusionary. Finally, we turn to consider the importance of acknowledgement for victims and survivors of forcible displacement as a means of providing symbolic reparation for harm suffered. We note the role of softer, non-judicial transitional justice approaches such as storytelling, art interventions, and theatre, and provide an insight into their reparatory potential in providing some form of acknowledgement for those who experienced forcible displacement.

Many interviewees suggested that they have been able to live 'normal' lives following their moment of rupture, albeit within the context of the enduring abnormality of living throughout the Troubles. However, many others experienced further instances of forcible displacement, struggled with issues relating to loss of labour, family break-up, and on occasion went on to experience the loss of a loved one due to a conflict-related incident. In seeking to address the legacy of the past, and building upon the existing platform for dealing with the past in Northern Ireland, we argue the case for some form of reparations for those who were displaced are better served by way of invoking a public moment of recognition, a symbolic form of reparatory justice – one that gives this form of victimhood appropriate recognition and acknowledgement within the wider discourse on the experiences of victims and survivors in the Northern Ireland conflict.

Theorising Reparations

As a foundational principle of transitional justice, providing reparations for those who have suffered harm during a 'conflict' is often viewed as important for ensuring a successful period of 'post-conflict' transition. Reparations are often conceived as the monetisation of an apology, a fiscal form of recognition that the individual or group harmed by a previous regime are entitled to have this harm acknowledged by the perpetrator, in the language of transitional justice, the incumbent state. The International Center for Transitional Justice (ICTJ) assert that reparations ought to

> [s]erve to acknowledge the legal obligation of a state, or individual(s) or group, to repair the consequences of violations – either because it directly committed them, or it failed to prevent them. They also express to victims and society more generally that the state is committed to addressing the root causes of past violations and ensuring they do not happen again.

That there exists a legal obligation to repair harm caused as a result of state-sponsored violence has been reaffirmed consistently at the highest international level, including by the United Nations General Assembly (UNGA) in its 'Basic Principles and Guidelines on the Right to a Remedy and Reparation for Victims of Gross Violations of International Human Rights Law and Serious Violations of International Humanitarian Law' (UNGA Res 60/147). As our previous chapters have revealed, delineating the actual cause of forcible displacement during the outbreak of the Troubles is challenging, particularly when we note that the experience of direct or actual violence was not the only driver for forcible movement, nor is it possible in many instances to discern who should be held accountable. As a result, understanding what role the state should play when it concerns reparatory justice for forcible displacement is not immediately obvious. Or, in other words, where it is difficult to prove the guilt of one party at the expense of another party's victimhood, the rationale for some form of reparatory justice is less clear. As a result, unpacking what role (if any) the state played in facilitating or failing to prevent the forcible transfer of civilians during the outbreak of the Troubles in Northern Ireland leads to further questions as to how to acknowledge responsibility and repair the harm suffered by individuals.

Across the broad spectrum of our research participants, there was little by way of consensus on what should amount to reparations for those who were forcibly displaced. However, there was a consensus against receiving monetary compensation to recompense for their loss based on a fervently held belief that there were more worthy victims who required support. There was, as we have shown above, an acute sensitivity to the purported hierarchy of victims and conflict-related suffering. However, there was a strongly held view that the stories of displacement and the personal experiences of the families who suffered during this time were worthy of greater acknowledgement among the public at large. 'Official', state acknowledgement and wider public recognition of the harm suffered because of displacement, would help counter a perceived sense of silence that had come to exist around the issue. What form this acknowledgement ought to take was subject to various viewpoints with some suggesting that the most appropriate way to acknowledge the harm suffered would be to log stories of forced movement in some form of public archive to ensure that the stories did not die out as time passed. Other suggestions ranged from film documentaries, exhibitions, and artwork to a possible national day of reflection. Others noted that an appropriate way of repairing the harm would be to ensure that Northern Ireland does all it can to reverse the effects of entrenched segregation and division, one of the unfortunate consequences of the forcible transfer of civilians during the conflict.

Within the field of transitional/post-conflict justice a fulsome body of scholarly research has emerged that considers the role of reparations for victims and survivors of state-sponsored violence, including significant contributions from scholars working in and on post-conflict Northern Ireland. In more recent times the language of reparations has been popularised, moving beyond the preserve of academic and legal discourse, mainstreamed through high-profile published works by scholars and activists in the United States, those committed to addressing social inequalities and combating racial injustice. In his oft-cited essay in *The Atlantic*, academic, activist, and public intellectual Ta Nehishi Coates (2014) presents 'the case for reparations', noting that for those who are descendants of slavery, systemic racism continues to be the defining feature that shapes the inequitable development and maintenance of modern-day America. Although his position has been publicly criticised by fellow public intellectual Cornel West, Coates argues persuasively that without a meaningful engagement with some form of reparatory justice, the United States of America will continue to be plagued by the externalities of severe inequality and segregation. Coates's intervention is important in that, rather than being mythologised or viewed as hypothetical, the language of reparations now enjoys a visible place within public discourse, being elevated to a position of everyday parlance. Pioneering voices in the field of transitional justice whose work has focused on reparations include de Greiff (2006), whose analysis has helped develop its theoretical underpinnings particularly when it comes to assessing how to provide redress when the number of victims of human rights violations is significant. In his highly cited chapter in the *The Handbook of Reparations,* de Grieff (2006) argues against applying a formula of monetary compensation that is in proportion to harm suffered; rather he maintains that reparations programmes established in post-conflict spaces ought to focus on achieving recognition for harm suffered by victims and survivors to generate a greater level of civic trust, and in turn develop social solidarity. As we have outlined in previous chapters, the forcible transfer of civilians during the Troubles in Northern Ireland impacted a vast number of civilians and cut across the sectarian divide. As such, De Grieff's (2006) understanding of reparations as recognition is perhaps an appropriate way of tackling the issue of state-led acknowledgement for victims and survivors.

Laplante (2014) argues that, while traditional practices of transitional justice are rarely victim-oriented, by combining theories of reparative, restorative, civic, and socio-economic justice, reparations programmes can have far-reaching societal implications and help to ensure that an individualised form of justice can flourish. Such an approach mirrors that proposed by de Greiff (2006) above, with Laplante (2014) arguing that the result will be a more equitable outcome for victims and survivors in the long term. Work that has focused on the more traditional legal dilemmas around reparations includes that done by leading transitional justice scholar Naomi Roht-Arriaza (2004) whose analysis attempts to situate a right to remedy and reparation for victims of gross human rights violations within the framework of international humanitarian law. In identifying reparations as the most tangible and visible expression of justice, Roht-Arriaza presents three overlapping 'models' for what might constitute some form of collective, societal reparation for victims and survivors: reparations as development, reparations as community-level acknowledgement and atonement, and reparations as preferential access to services and public goods. Kutz (2004) argues that any reparatory justice programme proposed by new political regimes following the end of a protracted period of conflict will inevitably struggle to generate legitimacy. This, it is argued, is because the shifting of blame on to past regimes will not be enough to meet the needs of victims and survivors in the present day. Acknowledgement of past state failings without any structural change will be toothless and a sustainable reparatory framework must ultimately be forward thinking. This need for reparations programmes to be 'forward thinking' is a view shared by Roht-Arriaza and Orlovsky (2009) who note that reparations programmess ought to create sustainable and long-term change while also taking into account the root causes of conflict in the first instance and attending to victims' and survivors' immediate economic needs. The authors argue that, while reparations programmes cannot replace long-term development strategies, they can create habits of 'trust', therefore helping to foster and develop positive relations between victims and survivors and the state. Wenar (2006) has suggested that valid reparative demands made by victims and survivors ought to be forward-looking to repair historical injustice. The tension between the right of the individual to receive redress, reparation, and restitution versus the greater need for society to move beyond the past is commonplace in many spaces undergoing a period of post-conflict transition. In the context of our present argument, and in noting the sustained legacy of segregation and division that has endured in post-conflict Northern Ireland, any reparations discussion that does not seek to provide long-term solutions to our legacy of residential segregation, we maintain, will be time limited and thus incomplete.

More general critiques of the role of reparations in transitional/post-conflict societies include that offered by Moffett (2017) in which the author provides an overview of the theoretical foundations and logistical implications of reparations as a potential measure of victim-centred transitional justice. Moffett's (2017) fundamental principles of reparation measures, and their potential efficacy for societies transitioning from sustained violence or human rights violations, is a useful introductory framework. Verdeja (2006) points to the crucial role played by reparations in post-conflict as being the ability they possess to help to strengthen public trust in state institutions, particularly those that have caused harm to victims and survivors in the past. Such an aspirational goal of reparatory justice is powerful inasmuch as it helps transitioning states strengthen their commitment to more peaceful, democratic practice and reform. The more technical, legal arguments around reparations and how they might operate in practice are discussed by Ferstman (2017) who provides analysis of the mandates, rules, and procedures, and practice of international criminal courts in relation to reparations. Availing of case-study examples from Cambodia and Lebanon, the author discusses how victims and their representatives access entitlements to reparations, and the legal challenges that have arisen to this practice. Related to the issue of design, Suchkova (2011) draws attention to the crucial need to ensure meaningful involvement of victims and survivors when seeking to design and implement reparations programmes. While focused specifically on developing reparatory practices through the work of the International Criminal Court, the general point regarding victim and survivor input when designing appropriate reparations initiatives is one that the authors consider particularly important when it comes to better acknowledging the harm associated with forcible displacement during the Troubles.

Focusing more on the role of reparations to help foster meaningful reconciliation between victims/survivors and perpetrators, contributions from Adhikari, Hansen, and Powers (2012), Firchow (2017), and Lu (2018) are all particularly useful. Adhikari et al. (2012) argue that although normative explanations of why reparations are granted in the aftermath of regime changes are helpful to understanding the need for reconciliation, these narratives are inadequate for understanding victim demands for compensation. What is particularly important is to understand the impact of loss and the risk factors that led to this loss in the first place, before seeking to develop specific elements of any reparations process. Moon (2012) argues that reparations can function to placate a victim's demands for criminal justice and to effectively regulate the range of political and historical meanings with which the crimes of the past are endowed. Although programmes of reparations by the state often serve to control social suffering, situations also arise whereby reparations made can intensify suffering. All of which may ultimately undermine the long-term goal of using reparatory justice to heal post-conflict wounds and draw a line under the past. In Firchow's (2017) case-study analysis of reparations and reconciliation in Colombia the author compared two communities who were demographically similar with congruent histories of violence, but who had received starkly different levels of reparations for past harm suffered. The author noted that both communities have low levels of overall reconciliation, concluding that in order to be effective, greater emphasis must be placed on an education surrounding the meaning of reparations if there is to be meaningful community healing. Deriving from the 'Peace Studies' tradition, Firchow and Mac Ginty (2013) focus on the nexus between peacebuilding and reparations and propose ways in which reparations can play a key role in building what Peace Studies scholars routinely refer to as a 'positive peace' (Galtung 1969)[1].

In noting the potentially nefarious aspect of state-sponsored reparations programmes, García-Godos (2008) draws attention to the social and contested character of reparations programmes, arguing that reparations programmes should be seen in relationship to the political project they support. In much a similar vein, Pradier, Rubin, and van der Merwe (2018), through their analysis of South Africa's transition beyond Apartheid, draw attention to the fact that reparations programmes are often highly susceptible to political instrumentalisation. Moreover, the authors note that short-term political interests are often put ahead of the rights of victims and survivors to meaningful reparatory justice. The extent to which reparations are useful as a means of holding states to account for past violations has long been debated, with Marks's (1978) analysis of the failures of reparations imposed upon Germany following the end of the First World War regularly cited. The author points to the manner by which reparations programmes can in fact become a polarising issue and can lay the foundations for a future period of conflict and instability.

Other scholarly interventions around the issue of reparations include case-study analyses of the recommendations made by the South Africa Truth and Reconciliation Commission programme (Colvin 2006). Colvin highlights the disconnect between the ambitious and comprehensive proposal for reparations recommended by the TRC, and the inaction of the South African Government to adequately respond and implement said recommendations. This disconnect between recommendation and implementation is a critical insight and one that has broader international lessons to be shared. Similarly, Laplante (2007) draws attention to the negative impact of Peru's government conflating post-conflict development with a traditional reparations programme. While focused primarily on transitional justice efforts in Colombia, a recent report written by Moffett, Lawther, McEvoy, Sandoval, and Dixon (2019) spotlights many universal issues facing reparations programmes, particularly those dealing with non-state actors and societies who are unable to command the resources necessary to make meaningful contributions to victims and/or survivors. In their comparative analysis of reparatory frameworks implemented in Canada and Argentina, Bonner and James (2011) define the three important goals of transitional justice as being reparations, responsibility, and reframing, and argue that Argentina has been more successful at placing emphasis on social and political accountability when dealing with issues of its troubled past than Canada has when it comes to issues related to anti-Indigenous colonialism. For the purposes of our own analysis, this identification of three 'r's'– reparations, responsibility, and reframing– feels particularly important when considering reparatory justice for victims and survivors of forced displacement during Northern Ireland's Troubles.

Rubio-Marin and de Greiff (2007) outline the need to ensure that the procedural and substantive components of reparations programmes are gender appropriate. They are particularly interested in noting that a gender perspective must be taken into account during the conceptualisation of victims, beneficiaries, and the benefits that ought to be transferred during any reparatory justice framing. However, Walker (2015) calls into question whether gender-just reparations should be 'transformative' rather than corrective or restorative and argues that this conception of reparations threatens to bypass reparative justice as a distinctively victim-centred process. Such a view is particularly pertinent when we consider the fact that in many instances the mass evacuations that took place during the forcible displacement of civilians during the outbreak of the Troubles involved primarily the movement of women and children (as outlined in Chapter Three), with the expectation being that men stayed behind to defend the areas under attack, as we have noted above. Moffett (2015) further focuses on the issue of providing reparations within a conflict where there exists a blurring of the line between perpetrator and victim. In what he defines as 'complex victims', Moffett argues that the need to be defined as one or other should not be used as a means of limiting the use of reparations to ensure accountability. Roht-Arriaza (2014) argues for the expansion of the mainstream transitional justice agenda to incorporate the protection of economic, social, and cultural rights. She focuses on violations of economic, social, and cultural rights arising from displacement and dispossession of property, offering suggestions as to how reparations programmes could be more effective when dealing with violations stemming from systematic discrimination and exclusion.

While the international literature has provided much by way of theorising the role of reparations for post-conflict societies, and thus is an important theoretical framework upon which to build, it is the work of scholars closer to home, including Kris Brown (2013) and his theorising on the role of commemoration as symbolic reparation and Kevin Hearty (2020) on problematising symbolic reparation, which we believe offers up a potential avenue when it comes to how best to meaningfully address the issue of acknowledging and repairing the harm experienced by those who were forcibly displaced during the Troubles. In differentiating between monetary and symbolic reparations, Hearty (2020: 337) notes, 'Whereas material reparations seek to repair any past harms in a pecuniary sense (De Grieff, 2008), symbolic reparations are predicated on offering redress where particular harms cannot be repaired in a pecuniary sense or where there was a collective suffering of harms (Mégret, 2009).' The purported benefits of symbolic reparations lie in the belief that they are better suited to addressing the causes and consequences of harm rather than material reparations that are, on many occasions, deemed insufficient to meaningfully redress structural issues (Hearty 2020). According to Brown (2013: 275):

> Symbolic reparations take a variety of forms and can comprise the renaming of public spaces, the construction of museums, processes of physical memorialisation, public apology and atonement, the rededication places of detention transforming them into sites of memory and the establishment of commemorative events. What all the forms have in common is an explicit aim to carry meaning and shape narratives.

While accepting the limitations associated with symbolic reparatory justice, which Hearty (2020) links to the issues associated with designating victim hierarchies, that is, who ought to be considered as legitimate or non-legitimate victim, it is the symbolic reparations approach that we consider to perhaps be the most appropriate route to consider when seeking to acknowledge the harm associated with being forcibly displaced because of a conflict-related incident during the Troubles. This is even more reasonable, we suggest, when we consider that the vast majority of those with whom we met were uncomfortable with the notion of receiving compensation for the harm suffered as a result of being forcibly displaced. Taken alongside the further logistical limitation being the fact that there were simply so many persons who experienced the violence of being displaced, we argue there is merit in examining the role that symbolic reparation might play in this instance, including by considering the various forms proposed by Brown (2013) above. However, we also share Brown's (2013: 286) concern that the challenge lies in ensuring that symbolic reparations – in whatever form they are conceived – are thick enough to 'capture complexities and commonalities whilst also making them accessible to a range of groups and individuals across an ethnically divided society'.

As this necessarily succinct sweep of the literature on reparations in an international context demonstrates, interest in conceiving of how reparatory justice ought to be considered in any society transitioning from armed conflict is burgeoning and complex. However, beyond the monetisation of repairing harm, state-sponsored acknowledgement of the harm experienced by victims and survivors and the implementation of varied forms of symbolic reparations can help to ensure that the voices of those who were displaced are afforded the opportunity of public recognition, amplified rather than confined to the annals of history.

Compensation and State Support

As noted above, the right to receive reparations (however conceived) for those who have experienced violent displacement during a conflict has been readily affirmed, with Duthie and Seils (2016: 3) highlighting, 'State attempts to support the resolution of displacement through repatriation, resettlement, or local integration may have reparative value if they are undertaken as an expression of the state's responsibility for generating, or failing to prevent, displacement crises' in the first instance. Despite the vast array of transitional justice research that has emerged from Northern Ireland, questioning the impotence of the state response to preventing the forcible displacement of citizens across the north (and further afield) and in providing compensation as a form of redress has yet to be meaningfully considered. Moreover, within the myriad options for dealing with the past in Northern Ireland (as detailed above) considering reparations and redress for those who suffered violent displacement as a result of the outbreak of the Troubles is notably absent.

As we have shown, for many of our research participants it is the shock associated with the sudden and dramatic change in living conditions that remains one of their strongest and most enduring childhood memories. On many occasions individuals went from homeowners to homeless overnight. In addition, it was not uncommon for families to leave urban spaces in and around Belfast and relocate to perceived safer rural towns and villages, such as Downpatrick or Ardglass. Seamus Magee, who grew up in a Catholic household in a Protestant area in outer East Belfast with his four siblings, recalled the moment that his family were forced from their home and relocated to the fishing village of Ardglass. He notes the dramatic change in lifestyle, moving from a relatively comfortable, middle-class family home that the family owned outright, to a Housing Executive house in a fishing village:

> The Housing Executive bought the house; they had a scheme called the SPED scheme or something ... I can't remember, but it was against my dad's will ... He wanted to stay; his view was no-one was putting him out of the house ... But the scheme was there and so, so on St Patrick's Day 1975 we moved. I remember it very clearly. I was doing my A levels that year, and overnight we moved from East Belfast, an urban area, to a fishing village called Ardglass 30 miles from Belfast ... like overnight ... We moved from a house we owned with four bedrooms, to a Housing Executive house in Ardglass where I now stayed in the same room as my three brothers.. It was surreal really.

Across the sectarian divide, becoming homeless overnight meant that families turned to the state for support in providing social housing as a result of having their own property destroyed or rendered unliveable (as the testimonies outlined in greater detail in Chapter Two reveal). However, state support at the time was ad hoc and not always as forthcoming as one might expect, with the process of applying for support considered by many respondents to be a laborious, bureaucratic, and drawn out one. At a time when the need for housing was a particularly sensitive issue, victims and survivors of displacement were left in the position of having to depend on their wider family network or the burgeoning networks of community and voluntary organisations who were emerging in the void left by the state, to rehouse them in the interim. Paul Browne grew up in a Catholic family home on the Garnerville Road in outer East Belfast with his three siblings, mother, and father. Their home was attacked following an increase in tension over a period and eventually the family moved out of the house, seeking refuge within the wider family network: In documenting the last time he was in the house, Paul recalled:

> I remember going back over to the house after it had been burnt ... we had got a call from Mrs XXX and she had said we should come over and so we came across in one of those flatbed lorries and gathered up as much as we could. My mother and father went around the house and said, take that, leave this, OK take that ... and that was it. Then there was a gunshot that came from the top of the road and that was it ... that was the signal that said, you've got enough, time to leave.

One of the most pressing challenges that many of our respondents recalled was that associated with trying to find alternative accommodation. Paul was one of several respondents who noted the desperation that there existed in trying to bring the family unit back together and recounted the time that the family received word of a property that was becoming available in West Belfast and the associated scramble to try to secure the house before it was no longer available. Far from there being any state support, it was the support of the wider family network as we noted before, who played a key role in keeping an eye on what houses were potentially becoming available. The speed with which you had to move to try to bring the family back under the one roof was shared during interview:

> So, we were on the lookout for a house. In fact, we nearly had a house on the Glen Road that we were going to go and live in and my mother went round, and she actually cleaned it, and then when we went round and had a look at it, and it was a shocking house ... It was sheer desperation on her part to get us all back as a family. And we were all over the place at the time. And it was horrible. Uncle George was on the lookout – everyone was on the lookout – for a house for us ... It

was desperate times, and you weren't waiting on help from anywhere else, the state, the government, or anyone … It just wasn't there. Then word came back that a Protestant family in Ladybrook Parade were about to move out and that we were to move. Get moving, and get moving quickly … and again … And so that's how we ended up in the house in Ladybrook … As the Protestant family came out, the Catholic family went in.

In discussing the compensation and fiscal support that displaced families received at the time, Side (2018: 29) notes, 'Initially, short-term, non-monetary assistance was provided to affected households charitably as a temporary form of relief … displaced residents used volunteer removal services to leave their houses and neighbourhoods.' As we have outlined in detail in Chapter Three, the Herculean task of evacuating thousands of civilians who were at risk of sectarian violence, or who had experienced actual violence, was left to civic society, including charitable organisations and volunteer groups. The physical movement of furniture and the setting up of temporary accommodation in schools, church halls, and across wider family networks rarely, if ever, involved support from the state. When the state did engage in providing support for civilians, it is not controversial (as our research has shown) to argue that it did so in a way that was selective, demonstrating which side of the community was entitled to some form of, albeit limited, state support. Therefore, the issue of how compensation and the provision of post-displacement fiscal support was administered is worth placing under further scrutiny.

Several interviewees noted that the process that had to be followed when seeking to gain compensation for the loss of personal affects was arduous, bureaucratic, and therefore fundamentally flawed. To make a claim, an application had to be submitted to the Northern Ireland Office. Several respondents noted that there was a compensation procedure that had to be followed in order to try to recoup some of the losses suffered. Paul Browne said:

There was compensation … Well … it was money for when the house was burned and after it was sold … My mother had to itemise everything that was in the house; she had to make a list of everything and make a claim off the Northern Ireland Office … She's just lost her house and everything inside it and now she's having to scramble and think of the items that we might need. Remember we were all still at school. And so after she made the claim, we all had brand new duffle coats, and we all had so many pairs of trousers and so many pairs of this, and all the things that were destroyed. But it was a long process, and it must have been tough to sit and go through everything like that. It wasn't straightforward, and there wasn't any guarantee you'd get anything. Of course, we weren't getting the house back.

When it comes to unpacking and critiquing the response of the state in terms of how it chose to respond and manage the crisis of forced displacement that was developing at the time, including to ascertain what, if any, steps were taken to provide redress for victims and survivors of displacement, only a very limited body of scholarly work exists, including research done by Side (2018), Browne and Asprooth-Jackson (2019), Gilmartin (2021), Moffett et al. (2020), and Lawther and Moffett (2021). In considering the availability of compensation for those who were forcibly displaced at the outset of the Troubles, Moffett et al. (2020: 242) note:

> There were a number of schemes that aimed to alleviate and remedy some of the harm victims faced as a result of being displaced or intimidated out of their homes. After the mass displacement in August 1969 the government introduced a 'special extra-statutory grant' of £50,000 to provide compensation for individuals who suffered financial loss or hardship not covered by other schemes and distributed by voluntary organisations sheltering those displaced.

Moffett et al. (2020: 242) further affirm the ad hoc nature of compensation that was provided, noting that many short-term schemes were established as an emergency response, including discretionary grants that were designed to cover the cost of food, and some resettlement grant opportunities that assisted in providing support for furnishings. The authors note that temporary wooden houses and/or caravans were often provided to rehouse evacuees (2020: 243). However, as we have noted previously, the provision of fiscal support for those who were displaced was often more readily available, or more accessible, from charitable organisations who had fundraised for those who were being evacuated as a result of the outbreak of the conflict. More recently, Moffett and Lawther (2021) have drawn attention to the fact that some £990,372,313 was paid out in criminal damage from 1968 to 2003 by the United Kingdom Government. While some of this compensation may have been allocated to those who had been forcibly displaced, given the all-encompassing nature of the scheme (which included damage done to houses, businesses, cars, and other property) it is unclear as to how much of this would have been made available to those forcibly displaced. Moreover, during the course of our own interviews, few of our respondents shared their knowledge of the various compensation options available.

Katherine Side's (2018) analysis of the state response to violent displacement – a process she refers to as 'ungenerous, though not mean' (25) – is by some distance the most detailed and useful for the purposes of the present analysis. Known as the Scheme for the Purchase of Evacuated Dwellings (SPED), a British-funded programme for partial 'compensation' for those who were violently displaced, or facing the prospect of violent displacement, was introduced in 1973 under the auspices of the Northern

Ireland Housing Executive (NIHE) and 'administered in Britain and Northern Ireland, for the purpose of providing, on evidence of proof, limited financial compensation to homeowners and residents who lost their houses due to conflict' (Side 2018: 25). The legal basis for the SPED scheme, as Side's (2018: 26) research has revealed, derived from a range of existing legislation, including The Conspiracy and Protection of Property Act 1875, the Criminal Injuries to Persons Act (Compensation) (c.9, N.I.) 1956, the Criminal Injuries Act to Property (Compensation) Act (Northern Ireland) 1973, the Protection of the Persons and Property Act (Northern Ireland) 1969 (amended under the Northern Ireland (Modification of Enactments No. 1) Order 1973, and the Northern Ireland (Modifications of Enactments- N.I.) Order 1973. To view SPED as some form of reparations designed to compensate victims and survivors of violent displacement would be to grossly over-exaggerate the objective of the programme and the relatively paltry sum offered to successful applicants in terms of award made. More significantly, to view SPED as compensation downplays the significant barriers to accessing support due to the many bureaucratic obstacles that prevented applicants from being successful. Side (2018: 26) elaborates:

> The application process for SPED was onerous. Applications had to be made through solicitors, and necessitated an extensive knowledge of the property, a Certificate of Verification of Intimidation from the Chief Constable, Royal Ulster Constabulary (RUC) or British security forces, and confirmation of inclusion on the Emergency Housing List (DED SPED). Successful awards were made at levels significantly below the property values. Under SPED, a maximum purchase price, by the Northern Ireland House Executive, of £5,000 was payable to the head of household.

The SPED scheme was an attempt to assist homeowners/occupiers across Northern Ireland who had been forced to abandon their homes as a result of violence or the threat of violence and were subsequently unable to sell their property on the open market due to local adverse conditions arising from the Troubles. However, the legislation listed above empowered the Northern Ireland Housing Executive (NIHE) to acquire, by agreement, houses owned by persons who, in consequence of acts of violence, threats to commit such acts or other intimidation, were unable or unwilling to occupy those houses. At the time, it was the responsibility of the Royal Ulster Constabulary (RUC) to determine the nature and extent of the threat to the individual family in question, with the NIHE absolved from making any assessment as to whether or not such a threat would be considered 'conflict related'. In practical terms, those who were facing displacement were required to have their fears and apprehensions upheld by an RUC investigation at the time. Only then were they able to engage with the SPED initiative and have their property assessed by the Land and Property Services to determine its potential value. What must be considered therefore is the fact that for a significant portion of the population in Northern Ireland, predominantly those coming from a Catholic/nationalist background, turning to the RUC for support at this time during the conflict was not something that would have been readily encouraged nor willingly engaged in. The SPED scheme worked on the assumption that the RUC would act as a neutral, rational assessor of these applications. As noted above, many Catholic homeowners had serious issues in turning to the RUC in general, not solely when it came to assessing the potential risk they faced in terms of intimidation or threat to their household. 'Gerard', who was brought up in a Catholic household in East Belfast, recalled his father asking for police support to designate the threats against their family as being of a sectarian nature and thus allowing the family the opportunity to begin the process of moving out:

> We actually had the police out on one occasion before we moved and said to them that we were fearful that we would be attacked in the house if we stayed. Ultimately, we were wanting them to determine that we weren't safe anymore in the house so that we could at least get on to the list of those looking houses. Even though the windows had been broken, the police didn't say that we were under threat.

Martin McAleese's family lived in the loyalist hinterland on the boundary of Ballymacarrett in East Belfast. Unlike those in nearby enclave of Short Strand, the McAleeses were the only Catholic in their entire neighbourhood, where everyday occurrences such as going to the shops or school were fraught with fear, tension, and often violence. As the violence of the Troubles increased, the McAleese family home was under sustained attack. The family was eventually forcibly displaced when a large crowd of loyalists kicked in their front door and told the family that they had 20 minutes to pack up and leave. Martin described his engagement with the RUC in the run up to their displacement:

> When we got to Internment, 9 August 1971, in the year in the run up to that, one of us, one of the family had to sit up every single night with these wire mesh as shutters for the back windows of the house in case a petrol bomb came in the window. And I remember one night there was a lot of activity out the back of the house and we were frightened the mob was going to come in and put us out and so I went to Mountpottinger Police Station and told this guy what was happening and the guy laughed and said, 'You're on your own' and I just turned with my coat and went home and told my mother and father that we would not be getting any assistance from the police. So that sitting up every night went on through 1970 and 1971 and then in '71 I was working

in Blackpool for the summer holidays and I got a call to say that all my mother and father got were two suitcases out of the house... now the police came but they would not assist them [in preventing their forced eviction by loyalists] and they were spat at [by loyalists] and the house was wrecked and they defecated and urinated all over the house.

However, what was also gleaned during interviews with a number of Protestant participants who were displaced during the conflict was that they too had serious frustrations with the RUC who they felt were unwilling or unable to adequately tackle the source of republican threats to their family and properties. This was acutely felt in many of the border communities and, in particular, parts of Derry. In addition, during several interviews it was further revealed that the RUC and/or the British Army were, on occasion, the source of the family's displacement. Several republican-aligned families pointed to the fact that the constant raiding and harassment at their home by members of the RUC/British Army singled their family out and resulted in them having to leave the area. This was most acutely and disproportionately felt by family members who, while aligned by virtue of birth or marital status, were not necessarily involved in the republican movement.

The 'official' figure attributed to the number of people who were subsequently re-housed under the SPED scheme pre/post the 1998 Good Friday Agreement is difficult to discern. Browne and Asprooth-Jackson (2019) note in their analysis of SPED that the NIHE's computerised records for SPED cases were only operational from 1998 and as a result only manual records up to 1998 were retained, and they indicate that there were approximately 4,700 SPED cases filed in total. When we compare these 'official' figures with the numbers of those who were displaced overall it is clear that a disparity exists, and while the reason for such a disparity is difficult to discern, one could draw the tentative conclusion that it is due to a perceived lack of awareness among the general public concerning SPED or, and perhaps more likely, an unwillingness to engage with the process among a significant portion of the population. Browne and Asprooth-Jackson (2019) further note that an overall assessment of the effectiveness of the scheme has never taken place. When pressed during interview over whether the SPED scheme could be viewed, in the modern parlance of transitional justice, as an attempt to provide compensation or some form of reparation for victims and survivors of violent displacement at the time, a member of the NIHE noted that SPED was not to be viewed as such. SPED was merely a way of ensuring that a willing buyer for the property could be discerned where it may have proven exceptionally difficult for a person who was facing intimidation to sell his or her home on the open market. Fiscal support that was provided by way of a SPED application should therefore not be viewed as a form of compensation or even as an acknowledgement that the state failed in its duty of care to protect those who were intimidated and forced to flee their homes due to the threat of or actual experience of violence. All of which, we suggest, leaves the door open for a more considered, reparatory response (however conceived) for those who were forcibly displaced.

In assessing the long-term impact of the introduction of the SPED scheme as a means of responding to the displacement crisis that erupted at the outset of the Troubles and that subsequently transformed the spatial reality of Northern Ireland, Side (2018: 34) succinctly concludes:

> The effects of conflict-instigated housing displacement are marked indelibly on Belfast's streetscapes. They are evident in its rebuilt houses and neighbourhoods, in its peace walls, motorways, public art displays, and in the maintenance of physical and social boundaries. Their permanence is also recorded in archival documents that recount particular versions of the conflict and record SPED's development and its opportunistic operation to curtail emigration, bolster state securitisation, and rebuild a Victorian-age city.

SPED, and more appropriately its application, we argue helped to cement the deep-rooted issue of segregation and division that has endured in the present day, a view that has been endorsed by previous conclusions reached by both Side (2018) and Browne and Asprooth-Jackson (2019). While it remains difficult to definitively conclude what role the state played in helping to facilitate the mass displacement of its citizens during the outbreak of the conflict, it is reasonable to question whether or not a more appropriate response of the state ought to have been to provide greater protection for its civilians who were being intimidated from their homes, rather than helping to facilitate population transfer, and the subsequent entrenchment of segregation through the drafting of policies designed to purchase toxic properties. Undoubtedly such a position is only ever reached with the benefit of hindsight. However, it is hard to conclude anything other than, far from being a form of compensation or even some sort of reparatory justice (however conceived), SPED operated as a blunt instrument during a time of perceived chaos. Its bureaucratic procedures ensured that barriers existed to gaining access to fiscal support for those who needed it most, and for many at the time, the barriers to accessing the support available were insurmountable and potentially dangerous. Far from preventing fear, intimidation, and the ultimate forcible displacement of its civilians, the state facilitated, encouraged, and helped to manage the mass movement of those who ought to have been entitled to protection. It is hard to reach any other conclusion than, when it comes to the protection of civilians, the state ought to have done better.

Uncovered during many of the interviews with victims and survivors who were forced to evacuate their homes due to violence or the threat of violence was the perceived lack of support received from members of the security forces at a time of uncertainty and vulnerability. Far from being offered guarantees with regard to their safety, several of those interviewed alluded to the role that the police played in encouraging their families to consider relocating, proposing that the family would be best moving to areas where their perceived 'otherness' was not an issue. Seamus Magee, whose family eventually moved from East Belfast to Ardglass following a gun attack on the family home, recalled the moment that the police arrived to discuss the various 'options' available:

> When they [the police] came to the door after we reported a petrol bomb attack one Sunday evening, the police said to my dad, look Mr Magee, why don't you move the family out to Antrim or somewhere else. [Laughing] A police officer at the scene actually suggested Carryduff would be a good place because all the Catholics were moving there!

Others noted that it was their lack of faith in the ability of the security forces, namely the RUC to protect them and their family, that was the main driving force behind the family deciding to leave their home. As a recent report by Moffett et al. (2020: 18), referencing the work of Boal (1976: 87), has noted, 'In the most part the pattern of population movements often followed a defensive one, wherein mixed families or minority Catholic or Protestant families often moved to majority dominated estates of their own community.' 'Ciaran', who grew up in a predominantly Protestant area and whose family subsequently chose to relocate to a Catholic area in Lenadoon in West Belfast, notes that the decision was relatively straightforward despite the awareness that such a move would increase the likelihood of being closer to what they referred to as 'the war':

> We knew that we were leaving an area that was more middle class so to speak and moving into a part of town that was getting a lot of bad press because of the Troubles being on the doorstep … but there was little choice in my dad's eyes. If the RUC weren't going to protect us in our own houses, then we had to move to a place where we knew we wouldn't be targeted because we were Catholic. We may have been moving towards the eye of the storm in some ways, but there wasn't a lot of choice.

In stark contrast and reflecting the fact that the experience of violent displacement at this time crossed the sectarian divide, a number of respondents from the Protestant/unionist community in Derry recalled the positive engagement their families had with members of the RUC who helped to facilitate their moving from the predominantly nationalist area of the Bogside to an area known as Newbuildings. Several Protestant respondents stated that following their evacuation their families were able to briefly return to their homes and collect belongings, furniture, and any other valuables due to having relatives or friends in the B-Specials. This provided armed protection for Protestant families to return to the space where they had been forced to flee and to load up their flat-bed lorries (as detailed earlier in our chapter on flight and evacuation). Although for some there was an inherent sadness about leaving the area they had grown up in (and in relative peace and harmony with their Catholic neighbours) there was a sense that the RUC were genuine in their desire to ensure the well-being and safety of the Protestant residents, and for that they were grateful. 'Betty', who grew up in a Protestant household in the predominantly Catholic Bogside area of Derry, recalled:

> We actually lived in the Bogside and we had Roman Catholic friends and neighbours. We had Roman Catholic tradesmen coming in to fix things in the house if they were broken. Things were all very calm, but that started to change around the mid-1960s when things outside started to really get tense. The day that we ended up moving to Newbuildings the police came to our house and helped us load up things and move us out of there. We never thought it would be a permanent move, just a while to allow things to get less tense.

Whether the RUC and the state security forces played a nefarious or enabling role in helping to facilitate the forcible transfer of civilians during this period is not necessarily the point, and as with most things pertaining to the conflict in Northern Ireland, is largely untestable and open to divergent views. Some will argue that the actions of the RUC at this time were those of a police force responding under extreme pressure and, as such, to view their response as being distinct from the context in which it occurred is to apply an unfair revisionist standard. However, for others, including several respondents with whom we met, as an emanation of the state and an enforcer of law and order, the RUC had a duty of care to ensure the protection of all its citizens. In referencing an earlier report by Darby and Morris (1974), Side (2018: 29) notes that the RUC and the British Army were often accused of being responsible in deliberately delaying assistance to, or indeed refusing to assist some households who were seeking to leave their homes due to the threat of violence. The response of the police force, some would argue, ought to have been to pursue perpetrators of violence and intimidation as opposed to helping to facilitate the displacement of large swathes of the population. As a result, when it comes to considering reparations and redress for those who experienced violent displacement as a result of a conflict-related incident in Northern Ireland, apportioning blame is much less straightforward than may be the case in other post-conflict/ transitional spaces.

For some interviewees, regardless of where the blame lies, the importance when it comes to reparations and redress centres on an acknowledgement of harm suffered as a result of their violent displacement and the enduring impact that this moment of rupture had on their life trajectory. Such a public acknowledgement would go a long way in recognising the legitimacy of their own 'victimhood'. In discussing the issue of reparations or the need for some greater acknowledgement for the harm suffered, 'Sean', who grew up in a Catholic family in East Belfast and who subsequently moved to the Belfast suburb of Carryduff, noted:

> Look, see to be honest, I'm not looking for someone to come and tell me that I am due money or anything. I just want someone to say that what happened to our family at that time, even though it happened to loads of families, wasn't right and shouldn't have happened. The experience wasn't inconsequential. I've done OK, but others didn't – families were broke up because of it. In some cases there were jobs lost. Marriages broke down. It shouldn't have happened and acknowledging that takes nothing away from anybody.

While there has been nothing by way of acknowledgement by the state for its actions that may, or may not, have resulted in facilitating the harm suffered as a result of being forcibly displaced, and thus no consideration of reparations (however defined) provided to victims and survivors of displacement within the borders of the six counties of Northern Ireland, conversely the southern government in the Irish Republic have spotlighted the significant impact that forcible displacement had on those individuals who were forced to flee across the border. In 2003 the Irish Government announced a Scheme of Acknowledgement, Remembrance, and Assistance for Victims in this Jurisdiction of the Conflict in Northern Ireland, and established a Remembrance Commission and Fund in the Republic, towards restorative ends in the spirit of the Good Friday Agreement, which included, for the first time, an acknowledgement of a special category of victim, namely those who experienced a 'conflict'-related incident in the north and who subsequently fled across the border. In addition to offering payments for the families of those victims who had been killed as a result of the conflict in the north, on the condition that said victim was a resident of the 26 counties at the time, the scheme extended its reparatory scope to include a category of restitution for 'Northern refugees', detailed under the heading 'Displacement from Northern Ireland': payments of up to €15,000 were to be made, subject to certain conditions, to anyone who was a victim, or who is the surviving family member of such a victim, who had to flee from Northern Ireland across the border to the south, as a direct consequence of the conflict in Northern Ireland and who now wishes to return to their original jurisdiction (Department of Justice, Equality and Law Reform 2003: 4).

Rather than being viewed as 'refugees' (for reasons that have been outlined in previous chapters) those who were forced from their homes due to intimidation or actual violence, and who remained within the six counties that make up Northern Ireland, were not afforded the same 'state-sponsored' care one would expect to receive when being transported across an 'international border' due to their designation (albeit retrospectively) as an 'Internally Displaced Person'. Thus, what is immediately apparent is that when it comes to considering reparatory justice for victims of violent displacement during this post-conflict/transitional phase, the issue of crossing a recognised border also yields a disparity in terms of acknowledging suffering and harm. The significance in crossing an internationally recognised border, and thus becoming entitled to a refugee status, appears to (rightly or wrongly) sharpen a governmental response towards some form of reparatory justice. This acknowledgement of the victimhood status of those who were violently displaced in Northern Ireland and the subsequent offer of reparations for harm suffered is highly significant in that it suggests that, by virtue of gaining 'refugee status', rather than being an 'Internally Displaced Person', the designation of victimhood appears more easily adopted. Such a view is, of course, problematic, particularly when we take into consideration the fact that most individuals displaced remained within the six counties of Northern Ireland and the fact that for many, recognition of the existence of the border itself is a politically charged issue and as such, the language of refugee is wholly inappropriate.

The emphasis on the displaced found in the Scheme of Acknowledgement, Remembrance, and Assistance for Victims in this Jurisdiction of the Conflict in Northern Ireland is notable in that it is the only aspect of the Commission's efforts explicitly aimed at citizens of the north. As a form of an official acknowledgement that constitutes formal recognition of Northern-born displacement to the south caused by the Troubles in language that was hitherto unused since the early 1970s, the scheme is significant. Rather than sweeping the experiences of victims and survivors of conflict-related displacement at the time under the carpet, the scheme acknowledges the issue explicitly and recognises the harm, suffering, and loss that was experienced. Finally, and most importantly, in terms of reparatory justice for victims and survivors, it represents the only meaningful form of restorative legislation designed with the discrete purpose of repatriating and providing restitution for those who were forcibly displaced during the Troubles in Northern Ireland. Although a review of the individual uptake of the scheme was never published, Browne and Asprooth-Jackson (2019) have noted that the Commission's term of appointment was twice extended, running from 2003 to 2008 and distributed approximately €6.5m of the €9m allocated for victims and their families (Department of Justice, Equality and Law Reform 2008).

Truth, Denial, and Acknowledgement

As a case study, Northern Ireland shows the extent and the limitation of forensic truth as a viable mechanism capable of addressing a plurality of harms in a way that is conciliatory and transformative. According to Elazar Barkan (2016), even in a relatively small conflict like the Troubles, the resources needed for criminal investigations are enormous, and even when the goal is relatively limited, the results are often frustrating, leaving many unsatisfied. The predominance of attention afforded to 'conventional' forms of physical violence such as shootings and bombings often over-shadow other forms of conflict-related harms and loss. Conventional ideas within international relations typically understand violence as a deliberate, direct, physical act where one or more agents inflict harm onto another – a 'manifest' or actor-based form of violence. Such empirical-based approaches to violence and conflict assume that violence is both visible and measurable (Baron et al. 2019). The school of realism within IR studies assiduously nurtures a relatively limited understanding of violence as something conducted by state and non- state actors in the pursuit of political objectives, therefore embedding violence in conventional, statist terms, and equally as important, as a causal practice involving protagonists and victims. Such a reductive framework therefore 'measures' violence solely by limited and crude forms such as body counts, injuries, and other forms of physical harms and in so doing, often precludes or conceals multiple forms of violence, domination, and insecurity, often situated outside the boundaries of seemingly orthodox understandings of violence and harm.

Given that the pluralised forms of violence and intimidation synonymous with forced displacement are situated outside the definitional boundaries associated with Troubles-related harm and loss, historically, violence connected with displacement often resulted in low levels of convictions. Despite the Scarman Report into the July and August 1969 riots and burnings, of the 431 complaints received by the police from families being forced from their homes, only 18 individuals were successfully prosecuted (Moffett et al. 2020). In instances of mass violence and violations such as forced displacement, the chances of individual accountability via judicial processes range from slim to non-existent. Where justice in the traditional, retributive sense is not possible, a minimal requirement should be the pursuit of acknowledgement and truth (Hayner 2001).

All interviewees were cognisant that there will be no state-led historical investigations, formal truth commissions, arrests, or criminal prosecutions of those involved in various forms of intimidation and attack. Despite this, the commonality across most was the quest for public acknowledgement and recognition, by the state, by representatives of the 'other' community, and in some instances, by members of their own communities. While memories of past violence such as displacement continue to be a prominent source of division and antagonisms, most respondents in this research framed their stories and their pursuit of acknowledgement in restorative ways rather than retribution. They seek accountability and responsibility in symbolic and restorative ways at a collective level rather than seeking individual forms of culpability. A range of arguments support the imperative to acknowledge or 'vindicate' victims to right the wrongs visited upon them during conflict, including the ability to restore dignity and self-esteem, recognise loss, while also holding the potential to build relationships based on trust and mutual accountability (Jankowitz 2017). Therefore, acknowledgement is decisive in the transitional dynamic.

Acknowledgment, particularly through hearing one another's stories, validates experiences and feelings and represents the first step towards restoration of the person and the relationship. While accountability via a judicial court case can in some instances mitigate feelings of anger and animosity regarding past injustices (Biggar 2001), public acknowledgement can be effective in repairing many broken relationships in Northern Ireland by conferring public recognition of pain, trauma, and loss. Such public expressions can be symbolic forms of reparations, including apologies, museums, and monuments. The need to tell, record, and publicly dissem- inate their stories of displacement emerged as the overarching demand among participants; in other words, acknowledgement, recognition, and validation were identified as key transformative outcomes and objectives. Perceptions that many episodes of displacement are being denied, dimin- ished, or at best, deliberately obfuscated, has compounded the sense of loss and pain, at both an individual and collective level. Denied the public space for trials, truth recovery, and physical sites of commemoration, many of those displaced seek public acknowledgment and recognition of their experiences, through storytelling, oral testimony, and the public dissemi- nation of displacement narratives and experiences.

Far from being a matter solely of individual experience, however, story- telling and memory is a social phenomenon. What and how we remember is shaped and moulded by our experience and interaction with significant others, our participation in social discourse, and our interactions with meaningful symbols, surroundings, and landscapes. Nor is memory purely a record of the past. While memory is indeed about the past, perhaps memory's defining feature is its presentism (Misztal 2003). As an active and dynamic process, recalling and narrating past experiences are shaped and filtered in light of the present and, moreover, the content of what is recalled or not is situational and contingent on the audience and narrator and the power relationship between them. Testimonies of tumultuous and violent 'life experiences' such as forced displacement should therefore be considered constructions and products of active agents and 'experiencing subjects' seeking to make sense of violence and turbulent change, paying particular attention to the ways in which experience is framed and articu- lated (Eastmond 2007). Thus, the caveat here is that stories and recollections cannot be seen as simply reflecting life as lived through some rational, objective, value-free lens; on the contrary, narrations should be seen as creative constructions or interpretations of the past, generated and shaped in specific contexts of the present (Misztal 2003: 250). In the context of a region transitioning from protracted armed violence, recollections of the past are also embedded in a wider, adversarial framework of 'memory politics' as the social action of collecting and recording stories become sites of struggle and resistance regarding legitimacy, morality, blame, and culpability. Ruti Teitel (2003) contends that all recollective accounts generated in transitional times are never autonomous and often anchored in national narratives, therefore, transitional truths are socially constructed within processes of collective memory' (70).

Notwithstanding the opportunity and ability to narrate one's own story, as a means to secure recognition has become associated with a transition from the condition of being a (passive) victim into that of an (active) survivor (Dawson 2017). The agency and cathartic outcomes of articulating conflict-related harms are of course tempered by the reality that such endeavours have the potential to exacerbate or reignite feelings of pain, loss, and hurt, as well as the obvious danger of exacerbating already polarised conflict narratives (Hayner 2001). The growth in giving testimony has also been linked to the evolving culture of rights internationally, with some arguing that the collection of stories of violation and the development of publicly accessible archives could help cement and consolidate human rights in the present and ensure non-repetition in the future (Hamber and Kelly 2016).

While the previous chapter contends that displaced persons need to be considered within the spectrum of victimhood and harm, nevertheless, it is important to look beyond the 'passive' connotations often associated with victimhood and highlight that many respondents are agents seeking individual recognition, truth, and restoration, and in some instances, agents seeking to engage in processes that advance wider societal healing through various forms of inter-communal dialogue and engagement. With regards to enhancing community relations, respondents in this research stressed the need for members and representatives of the 'other community' to hear their stories, acknowledge them, and seek to address the hurt through dialogue. Some of the research participants from the Protestant community in Londonderry, such as Brian Dougherty, have been active in the community sector for many years and have engaged with nationalists and republicans on the issue of Protestant displacement but are often confronted with a sense of denial.

> [It's] not only because of the physical attacks and murders and intimidation but the lack of recognition; almost like a cruel thing that that movement and the impact and trauma of that has never been recognised never mind appreciated or dealt with. Derry has been a model of good practise in so many ways and like there is this idea then of celebrating

diversity and culture, and so if you're Chinese or Romanian, you are welcome here but if you're a Protestant 'fuck off'. The Exodus, as we call it, runs very deep in the DNA of Protestants in this city and we felt that we got a raw deal in terms of how that has been dealt with or not addressed and the things thrown at us is 'oh you're just whinging Protestants' or 'we don't believe you' and that is why it is so important to have an honest narrative. And you're not attacking anything; you're just saying, 'This is my story and this is my truth.'

Defining denial as information that is too threatening or disturbing to be publicly acknowledged, and so, must be repressed or reinterpreted, denial is inherent to the practice of social exclusion (Cohen 2001) – denial of others' suffering creates the framework for legitimising violence against the other. All respondents articulated a view that denials and downplaying of intimidation have impacted negatively on community relations despite the advancements of the last 25 years of the peace process. For Lederach (1997), reconciliation is not a process or a policy, but a social space where encounters between former enemies can engage in issues of truth, justice, mercy, and peace. For reconciliation to be effective, the humanity of the 'other' group must be recognised; a new moral order needs to be created that reflects cooperation between two competing groups; stereotypes and gener-alisations need to be adjusted; communicative purposes that build trust and facilitate mutually beneficial cooperation are required (Ellis 2006). Many Protestant participants believe the nationalist and republican community will not countenance an acknowledgment of the loss and trauma caused by intimidation and displacement; an acknowledgment would signify as admission of culpability, thereby undermining republican narratives of the nature of the conflict.[2] While some respondents stated that an acknowl-edgment from the 'other' community was unlikely, most continued to invest much energy into communicating their displacement narratives through the means of storytelling. Jonathan Burgess's family lived close to the nation-alist Bogside area of Londonderry but left in 1972 after years of growing fears for their safety as a Protestant family. Jonathan has devoted a lot of time and work into documenting and communicating Protestant stories of displacement both within his community but also to Catholic communities through a variety of methods, including books, plays, and inter-communal workshops, which he contends is a more effective way of communicating displacement narratives:

The residual pain is still there, and until you lance that, lance that boil, it won't heal. I believe everyone in society needs to have their voice heard because when you don't you will always have people stuck in the house screaming at the wall and that is not a healing society. What I'm trying to do here is tell the stories [of the Exodus] so people from outside can empathise on a global basis and also the Catholic Community here who are ignorant of a lot of aspects of my community, and some of those reasons are also as much the fault of my own community. They've been silent as much as they have been ignored and that is something that has to be rectified and so that's how I see the future going.

While respecting the diversity of memories, meanings, and needs of the research participants, all contended that 'story telling', 'oral testimony', and 'putting our stories on the public record' was their overarching preference for ending the silence and marginalisation regarding their displacement experiences. Cillian McGrattan (2016), however, situates the recent rush towards 'story-telling' as a deliberate political act to displace highly contentious legacy issues away from the formal political arena into the more amicable community setting of oral testimony. While acknowledging the important role of testimony, the emphasis on 'grassroots' truths' may work to hamper the stated policy goals of transparency, proportionality, and accountability in this area of dealing with the past. In other words, the traditional law-and-order apparatus of due process and forensic evidence will be substituted with an approach to justice based on relative and subjective forms of 'truth' that intuitively feel to be (in)correct, regardless of facts and evidence. While there is indeed validity to McGrattan's contention, time and again however, Northern Ireland's endeavours with rigorous, forensic investigations that collate 'hard data' rarely bring about the desired outcomes sought by victims and survivors. Moreover, given the diversity of needs and interests among victims, any approaches to dealing with the legacy of violence must eschew the idea and pursuit of a one-size-fits-all approach. There is also an epistemological point of contention. While it is clearly possible and constructive to establish 'facts' about a particular incident or events, nevertheless, memories, perspectives, and meanings attached to those events are malleable and profoundly shaped by social interactions in the present, furnishing a plurality of truths as opposed to constituting a singular, value-free account.[3] Furthermore, the idea of a forensic, systematic examination in pursuit of objective facts is not identified by those affected by displacement as an effective mechanism capable of addressing their particular aspirations and demands for recognition and acknowledgement. Given this, localised forms of truth recovery can and do play an important role in transforming societies emerging from conflict and Northern Ireland's vibrant civil society has widely used storytelling, oral recordings, and archives, as well as witness programmes as important means in the quest for public acknowledgement. Many victims have regarded the telling of such stories as essential, either in terms of their recovery and healing or in terms of bearing witness to atrocity so that future atrocities can be avoided, and so storytelling offers effective and practical ways of dealing with the horrors of the past (Hackett and Rolston 2009). One of the cornerstones of modern-day psychology is the belief that expressing one's feelings, and especially talking out traumatic experiences, is necessary for recovery and for psychological health. It is often asserted that following a period of massive political violence and enforced silence, simply giving victims and witnesses the chance to tell their stories in ways that are respectful and non-confrontational can help them regain their dignity and begin to recover (Hayner 2001). This is especially pertinent in the cases of previously denied events.

In many cases of displacement, there is no paper trail, no chain of evidence, no organisational admission of responsibility, therefore, victims and survivors of displacement look towards alternative and more innovative mechanisms that provide not only recognition of their experiences but offer the development of meaningful voice and participation in wider conversations regarding peacebuilding. As articulated by Jonathan Burgess, most of the research participants look towards various communicative platforms for 'storytelling', including direct dialogue, oral testimony, plays, books, documentaries, among others, not only as a means of seeking acknowledgement but also by way of giving voice to the displacement experience. For the Protestant community in Londonderry, the Exodus has emerged as a central conduit of communicating the collective Protestant experiences of the Troubles in the city with a view to seeking recognition and acknowledgement as part of a suite of measures to address the individual and collective legacy of forced displacement. Narratives are critical for peacebuilding processes because they are the primary way in which people make sense of the world, produce meanings, articulate intentions, and legitimise actions. When people who have experienced conflict or violence narrate their everyday stories, they articulate the type of loss they suffered, the myriad ways such loss affects their lives, and how they are coping. In doing so, their narratives reveal individual interpretations of conflict and peace and illuminate the differentiated requirements that people need for justice or reconciliation to take place (Parry 2020).

Despite the slippery nature of the concept, reconciliation according to Lederach (1997), suggests meaningful engagement and discernible changes in previously adversarial relationships. Reconciliation, therefore, requires an acknowledgement of trauma, in all its manifestations, and genuine endeavours to seek truth recovery in ways that build towards healing that trauma. To marginalise or deny (and that includes silence) is to increase social exclusion and thus denial becomes a practice that re-enforces harm. However, many of Northern Ireland's endeavours to address the past, though by no means all, are embedded in processes of assigning culpability and blame, rather than reconciliation and transformation. According to Daniel Bar-Tal (2003), groups in conflict tend to form selective 'collective memories' of violence, ones that 'focus mainly on the other side's responsibility for the outbreak and continuation of the conflict and its misdeeds, violence, and atrocities' while simultaneously focusing on their own self-justification, self-righteousness, glorification, and victimization' (78). Therefore, the potential benefits of sharing personal and communal stories of past violence are also weighed against the likely prospect of denial. Jeanette Warke recalled a time when she told her story in front of a group of nationalists and republicans as part of a cross-community exchange in Londonderry. When she finished telling her story a member of the audience asked, 'What fairy tale book did you get that story from?' which Jeanette found hurtful and incredibly deflating, yet nonetheless she still believes that storytelling through inter-communal dialogue has the potential 'to get our story out there and educate people'. The focus on reconciliation than retribution through an array of mechanisms is fraught with dangers of encountering animosity and antagonistic opposition. Nonetheless, it also offers potential not only for individual restoration and well-being but also the advancement of repairing societal harms.

Additionally, it is now widely recognised that telling stories can repair the ruptures to the identities of refugees and IDPs, thereby assisting them to recreate new and more acceptable self-identities, restore order in the aftermath of disruption, gain control of their present lives, and find meaning in the incomprehensible (Puvimanasinghe et al. 2015). Marian Kane's family were forced from their homes by loyalists in North Belfast on two occasions in the early 1970s, and she believes it is time that the experiences of displacement be heard:

> Yes we are victims, of course we are. Like the trauma I went through thinking that you'd never see your husband, your family and your house and the fear. You need to listen to peoples' stories and if you don't that trauma is never going to go away.

The connection between the two aspects of storytelling – as a private tool for processing and a public tool for reshaping collective memories – is what may allow the practice of recording oral testimonies to act not only as a historical document, but also as a mechanism for transition out of conflict through its creation and dissemination (Anderson 2019). Acknowledging and listening to overlooked or marginalised perspectives and experiences can only enhance our comprehensions regarding conflict and its many harms, and furthermore, challenge some of the orthodoxies within conventional or accepted narratives, thus forcing us to revaluate our understandings of violence and legacy and our endeavours for addressing it.

Furthermore, some participants have used art and drama as practices of both dealing with and communicating the loss and non-recognition of displacement. The development of the arts in transitional justice reflects a broader trend in peacebuilding scholarship and practice where the arts have gained increasing attention as an instrument to promote dialogue, reconciliation, and conflict transformation (Fairey and Kerr 2020). It has been noted that some displacement service providers are using innovative therapeutic projects such as 'theatre of the oppressed' or 'art therapy' involving enacting one's life story through body movements or via the medium of art respectively, when talk therapies were less successful. According to service providers, non-verbal devices could be more culturally familiar and hence more acceptable; or they circumvented the need to be exposed to emotional turmoil in order to hear (Puvimanasinghe et al. 2015). Christina Bennett has conceived and created a number of public art exhibitions that document her visualisation of displacement through a variety of media including paint, print, found objects, and short films, which she contends is about exploring layers of personal memories and 'represents my wish to acknowledge, to state, this movement of community, and the individuals within'.[4] Jonathan Burgess has been involved in writing and producing plays about Protestant experiences of the Troubles including displacement and he contends it is all motivated by a desire to provide access to these stories in a way that is effective and meaningful. He states:

> In terms of the guy sitting in the housing estate, he is not going to sit down with a 400-page report with big language. So we did that [play], and we toured it, took scenes from it and brought it to community centres. So that led to workshops: play a scene, then get people to talk about it, talk about the impact.

By communicating their experiences to the 'other community' and wider society through oral testimony, plays, drama, documentaries, workshops, as well as the production of art and short films, many participants see the restorative and healing potential in such endeavours.

In the spring of 2019, one of the authors, Brendan Ciarán Browne, along with Casey Asprooth-Jackson produced a research-based artwork exhibition at the ArtCetera Studio in Belfast exploring the history and impact of displacement in Northern Ireland. As a result of a long-term collaboration between Casey and Brendan, their project used documentary interviews with people burned from their homes during the riots of 1969 and early 1970s, and using visual displays of primary evidence, sought to provoke reflection on the scale and legacy of displacement. The innovative methods used in the exhibition combined visual, textual, and audio representations of interviews with victims and survivors of displacement, alongside objects related to their displacement. As was the case in 2009, in 2019 residents of West Belfast organised a series of events to commemorate the 50th anniversary of the mass violence and burnings of 1969. Under the auspices of the Belfast 1969 Pogroms Commemoration Committee, a series of events in the worst affected areas – Ardoyne in North Belfast and the Lower Falls and Clonard districts of West Belfast including documentary screening, anniversary Mass, panel discussions, photographic exhibition, new murals, finally culminating with a march to Clonard Memorial Garden in Bombay Street.

The reality is that despite the pain and loss, all research participants were keen to speak about their experiences through this research. For some it was the first time articulating their memories; for others, they had spent much of their adult lives endeavouring to process, record, and communicate what they see as 'silenced voices'. Many believe they are forgotten victims of the Troubles and to date there has been no state-led recognition of Northern Ireland's mass displacement during the Troubles. The legacy of diminution and denial of displacement by sections of opposing communities remains a formidable issue within inter-communal relations in Northern Ireland. For peacebuilding to be a truly transformative process whereby society moves towards sustainable relations, the legacy of displacement and the needs of its many survivors must be incorporated as part of the peacebuilding process. While the notion of oral testimony is tempered by the reality that conventional forms of justice, guilt, and accountability are effectively dispensed with, nevertheless, in certain instances such as historical displacement, the role of 'storytelling' and other bottom-up acknowledgment projects is seen by victims and survivors as an effective vehicle to 'end the silence', challenge denial, and offer a counter-narrative for those displaced during the conflict. According to Lederach (1997), the idea of reconciliation suggests meaningful engagement and discernible changes in previously adversarial relationships. Reconciliation, therefore, requires an acknowledgement of trauma, in all in its manifestations, and genuine endeavours to seek truth recovery in ways that build towards healing that trauma.

Conclusion

Though the experiences, needs, and interests of those displaced are heterogenous, the thread of commonality running throughout was a quest for public recognition of their long-standing losses. The visceral sense of being silenced, ignored, or marginalised are the outcomes of reductive discourse and policy outputs that continue to frame loss, suffering, and victimhood solely as those acts associated with conventional forms of physical, armed violence, thus cultivating a hierarchy of harms and victims. This chapter closes therefore by offering some recommendations that may be considered appropriate in seeking to address the dearth of attention and quest for recognition for the displaced. First and foremost, those who suffered and survived displacement because of political violence constitute a category of victims consistently overlooked and therefore their conflict-related experiences warrant their inclusion on the spectrum of victimhood. Second, their diverse testimonies and perspectives provide an important yet relatively under-explored aspect of the conflict. The unique circumstances of their displacement therefore expand our understanding of harms and loss and so they offer important new perspectives and inputs on possible transitional justice mechanisms. Third, the issue of displacement has the potential to motivate cross-community engagement and dialogue, already evidenced by engagements in Londonderry and with some of those community representatives in the Clonard area of West Belfast. Finally, as the testimonies of our respondents have suggested, oral testimony, public dissemination, and the creation of a historical archive offers an effective means for recovering the silenced voices of displacement. Such an archive could come in the form of a stand-alone project or as part of the proposed Oral History Archive, which forms an important pillar of the 2014 Stormont House Agreement, which set out a range of strategies and frameworks for dealing with the legacy of conflict. While storytelling processes are of course vexed and complicated by the perennial epistemological battle between positivist and constructivist accounts of armed violence, nevertheless, they were consistently identified by participants as an effective mechanism capable of addressing what they feel have been 'forgotten victims' of the Troubles.

There is also a pressing need for a wider debate regarding forms of symbolic reparation and public, state-sponsored acknowledgement of the harm suffered. Given the vast levels of forced movement, the state and wider Northern Irish society should consider additional forms of symbolic reparation to symbolise and acknowledge the suffering and loss, akin to those proffered by Brown (2013) above. While the UN 'Basic Principles' categorise reparation as rehabilitation, restitution, assurances of non-repetition of harm and satisfaction, symbolic forms of reparations are increasingly looked to as a form of justice and redress for victims of complex, protracted armed conflicts. This is all the more pressing when you take into consideration the state's abject failure to prevent past displacement and, moreover, its continuing failure to address its legacy in the present. As a result, we suggest that any future state-led endeavours to address the legacy of conflict need to incorporate displacement as a source of harms and should consider some form of symbolic acknowledgement as an important means of recognising the high levels of displacement experienced by its citizens.

Public acknowledgement of forced displacement is therefore more than simply being mindful or knowing about past hurts; it is about conferring public recognition on an injustice that was committed in the name of a specific political unit or collective. In doing so, it validates the hurt and suffering of those forcibly uprooted and has the potential to establish new relations and understandings regarding conflict-related harms and their long-term impacts. The eclectic initiatives through which victims and survivors articulate their memories, needs, and perspectives are, of course, anchored in practices and processes that are often confrontational and selective and serve to reinforce the antagonisms and divisions central to the conflict. Despite this, confronting the past, with all its pain and complexity, holds the potential to create new forms of dialogue and understanding that can lead to re-evaluations and new comprehensions that are truth-seeking in genuinely non-adversarial ways, all of which can be genuinely reparatory in their outcome. Those who were displaced as a result of the outbreak of conflict in the north of Ireland have lived with their experience with stoicism, with many silently holding on to their experience of victimhood. It is about time that their voices be afforded a dignified platform and their loss, suffering, and harm recognised as unjust.

Notes

1   Positive peace refers to a peace that is more than the absence of violence and one that is focused on, inter alia, the repairing of inter-personal relationships, and the creation of social structures that have been damaged by conflict and whose repair is for the betterment of the post-conflict society as a whole.

2   Typically, republicans are accused by unionists and others of attempting to 'rewrite' history to justify their violence as non-sectarian and a 'war of liberation'. Many nationalists and others accuse the British state, unionists, and loyalist paramilitaries of concealing their role in the conflict, particularly committing human rights violations and social exclusion against Catholic citizens. For an insightful overview of this complex debate, see Kieran McEvoy and Kirstin McConnachie, 'Victims and Transitional Justice: Voice, Agency and Blame', *Social and Legal Studies* 22 (4) (2013): 489–513.

3   Take, for example, the events of Bloody Sunday in Derry on 30 January 1972. Broadly, the Saville report released in June 2010 (Hoyt, Toohey, and Saville 2010) uncovered what are generally accepted facts about the events of the day and, most importantly, affirmed the innocence of the victims and wounded. However, within the hundreds of testimonies across an eclectic range of witnesses, there emerged both complimentary and contrasting memories, some nuanced, others vast. Across the inquiry, there were, therefore, undeniable facts that were backed by rigorous evidence, but there also existed a wide range of experiences, perspectives, and memories of events that day.

4   Christina's portfolio of artwork, including her work on displacement, is available to view at her website: http://christinabennett.ie.

Chapter Six

Conclusion

In Northern Ireland we have developed a remarkable ability to normalise the abnormal, to sideline residual, conflict issues and dismiss their impact as being par for the course in our transitional context. We laud our transition from conflict to imperfect 'peace' as remarkable (Coulter and Murray 2013) and in so doing, applaud those who took the great leap of faith needed to bring an end to a bloody, murky, and wholly destructive conflict. We have much to be positive about, and since the onset of 'peace' following the signing of the GFA in 1998, Northern Ireland has been designated and strategically marketed as a 'post-conflict' society. The persistent exaltation of Northern Ireland's ambiguous encounters with peace as a 'model of conflict resolution', however, withers in the face of a society imbued with many forms of deep-seated conflict, violence, division, and inequality. Despite the undoubted political progress and the ostensible semblances of peace and prosperity, the scars and long-term consequences of our violent past remain visceral and pervasive. The magnitude of our forced displacement story certainly weighs heavy with large-scale residential segregation widespread across the six counties. As beneficiaries of a hard-fought peace and as scholars committed to platforming the impact of forcible displacement on victims and survivors, it is incumbent that we engage in an honest appraisal of the progress thus far, to spotlight the successes but also to call into question the flaws and failings, particularly at a time when post GFA optimism appears in short supply. Many of us who call the north of Ireland home have grown up conditioned by the scourge of segregation and division, acutely aware of areas that are characterised as 'safe' or 'risky'. Our residential division is accompanied by a preference to engage and promote single identity cultural, sporting, and 'other' recreational activities. Despite pledges and affirmations by political leaders to tackle segregation in all areas of life, particularly housing and education, words have not been matched with deeds to take steps towards embracing a genuine, shared, integrated reality.

The 'temporary solutions' that were hastily erected at the outset of the Troubles, the oxymoronically named 'peace lines', remain in place – an enduring symbol of entrenched segregation, where their dual purpose now comprises a necessary segregation security measure and, more bizarrely, a 'must-see' tourist attraction. Their increase in both quantity and size since the signing of the 1998 peace accord acts as a cold reminder of our failure to develop meaningful, positive peace.[1] This expanding network of about 100 semi-permanent barriers more than 34km long and reaching, at their highest point, 7.5m tall did not emerge in a vacuum and for many who live on or alongside the walls, they continue to represent the legacy of forced displacement that erupted during the outbreak of the Troubles. Since the signing of the GFA, Shirlow and Murtagh (2006: 60) note that about 98 per cent of Northern Ireland Housing Executive (NIHE) estates remained segregated according to religious designation, with this figure only marginally falling in the intervening 20 years (Browne and Asprooth-Jackson 2019: 24). Although levels of housing division from 1991 to 2001 were largely stable (Shuttleworth and Lloyd 2009) overall segregation in the urban spaces of Belfast and Derry remains particularly pronounced. The reason for this segregation is attributed to many factors, including the growth of non-integrated social housing estates (Shirlow 2003: 78) and the failure of shared-housing initiatives to receive any meaningful investment, both fiscal and public buy-in. Resultantly, in the absence of actual violence and the important reduction in ethno-sectarian conflict, as we have noted above, the majority of Catholic and Protestant communities in Belfast and other urban spaces in Northern Ireland remain highly segregated in terms of residential living space.

In Derry City, the Protestant population in the West Bank, which is home to the shopping and commercial city centre, has declined from 8,459 in 1971 to a paltry 300 today and shows little sign of being reversed. Moreover, the importance of demographics, territory, and power has not receded despite the 1998 peace accord. Brexit has reignited the constitutional question regarding the border and status of Northern Ireland, shifting it to the centre of politics in ways unimaginable only a few years back. Though the spectacle and daily reality of 'peace walls' and other forms of physical segregation remains an urban phenomenon, rural Northern Ireland, nonetheless, suffers similar levels of division and segregation, albeit with manifestations far more subtle and banal. While the movement of Protestants from the border regions has abated in recent years, relative to levels during the Troubles, nevertheless, the overall trend signifies a continuing movement of Protestants out of the western counties of Tyrone, Fermanagh, and south Derry to what are considered the 'safer' areas within counties Down and Antrim. Despite the plurality of identities that exist, the resurgence of debate and contestation regarding any future border poll is primarily given expression through the idea of the 'two communities' and the obligatory 'ethno-religious' head count. Changing demographics remains a prominent, albeit at times, unspoken feature of periodical elections to Westminster and the Stormont Assembly. Though the violence that characterised the Troubles has largely ended, formations of the conflict have dolefully mutated into 'everyday' forms of violence and sectarianism, typified by interface rioting; attacks on cultural symbols such as GAA clubs and Orange Halls; disputes regarding parades, flags, and emblems; language rights; and violence around housing and locations of schools. All of these indicate the prevalence of conflict and division that continue to centre on the zero-sum politics of territory, people, and power (Shirlow and Murtagh 2006). Concerningly, the issue of violent forced displacement and intimidation of supposed minority families in single-identity spaces remains a feature in the present-day, 'post-conflict' Northern Ireland. In this context, it is shocking though unsurprising nevertheless that these forced expulsions of persons and families based on their actual or ascribed ethno-religious identity remains a widespread practice designed to ensure that meaningful integration is marginalised. Thus, the issue of demographics and the antagonistic politics of territory, people, and identity has always been, and remains, the absolute essence of political, social, and economic life since the founding of the state in 1921 and beforehand.

The reasons for our inability to overcome segregation and division are complex and intersecting, including, we suggest, a lack of political will, a lack of meaningful investment, and flawed planning processes. Strategies for desegregation, we suggest, must move beyond the reductive and limited 'shared space' approach, which reflects a particular neoliberal understanding of urban spaces and aggressive urban gentrification. The construction of numerous sites of consumption, such as Belfast's 'premier shopping and leisure attraction', Victoria Square, or the Titanic and Cathedral Quarters while bringing jobs and investment, are often misinterpreted as an axiomatic signifier of peace and stability. Such polished sites of consumption, however, do little to foster meaningful, cross-community relationships between communities that remain residentially segregated. Importantly, the personal costs of displacement, the loss of homes, communities, families, friends, and employment, among others, as detailed throughout this book, remain deep-seated but largely unrecognised by the wider society.

On the Charge of Ethnic Cleansing

The testimonies gathered and shared in this book reveal the breakdown of the fabric of the northern state and its Janus-faced role in both failing to prevent, and at times helping to facilitate, the mass movement of its own civilians. While not wishing to engage in hyperbole, some of the recollections shared can only be described as deeply troubling, particularly when spotlighting the actions of a state that was, at times, choosing to act in its own interests over others. Some of our respondents noted that, in any other context, many of their own experiences would be designated as forms of 'ethnic cleansing' or 'pogroms'. Several respondents who designate as nominally Catholic contended that, although it might not be considered politically correct (or expedient in the context of our fragile peace), ethnic cleansing is exactly how they would view the actions of the state at the time. In a similar vein, all our Protestant respondents who lived alongside the border with the Irish Republic saw their displacement and the actions of the IRA as a deliberate strategy of ethnic cleansing. The term has been used before in academic literature when referencing the case of forced displacement in Northern Ireland, including work done by Patterson (2013), and Dawson (2007), and so our decision to interrogate further the usefulness of the language is not without precedent.

The practice of what would we now commonly refer to as ethnic cleansing is one that, according to Bell-Fialkoff (1993: 110), is as 'old as antiquity'. According to the United Nations, ethnic cleansing can be defined as 'a purposeful policy designed by one ethnic or religious group to remove by violent and terror-inspiring means the civilian population of another ethnic or religious group from certain geographic territory'. The practice of ethnic cleansing has only been universally condemned in the aftermath of the Cold War; in the 100 years prior to that, many states seeking internal stability and external security sought to minimise the political impact of ethnic minorities with affiliations to other, often neighbouring states and so they adopted policies and practices of forcibly expelling minorities (Wolff 2007). The post-1945 milieu witnessed the forced expulsions of millions of ethnic Germans from central and eastern Europe, while in the Middle East, the term 'ethnic cleansing' has been mainstreamed by the work of Ilan Pappe (2007) when referencing the policies adopted by the fledgling Israeli state to safeguard its territorial gains by forcibly removing an indigenous Palestinian population. However, it is the breakup of the former Yugoslavia that is most often associated with the terminology.

A United Nations Commission of Experts mandated to look into violations of international humanitarian law committed in the territory of the former Yugoslavia defined ethnic cleansing as 'rendering an area ethnically homogeneous by using force or intimidation to remove persons of given groups from the area', adding that the practice is 'a purposeful policy designed by one ethnic or religious group to remove by violent and terror-inspiring means the civilian population of another ethnic or religious group from certain geographic areas' (United Nations nd). The Commission of Experts also stated that the coercive practices used to remove the civilian population can include: murder, torture, arbitrary arrest and detention, extrajudicial executions, rape and sexual assaults, severe physical injury to civilians, confinement of civilian population in ghetto areas, forced removal, displacement and deportation of civilian population, deliberate military attacks or threats of attacks on civilians and civilian areas, use of civilians as human shields, destruction of property, robbery of personal property, and attacks on hospitals, among others. Petrovic's

(1994) analysis of the emergence of the terminology during the war in the former Yugoslavia, and his detailed listing of actions that may constitute ethnic cleansing, is particularly helpful for shaping our own understanding. Various measures that may amount to the practice of ethnic cleansing are listed, including administrative processes (also referred to as the bureaucratic elements of ethnic cleansing), terrorising measures (including attacks on places of worship and intimidation of minorities or undesirables in the street), and finally, military measures (summary executions, laying siege to villages, killing leaders).

According to Jenne (2016: 115) the process of ethnic cleansing can be broken down into two tactics that can either happen at the same time or follow on from each other. In the first instance, the group targeted is either subjected to intimidation, threats of violence, or actual force to initiate a process of flight from the area. The second phase involves a process of settlement whereby the 'other' group assumes the dominant position within the newly 'cleansed' land, generating a single-identity, homogenous group presence and embedding this presence by way of creating 'facts on the ground'. The arguments around what drives processes of ethnic cleansing vary. Some argue that the process is the violent outworking of state formation and an aggressive manifestation of self-determination. However, Jenne (2016: 117) also notes that alternative drivers include 'mutual enmities stoked by national symbolism (Kaufman 2001), mutual fears of victimisation during state transition (Posen 1993), and state institutions that can be used to mobilize people to engage in violence'. What is also worth considering is the fact that ethnic cleansing is not limited to war-time scenarios; slow, insidious practices of ethnic-cleansing have become a more prominent feature in peacetime, transitional societies.

The experiences of forced displacement in Northern Ireland shared in this book clearly map on to many of the descriptors provided above – in particular, the narratives of respondents who recalled destruction of their property alongside their everyday experience of intimidation (both from state and non-state actors). For many with whom we met, these were among the primary drivers for their family being forced from their home. According to Patterson (2013: 350) the language of ethnic cleansing was brought into mainstream discourse in Northern Ireland, perhaps unsurprisingly, following the outbreak of war in Yugoslavia. However, rather than being adopted by Catholics to describe their experience at the hands of the northern state, it was first proclaimed by Ulster Unionist political representatives to reference ongoing attacks against Protestants living on or alongside the border with the Irish Republic. Other reports, as Patterson (2010) notes, included one commissioned by the Church of Ireland diocese of Clogher, entitled *Whatever You Say, Say Nothing* (Patterson 2010: 350–51), in which it was suggested, by those who participated in the study, that there existed a campaign of ethnic cleansing against their community. The IRA's targeting and killing of off-duty army and police officers, commencing in the early 1970s, was consistently interpreted as a widespread communal attack upon the Protestant population. Many republicans refute allegations of sectarianism and point to the fact that first, they targeted security force personnel and were therefore targeting those in uniform and, second, they contend that the British Government policy of 'Ulsterisation' from 1976 onwards, which reduced the number of 'regular' British Army troops and instead pushed the RUC and UDR to the front-lines, was part of a deliberate strategy to change the narrative of the conflict to an inter-communal, sectarian squabble. Such debate does not of course deflect from the immeasurable loss of family members and the pain and harm caused at both an individual and communal level is discernible and palpable.

There is a strong perception, particularly within certain loyalist/ unionist communities, of terminal spatial and cultural decline, whereby episodes of Protestant displacement are upheld and understood to be the result of deliberate practices of ethnic cleansing by republicans (Shirlow and Murtagh 2006). During the Troubles, there is no doubt that border Protestants and unionists were subjected to a politics of intimidation and terror, but there is little to no evidence to suggest that this took place on a scale, nor with the consistency of a systemic pattern, to warrant the description ethnic cleansing (Dawson 2007). Despite this, as Richard English's analysis of the republican movement suggests, the IRA's actions had a significant divisive effect on local relations and, moreover, were perceived by the Protestant community as military endeavours to drive Protestants away from the border. However, universal acceptance of ethnic cleansing as an appropriate terminology in this context is difficult to discern. Patterson (2010: 351) highlights that many Protestants living alongside the border argued against its use when it became mainstreamed, suggesting that it gave far too much credit to the effectiveness of the IRA campaign and downplayed the resilience and determination of those who refused to be intimidated from their homes. Patterson (2010: 351) also points to the work of Graham Dawson who has conducted extensive work on the Protestant population living alongside the Irish border, and who subsequently concludes:

> In the course of the Troubles, border Protestants and Unionists have been subjected to a politics of intimidation and terror, but this has not taken place on a scale, nor with the consistency of pattern to warrant the description 'ethnic cleansing'.

As with the experience of some Protestants living on or alongside the border, many Catholics, particularly those who were living in vulnerable enclaves and districts, considered their experiences to have fallen within a framework of systematic 'cleansing' based on their religious or ethno-national identities. Mary McAleese has referred to her family's experiences and that of other Catholic families on the upper Crumlin Road near Ardoyne as a form of 'ethnic cleansing' by loyalists, recalling:

> Little by little, they picked off the Catholic neighbours – murdered them, intimidated them. Looking back it was obvious that we were next on the list … There was a design in our case, no doubt; they were designed to get rid of Catholics, to get us out, hoping that we would move across the border and take our nine kids with us.

Fulfilling the criteria of 'terrorizing measures' as a category outlined by Petrovic (1994) above, one of our Catholic respondents from East Belfast recounted the repeated and sustained acts of intimidation and threat that his family received over a period of years, all of which built up a sense of vulnerability and that amounted to a concerted campaign to force his family from their area. These multiple threats to his life included having a bomb left under his car at his place of work, followed up by a gun attack on the family home. He maintains that his experience of intimidation and continuous threat was because he lived in one of very few Catholic family homes who remained in their street and who refused to leave, akin to 'ethnic cleansing'. Other nationalist and republican respondents with whom we met used the language of ethnic cleansing alongside that of the term 'pogrom', most typically associated with attacks that were directed against Russia's Jewish community from 1881 to 1921 and that subsequently gave rise to an attempted purge and mass movement of people. Such a purge was allowed to occur due to the inaction and non-intervention of an apathetic state, and the failure of civil and military authorities to prevent such attacks from happening. For many interviewees the inaction of the northern state to prevent their forced displacement at the hands of loyalist paramilitary groups shared similar features to that of a pogrom. When it comes to situating their own displacement experiences in the late 1960s and early 1970s, for many Catholic respondents the history and experience of the Belfast Pogrom of 1920–22 loom large and their own experience is the natural outworking of a state policy of exclusion deriving from the time of Partition that failed to change over time. Such a view has been challenged by Prince and Warner (2019) who contend that, while there are some similarities between Russian pogroms and the events in Belfast in August 1969, there is simply not enough evidence to substantiate the use of the term to the latter. There is also little evidence to support the idea that the RUC, the Northern Ireland Government, John McKeagues SDA, and an assortment of non-affiliated loyalists constituted a homogenous bloc working towards the same objective, that being the 'destruction' of the Catholic community in Belfast.

Therefore, when it comes to advancing the view that what took place during this tumultuous period in Northern Ireland's recent history amounts to 'ethnic cleansing', there are several flaws in the veracity of claims made.

Most significantly, there is a clear lack of evidence showing the initiation and distillation of displacement as a deliberate and a purposeful policy and strategy of 'warfare' in Northern Ireland. Unlike in areas such as Palestine/Israel, where the work of historians, including Ilan Pappe (2007), points to a deliberate Israeli policy of 'ethnic cleansing' of indigenous Arab Palestinians from their homes under a strategy known as Plan Dalet, discerning anything similar in the case of Northern Ireland has not been possible. Regardless, through our qualitative enquiry, we have presented clear evidence of state actors being involved in helping to facilitate the movement of families from their homes, either by actively encouraging flight or failing to act upon threats to families and property and, as such, we feel comfortable in saying that there were many instances where the state assumed a role in actively shifting the ethnic demographics of given areas. What is also important to note is that these feelings of frustration at state actor inability to protect cut across the sectarian divide, with many Protestant respondents noting their anger at the state's failures to prevent IRA attacks on their areas.

Added to this is the incoherent patterns of displacement and the plurality of forms of causal violence and intimidation, suggesting as it does a lack of coordination or joined-up, strategic planning in terms of processes of ethnic cleansing. While forced displacement in Northern Ireland is extensive in relation to the population size and geographical area, it is unlikely to amount to an international crime; nevertheless, the use of language like ethnic cleansing, pogrom, and genocide, reflects a serious uneasiness and vulnerability of communities living in their area where they are at risk from purging by their neighbours. More significantly, by reducing displacement or intimidation down to simply ethnic cleansing, we fail to fully appreciate the complex reasons that people had for leaving their area, nor are we able to meaningfully countenance the reasons why those who remained chose to do so. All of this is yet further compounded by the lack of reliable data to measure population movements and demographic changes at the estate or village level (Moffett et al. 2020). What becomes increasingly clear is that there exists an evidential gap when it comes to unveiling a state-sponsored policy with regard to facilitating population transfer and, as such, the language of ethnic cleansing does not sit squarely.

While the charge of ethnic cleansing may be difficult to sustain, we can nonetheless suggest that it was the inertia of the state, both in terms of failing to meaningfully intervene at the time and by not providing for the welfare of those who were forcibly displaced, that was particularly impactful. This lack of support at the time, we argue, has played a major role in maintaining segregation and single-identity communities in the present day. Putnam (2000: 318) has previously noted that 'in areas where poor people have little economic capital and face enormous barriers in accumulating human capital, social capital becomes absolutely crucial to their welfare'. Leonard (2004: 931) has noted the 'strong network ties and social and economic support structures' that exist in single-identity communities where the Northern Irish state has been notable in its absence, particularly evident in republican/nationalist West Belfast. In the absence of support and protection from the Northern Irish state, those who fled to areas such as West Belfast from other parts of the city were able to draw on the support of what one of our respondents referred to as the 'state within the state'. While this form of communal support was necessary at the time, the legacy of distrust of the state has meant that communal boundaries remain as rigid and inflexible as ever. In the years following the signing of the 1998 GFA, a perceived lack of meaningful investment in those communities most directly impacted by the Troubles has resulted in an entrenchment of this societal division and gives a good indication as to how addressing the legacy of residential segregation, despite opportunistic soundbites to the contrary, is far from a priority for those in office.

Platforming Displacement Experiences

Across many testimonies shared was a complicated and complex relationship to physical space with several respondents revealing a distinctive sense of dislocation and lack of 'rootedness'. 'See after you're displaced', as one respondent noted, 'you never really know where you are from or like, where you call home. We moved to Ardglass, but I'm not from here. I never really feel like I'm from anywhere.' For many, this was a typical refrain, and their displacement experience had an impact on their sense of personal identity and fostered a sense of unresolved disconnection to place and identity. Memories of forced displacement remain entrenched in a terrain of hostility, fear, and recrimination and are unsurprisingly deeply entwined within competing narratives of victimhood and culpability regarding the 30 years of armed violence, despite the advent of the 1998 peace accord. The mass movement of civilians that took place at the outset of the Troubles altered the landscape of Northern Ireland dramatically and, in some instances, irreversibly. The bearing this has had on the individual who suffered harm, although difficult – nigh on impossible – to quantify, was colossal. To address the harm that these deeply traumatic events caused, we must seek to develop meaningful spaces and opportunities to open up frank conversations, to acknowledge, appreciate, and understand the impact that this forced displacement had on individuals, families, communities, and society as a whole. Only by honestly appraising the impact of these events do we become better placed to forge a genuinely non-sectarian strategy for moving forward. Addressing legacy issues has become the politically charged exercise in our transitional era and routinely plunges the Northern Ireland executive into crisis. In borrowing the words of Howe (2000: 1), like every aspect of the conflict in Northern Ireland, delineating your preference for how best to deal with issues of our past is 'to take sides in a long and bitter intellectual conflict'. Following this logic, history itself and associated facts have become both sectarian and generative in respect of how we choose to categorise and define political violence, victims, and perpetrators (Browne and Bradley 2021). When it comes to forced displacement, our normalisation of the abnormal has resulted in an all-pervasive silence and a sweeping of otherwise traumatic experiences under the carpet. While some of those with whom we met discussed the need to be more intentional about creating opportunities for proper integration, others were adamant that the harm they had experienced from displacement during the Troubles could never be undone, further demonstrating the heterogeneity of victims' and survivors' experiences of trauma and loss. Some interviewees were, in fact, slightly vexed when asked about addressing or undoing the harm they had experienced, particularly those who had suffered further loss and trauma following their displacement (this was noted among several participants whose parents had passed away shortly after they had been forced from their homes).

Many of those who were internally displaced continued to live with the trauma of the Troubles albeit in less familiar surroundings from where they had been brought up. The shift from urban to rural space was, for some, surreal and impactful, particularly in terms of shaping their life trajectory. Some respondents noted that following their forced displacement they went on to experience further conflict-related trauma, losing a loved one due to a conflict-related incident. All of those who were displaced along the border mentioned that they continue to live abnormal lives even after their resettlement, noting the impact of their trauma as being manifest in certain practices that remain a feature of life even in the present day, including checking under their cars every morning for suspicious objects and seeking out extra security. Others noted how displacement and segregation shaped their everyday (im)mobility, with many deliberately avoiding certain streets, certain districts, certain sites of leisure, and certain employment possibilities. One of the most harrowing aspects of Northern Ireland's displacement is that some experienced the loss of their home and community on more than one occasion. Additionally, those evacuated from places like Ballymurphy, Ardoyne, and Springmartin had to endure such disruption and anguish on several occasions in the early 1970s.

The 1998 GFA acknowledges the pain and suffering of victims, including their right to remember and a requirement to provide support to those victims and/or survivors who need it; there is, however, little to no mention of the category of those who experienced forced displacement. Nor is there such anywhere in the Agreement that outlines the processes and institutions required to address the legacy of displacement, residential segregation, and communal division, as Lawther and Moffett (2021: 143) have noted:

> The Belfast Agreement (1998) does not deal expressly with land or housing matters. The subsection on Reconciliation uses 'initiatives to facilitate and promote ... mixed housing' to exemplify 'the promotion of a culture of tolerance at every level of society', which is identified as an 'essential aspect' of the reconciliation process, but no institutions or processes were established to address displacement, resettlement, or redistribution.

Since the signing of the Agreement, various other mechanisms to address the legacy of the past have been developed, including the Eames–Bradley Recommendations, the Stormont House Agreement, and the Fresh Start Agreement, none of which have been fully implemented due to an inability to garner the requisite cross-party support needed. None of these subsequent attempts platformed the experiences of the many victims and survivors of conflict-related, forced displacement. As we have endeavoured to show in our presentation of the myriad flight experiences captured by this research, forced displacement and the physical movement of families took on a variety of forms. It is this nuance, we suggest, that has yet to be captured when it comes to appreciating the deep impact that an all-pervasive sense of fear had on many families living through this tumultuous period. There was a sense that, due to the sheer scale of what was happening at the time, you just had to 'get on with it'. The testimonies we have shared in this book are rich, powerful narratives that are nuanced, evocative, and traumatic, while simultaneously being inspirational stories that demonstrate remarkable personal and community resilience. At times they reveal the long-term, deleterious impact that forced displacement had on the individual and members of the wider family network and as such they are worthy of a much more prominent place in our broader understanding of the outbreak of conflict and violence and its impact on the everyday citizen born into the Troubles in Northern Ireland. Being forced from your home because of violence or the threat of violence ought not to be dismissed whimsically as a normal, everyday occurrence. Therefore, a pressing and key challenge is to recognise forced displacement as a specific but heterogenous form of conflict-related violence and harm, and thus devise processes and approaches that address their particular transitional rights in a meaningful and holistic way. Though our research focused on those forcibly moved, an additional and overlooked consequence of forced flight is the impact on those left behind. Across Northern Ireland, the decline of minority populations due to displacement, such as the Catholic community in Whiteabbey and Rathcoole and the Protestant community in Newry, exacerbated individual and communal feelings of isolation and vulnerability among those who remained. The experiences and perspectives of minority communities, such as that of the Protestant community in Newry, have yet to be told and undoubtedly warrants wider attention and research.

Repairing the Harm

In Northern Ireland, legitimacy around the concept of victimhood continues to be a major issue when seeking to move beyond the legacy of conflict. Polarising and unhelpful debates routinely lead to the conclusion that some conflict-related experiences are deemed less worthy of recollection, reparation, or redress than others. While we agree that drawing false equivalency between victims and survivors ought to be avoided, not least to ensure that finite support services are made available for those who need them most (Breen-Smyth 2012), through the process of conducting this research with a broad range of survivors from across the sectarian divide, it is abundantly clear that the impact of displacement for many, including the loss and trauma endured, was profoundly life-changing. As a result, we remain steadfast in our belief that greater attention must be given to uncovering and sharing these stories and narratives save they be left to dissipate with the passing of time. In bringing forward a call for greater acknowledgement of this form of conflict-related violence, we don't seek to further delineate valid or less valid conflict narratives. Similarly, we are sensitive to the fact that as a society we are already struggling to find the most appropriate ways of moving beyond the legacy of our past.

However, we do maintain that there is space for those engaged in transitional justice practices, including academics and practitioners whose work focuses on dealing with the past, to pay greater attention to the significant difficulties that families who were forced from their homes endured during what was a time of great upheaval. Among many interviewees, there was an acceptance that traditional forms of justice, such as securing convictions, would be practically impossible and, in many cases, undesirable. Duthie and Seils (2016: 5) note that, in many instances, when it comes to issues around providing reparations for those who have experienced conflict-related displacement, 'The scope and complexity... can also create resource and capacity constraints. Providing financial compensation to thousands ... for instance, may be impossible in many, if not most, countries.' Appropriating individual blame or staking a claim to monetary compensation for the loss that was suffered did not feature prominently in our interviews. Rather, justice, for many respondents, included the opportunity to share their traumatic experiences and to combat the silence that many felt had developed around their displacement. An acknowledgement that what happened to them and their families was impactful and traumatic would go a long way in helping to close this unfortunate chapter in our past. As we have noted above, the silence around the forcibly displaced has hindered our ability as a society to meaningfully address the scourge of segregation, but of equal importance is the fact that it has also asked a great deal from those whose extraordinary experience has been relegated to the back of the queue when it comes to unpacking the trauma and victimhood associated with the everyday citizen in Northern Ireland. The recent emergence of a small body of academic work (Side 2015; Browne and Asprooth-Jackson 2019; Moffett et al. 2020; Gilmartin 2021) is a welcome development that has sought to challenge this normalisation of conflict-related displacement by centring the conversation within the broader literature on dealing with the past. Alongside this academic engagement, the most recent attempts to legislate for dealing with the past in Northern Ireland have placed a greater emphasis on safeguarding and repositioning the voices of the everyday person who has a story to share.

One of the most significant aspects of the 2014 Stormont House Agreement (SHA) was its commitment to support wider reconciliation efforts, by recognising a plurality of conflict-related narratives. Although the agreement proposed a range of mechanisms and approaches to addressing the legacy of the conflict, a key institution of the SHA that is often overlooked is the proposal for an Oral History Archive (OHA), which could provide an important platform for personal storytelling and public acknowledgement, something that resonates with many of those who survived displacement. Calls for an archive to document these experiences in a way that is free from political interference could provide an opportunity for those who experienced forced displacement to have their story heard and recorded. While broadly in favour of an OHA that also captures stories of conflict-related displacement, we also urge caution and note the need to ensure that the stories that are captured are not decontextualised or documented in a way that fails to spotlight the detrimental role played by both state and non-state actors in causing the harm. Subsequently, we call on those who are involved in establishing an OHA in Northern Ireland to ensure they pay particular attention as to how such an archive is curated and to ensure it does not become an opportunity for a whitewashed, sanitised version of history to be retained. As we have shown throughout, it is necessary and important to critique the role played by the state in helping to facilitate displacement through its active support or non-intervention at the time and if curated properly, the OHA ought to capture this.

A proposed Belfast History Museum offers one potential further avenue for capturing and presenting these stories of forcible displacement in a way that ensures they no longer remain hidden from the public eye. A useful blueprint to follow in this regard is that of the 'Everyday Objects Transformed by Conflict' exhibition curated by Northern Ireland's leading non-governmental organization (NGO) for dealing with the past, Healing Through Remembering. According to their website, the 'exhibition reveals both unique and everyday stories through a range of loaned objects and their accompanying labels, all written in the words of those who own them'. The founders of the exhibition are guided by the principle that there does not exist one, single version of our history and visitors are invited to consider the objects as offering a glimpse into the everyday lives of those communities living during the Troubles, helping them to discern for themselves the true nature and meaning of the causes and effects of the conflict. We suggest that any future Belfast History Museum must pay particular attention to our legacy of conflict-related displacement, capture the voices of those who were displaced, and subsequently link these experiences to the ongoing issues of residential and social segregation in the present day.

When questioned specifically about how to document such forced displacement experiences, and how we as a society might platform, preserve, and showcase these stories so as to acknowledge the harm that many had experienced, a senior representative from the Northern Ireland Alliance Party noted:

> I think it's difficult. What I would say though is, I think there needs to be the story told a lot more anyway. I think that would be the first thing and I think maybe even in that point of view, it would be very helpful for people to know about that story. So, if we are having a Belfast Story Museum, that should be one of the things where we'll have those kinds of stories being told. Because at this moment in time, obviously, you focus on people who've been murdered or who died during the campaign, and all that sort of thing. But being burnt out did have a major effect, because as you say, it led to segregation and housing issues and everything else. So, there is a place for that story, yes – and I definitely think it should be in there.

The popular post-conflict refrain of 'never again' can only really be heeded when we are fully transparent and honest about what took place in the first place. Capturing displacement stories in dedicated oral history archives will also shine a light on the fact that, before the outbreak of conflict in the late 1960s, many spaces across Northern Ireland were, in fact, shared, mixed areas. This is a powerful message of hope when it comes to challenging those who see segregation and sectarian division as the norm. While we have been able to capture some testimonies cutting across the sectarian divide and have sought to ensure a broad geographical and religious representation, by virtue of the sheer volume of those who were impacted, many stories remain untold. Many of those with whom we met told us that it was the first time they had ever delved deep into their displacement experience. Equally troubling was that in some instances interviewees also noted a transgenerational impact of displacement where their own children have expressed feelings and narratives of 'not really being from here', despite being born long after their parents and grandparents were displaced. At times the interview process was emotional and challenging, yet further demonstrating the need to ensure that we can provide opportunities for those who wish to share their story. Failure to do so could mean that these stories of forced displacement become lost as successive generations pass away. While the overwhelming majority were pleased to be afforded the chance to discuss their experience, many did so with caution avoiding the drawing of a false equivalence by situating their 'story' alongside what they perceived to be a group of other, more deserving victims. At other times, some of our respondents, particularly those former members of the police and army, were understandably anxious and concerned about divulging identities, once again highlighting the presence of fear, threat, and insecurity some two decades after the 1998 peace accord. These testimonies should be and should always have been part of the rich tapestry of victims' and survivors' narratives to emerge from the Troubles, but we hope that they also challenge prevailing assumptions about being forcibly displaced while also adding to wider understandings of conflict-related definitions of violence and harm. It has been our intention to bring them to the surface in a way that is organic, and (we hope) sympathetic.

Condemned to Repeat It?

Throughout this book, we stressed the reality that forced movement pre-dates the Troubles, and more dolefully, remains a feature of life here despite the peace processes. A central logic underpinning the Northern Ireland peace process is the assumption that actor-based, manifest, direct violence constitutes the primary source of insecurity and volatility in modern conflicts. Much political and social capital has therefore focused, understandably, on those conventional forms of physical violence that characterised the Troubles. A direct consequence, however, is the marginalisation of other configurations of violence such as displacement. A common thread throughout this book is the silence and lack of recognition afforded to forced displacement. As a form of violence wholly neglected within prevailing approaches to peace, the violence of intimidation and forced displacement has therefore escaped the rigours of Northern Ireland's peace process, where it remains prominent and present today. Statistics from the Northern Ireland Housing Executive revealed that from 2013 to 2015, some 1,285 families were looking for homes due to housing intimidation (Wilson 2016). In 2017 *The Irish News*[2] reported that, since April 2016, the Northern Ireland Housing Executive was attempting to process 477 people who had presented as being homeless due to being intimidated from their homes as a result of paramilitary threats. Importantly, those most impacted by this present-day violent displacement are usually people living at the sharp edge of Northern Ireland's transition out of conflict. Following a freedom of information request submitted by the *Belfast Telegraph*[3] in 2019 it was revealed that from April 2015 to October 2018, some 2,017 households had presented themselves before the NIHE as being homeless due to intimidation. Of those 2,017 some 1,488 cases had been listed as being intimidation by paramilitaries. Within these figures, 135 cases were listed as being intimidation due to a sectarian incident and a further 80 were listed as being due to racial intimidation. These statistics make for grim and depressing reading and suggest, very clearly, that the issue of forced displacement is not something that can be consigned to the history books. Research published in *The New Statesman*[4] further points to the scourge of paramilitary groups in 'cleansing' residential areas from those they consider to be undesirable residents. What is also apparent in the statistical breakdown of victims is that, beyond the scourge of inter-communal sectarianism, issues related to forced transfer and racism have become more common place across Northern Ireland. This somewhat jars with the 'City of Sanctuary' title bestowed upon Belfast in 2013 when Northern Ireland pledged to open its doors to those who were fleeing conflict in the Middle East. It remains to be seen if this will continue to develop as an issue as Northern Ireland presents itself as a welcoming haven for refugees from other conflict-affected areas. What is evident, however, is that when it comes to forced displacement, the lessons from the past remain unheeded.

Moffett et al. (2020: 48) note, 'Efforts at integrated housing have struggled to take hold in the face of ongoing paramilitary influence in communities and more structural reform has lacked political will, so as to avoid upsetting electoral boundaries and representation in the Northern Ireland Assembly and Westminster.' In September 2017, a shared housing scheme designated in Cantrell Close, on the Ravenhill Road in East Belfast, made news headlines when a number of Catholic families who had opted to live there were forced from their homes due to perceived paramilitary intimidation.[5] Despite a broad outpouring of condemnation across the political spectrum, the largest political party in the North, including some prominent members of the Democratic Unionist Party, at the time refused to condemn the erection of paramilitary flags and emblems in a space that had been designated as shared, for fear of losing face among their traditional voter base. Similarly, Protestants in places such as Upper Ardoyne continue to express their fears of encroachment by a growing Catholic population, accompanied by a demonisation of their culture by republicans and a declining Protestant population due to continuing fear and insecurity. For all intents and purposes, housing in Northern Ireland remains fundamentally shaped by ethno-religious demographic concerns, rather than need, with the 2012 Girdwood fiasco an appropriate case in point.[6] While there have been some attempts made to desegregate urban spaces in Belfast and across Northern Ireland, which ought to be viewed as an important first step in addressing the legacy of violent displacement that occurred at the outset of the Troubles, to date these schemes have not been prioritised and have therefore been limited in terms of success. Until there is a more meaningful political buy-in towards tackling segregation, then shared residential housing schemes will exist in isolation.

It is Spanish philosopher George Santayana who is accredited with the saying, 'Those who cannot remember the past are condemned to repeat it', and as is the case in Northern Ireland, those families who were violently displaced are emblematic of the 'everyday' victim and survivor, whose experiences will remain hidden behind a mask of stoicism unless afforded a more prominent position within the wider discourse on dealing with the past. The rich tapestry of intuitive solutions, emanating primarily from a grassroots perspective, provide a useful blueprint as to how we might begin to acknowledge, capture, store, process, and learn from the forced displacement experience, to relegate it to history, and to ensure that we meaningfully make strides towards reversing its impact and engaging in a process of societal healing. Oral histories, public community led memorialisation, and shared cross-community schemes to acknowledge the harm of conflict are all potential avenues to explore in seeking to spotlight the impact of this specific type of conflict-related harm. What is clear among the views of those whose voices are present throughout this book is the desire to be heard; the challenge for the rest of society is our willingness and ability to listen.

Notes

1   A phrase coined by one of the fathers of Peace Studies in reference to a peace that is based on sustainability, through meaningful economic development that allows for structural reform to foster better societal relationships following a period of conflict.

2   https://www.irishnews.com/news/2017/11/07/news/rise-in-people-presenting-themselves-as-homeless-due-to-paramilitary-intimidation-1181044/.

3   https://www.belfasttelegraph.co.uk/news/northern-ireland/exclusive-2000-households-forced-out-of-their-homes-paramilitaries-blamed-for-73-of-cases-37676384.html.

4   https://www.newstatesman.com/politics/2021/04/how-northern-ireland-s-paramilitaries-exploit-social-housing.

5   https://www.irishnews.com/news/2017/11/07/news/rise-in-people-present-ing-themselves-as-homeless-due-to-paramilitary-intimidation-1181044/.

6   Girdwood is a former British Army barracks in North Belfast. Opened in 1970, it eventually closed in 2005. After years of deadlock over how the land should be redeveloped, in May 2012 the DUP and Sinn Féin agreed to develop the site for recreation and housing, with housing units allocated equally along ethno-national/sectarian lines despite the fact that the overwhelming demand for housing stems from the nationalist population. Under the auspices of 'shared space' and despite the potential to build 20,000 housing units, the 50:50 Catholic/Protestant deal between Sinn Féin and the DUP decreased that number down to 5,000 housing units alongside a cross-community centre The Girdwood Hub.

Bibliography

Acheson, Nicholas and Carl Milofsky. 2008. 'Peace Building and Participation in Northern Ireland: Local Social Movements and the Policy Process since the "Good Friday" Agreement'. *Ethnopolitics* 7 (1): 63–80.

Adhikari, P., W. L. Hansen, and K. L. Powers (2012) 'The Demand for Reparations: Grievance, Risk, and the Pursuit of Justice in Civil War Settlement'. *Journal of Conflict Resolution* 56 (2): 183–205. https://journals.sagepub.com/doi/abs/10.1177/0022002711421594.

Adhikari, Prakash. 2013. 'Conflict-Induced Displacement, Understanding the Causes of Flight'. *American Journal of Political Science* 57: 82–89.

Ager, Alastair and Allison Strang. 2008. 'Understanding Integration: Conceptual Framework'. *Journal of Refugee Studies* 21 (1): 166–91.

Aiken, Nevin T. 2010. 'Learning to Live Together: Transitional Justice and Intergroup Reconciliation in Northern Ireland'. *International Journal of Transitional Justice* 4 (2): 166–88.

Aldrich, Daniel P. 2012. *Building Resilience: Social Capital in Post-Disaster Recovery*. Chicago: University of Chicago Press.

Anderson, Benedict. 1983. *Imagined Communities: Reflections on the Origins and Spread of Nationalism*. London and New York: Verso.

Anderson, Michelle E. 2019. 'Community-Based Transitional Justice Via the Creation and Consumption of Digitalized Storytelling Archives: A Case Study of Belfast's Prisons Memory Archive'. *International Journal of Transitional Justice* 13 (1): 30–49.

Ardoyne Commemoration Project. 2002. *Ardoyne: The Untold Truth*. Belfast: Beyond the Pale.

Arvantis, E. and N. Yelland. 2019. '"Home Means Everything to Me ...": A Study of Young Syrian Refugees' Narratives Constructing Home in Greece'. *Journal of Refugee Studies* 34 (1): 535–54.

Barkan, Elazar. 2016. 'Memories of Violence: Micro and Macro History and the Challenges to Peacebuilding in Colombia and Northern Ireland'. *Irish Political Studies* 31 (1): 6–28.

Baron, Ilan Zvi, Jonathan Havercroft, Isaac Kamola, Jonneke Koomen, Justin Murphy, and Alex Prichar. 2019. 'Liberal Pacification and the Phenomenology of Violence'. *International Studies Quarterly* 63: 199–212.

Bar-Tal, Daniel. 2003. 'Collective Memory of Physical Violence: Its Contribution to the Culture of Violence'. In *The Role of Memory in Ethnic Conflict*, edited by Ed Cairns and Michael D. Roe, 77–93. New York: Palgrave.

Bean, Kevin. 2011. 'Civil Society, the State and Conflict Transformation in the Nationalist Community'. In *Building Peace in Northern Ireland*, edited by Maria Power, 154–71. Liverpool: Liverpool University Press.

Bell, Christine. 2003. 'Dealing with the Past in Northern Ireland'. *Fordham International Law Journal* 26 (4): 1095–147.

Bell-Fialkoff, A. 1993. 'A Brief History of Ethnic Cleansing'. *Foreign Affairs* (summer): 110–21.

Bielenberg, Andy. 2013. 'Exodus: The Emigration of Southern Irish Protestants during the Irish War of Independence and the Civil War'. *Past & Present* 218: 199–233.

Biggar, Nigel. 2001. *Burying the Past: Making Peace and Doing Justice after Civil Conflict.* Washington, DC: Georgetown University Press.

Bloomfield, Kenneth. 1998. 'We Will Remember Them: Report of the Northern Ireland Victims Commissioner'. https://cain.ulster.ac.uk/issues/violence/victims.htm (accessed 1 August 2022).

Boal, F. 1969. 'Territoriality in the Shankill-Falls Divide in Belfast'. *Irish Geography* 6 (1): 30–50.

Boccagni, Paolo. 2014. 'What's in a (Migrant) House? Changing Domestic Spaces, the Negotiation of Belonging and Home-making in Ecuadorian Migration'. *Housing, Theory and Society* 31 (3): 277–93.

Bonner, M. and M. James. 2011. 'The Three R's of Seeking Transitional Justice: Reparation, Responsibility, and Reframing in Canada and Argentina'. *International Indigenous Policy Journal* 2 (3): 1–29. https://ir.lib.uwo.ca/iipj/vol2/iss3/3/.

Borer, Tristan Anne. 2003. 'A Taxonomy of Victims and Perpetrators: Human Rights and Reconciliation in South Africa'. *Human Rights Quarterly* 25: 1088–116.

Bouris, Erika. 2007. *Complex Political Victims.* Connecticut: Kumarian Press.

Boyd, Andrew. 1969. *Holy War In Belfast.* Belfast: Pretani Press.

Bradley, Megan. 2012. 'Truth-telling and Displacement: Patterns and Prospects'. In *Displacement and Transitional Justice*, edited by Roger Duthie, 189–232. New York: Social Sciences Research Council.

Breen-Smyth, Marie. 2012. 'The Needs of Individuals and Their Families Injured as a Result of the Troubles in Northern Ireland'. Report for the WAVE Trauma Centre (Belfast).

Brewer, John D. 2010. *Peace Processes: A Sociological Approach.* Cambridge: Polity.

Brewer, John D. 2018. 'Towards a Sociology of Compromise'. In *The Sociology of Compromise after Conflict*, edited by John D. Brewer, Bernadette C. Hayes, and Francis Teeney, 1–29. London: Palgrave Macmillan.

Brewer, John D. and Bernadette C. Hayes. 2011. 'Victims as Moral Beacons: Victims and Perpetrators in Northern Ireland'. *Contemporary Social Science* 6 (1): 73–88.

Brown, Kris. 2013. 'Commemoration as Symbolic Reparation: New Narratives or Spaces of Conflict?' *Human Rights Review* 14 (3): 273–89.

Browne, B. and C. Dwyer. 2014. 'Navigating Risk: Understanding the Impact of the Conflict on Children and Young People in Northern Ireland'. *Studies in Conflict & Terrorism* 37 (9): 792–805.

Browne, B. C. and C. Asprooth-Jackson. 2019. 'From 1969 to 2018: Relocating Historical Narratives of Displacement during "the Troubles" through the European Migrant Crisis'. *Capital & Class* 43 (1): 23–38.

Browne, B. C. and E. Bradley. 2021. 'Promoting Northern Ireland's Peacebuilding Experience in Palestine–Israel: Normalising the Status Quo'. *Third World Quarterly* (May): 1–19.

Brun, Catherine. 2003. 'Local Citizens or Internally Displaced Persons? Dilemmas of Long Term Displacement in Sri Lanka'. *Journal of Refugee Studies* 16: 380–97.

Burgess, J. 2011. *The Exodus: The Story that Had to be Told*. Belfast, Nicholson and Bass.

Busteed, Mervyn. 2022. *The Sash on the Mersey: The Orange Order in Liverpool 1819–1982*. Liverpool: Liverpool University Press.

Cassidy, Kevin J. 2005. 'Organic Intellectuals and the Committed Community: Irish Republicanism and Sinn Féin in the North'. *Irish Political Studies* 20 (3): 341–56.

Cassidy, Kevin J. 2008. 'Organic Intellectuals and the New Loyalism: Re-Inventing Protestant Working-Class Politics in Northern Ireland'. *Irish Political Studies* 23 (3): 411–30.

Cederman, Lars-Erik and Kristian Skrede Gleditsch. 2009. 'Introduction to Special Issue on "Disaggregating Civil War"'. *Journal of Conflict Resolution* 53 (4): 487–95.

CGPNI (Consultative Group on the Past Northern Ireland). 2009. 'Report of The Consultative Group on the Past'. (Belfast).

Coakley, John. 2007. 'National Identity in Northern Ireland: Stability or Change?' *Nations and Nationalism* 13 (4): 573–597.

Coates, T. 2014. 'The Case for Reparations'. *The Atlantic*. https://www.theatlantic.com/magazine/archive/2014/06/the-case-for-reparations/361631/ (accessed 5 January 2022).

Cobain, Ian. 2020. *Anatomy of a Killing: Life and Death on a Divided Island*. London: Granta.

Cochrane, Feargal. 2013. *Northern Ireland: The Reluctant Peace*. London: Yale University Press.

Cochrane, Feargal and Seamus Dunn. 2002. *People Power? The Role of the Voluntary and Community Sector in the Northern Ireland Conflict*. Cork: Cork University Press.

Cohen, Stanley. 2001. *States of Denial: Knowing about Atrocities and Suffering*. Cambridge: Polity.

Colvin, C. 2006. 'Overview of the Reparations Program in South Africa'. In *The Handbook of Reparations*, edited by Pablo de Greiff, 176–215. Oxford: Oxford University Press.

Community Relations Commission. 1971. 'FLIGHT: A Report on Population Movement in Belfast During August, 1971'. https://cain.ulster.ac.uk/issues/housing/docs/flight.htm (accessed 1 August 2022).

Conroy, Pauline, Tommy McKearney, and Quintin Oliver. 2005. *All Over the Place: People Displaced to and from the Southern Border Counties as a Result of the Conflict 1969–1994*. Monaghan: ADM/CPA.

Corradetti, Claudio, Nir Eisikovits, and Jack Rotondi. 2015. *Theorizing Transitional Justice*. Farnham: Ashgate.

Coulter, Colin. 1999. *Contemporary Northern Irish Society: An Introduction*. London: Pluto Press.

Coulter, Colin, Niall Gilmartin, Katy Hayward, and Peter Shirlow. 2021. *Northern Ireland a Generation after Good Friday: Lost Futures and New Horizons in the 'Long Peace'*. Manchester: Manchester University Press.

Coulter, Colin, and Michael Murray, eds. 2013. *Northern Ireland after the Troubles: A Society in Transition*. Manchester: Manchester University Press.

Coyles, David. 2017. 'The Security-threat-community'. *City* 21 (6): 699–723.

Craig, Anthony. 2010. *Crisis of Confidence: Anglo Irish Relations in the Early Troubles*. Dublin: Irish Academic Press.

Crawley, Heaven and Dimitris Skleparis. 2018. 'Refugees, Migrants, Neither, Both: Categorical Fetishism and the Politics of Bounding in Europe's "Migration Crisis"'. *Journal of Ethnic and Migration Studies* 44 (1): 48–64.

Czaika, Mathias and Krisztina Kis-Katos. 2009. 'Civil Conflict and Displacement: Village-Level Determinants of Forced Migration in Aceh'. *Journal of Peace Research* 46 (3): 399–418.

Darby, John. 1986. *Intimidation and the Control of Conflict in Northern Ireland*. Dublin: Gill & Macmillan.

Darby, John and Geoffrey Morris. 1974. 'Intimidation in Housing'. Research paper for the Northern Ireland Community Relations Commission. https://cain.ulster.ac.uk/issues/housing/docs/nicrc.htm (accessed 1 August 2022).

Darby, John and Arthur Williamson. 1978. *Violence and the Social Services in Northern Ireland*. London: Heinemann Education Books.

Davenport, Christina, Will Moore, and Steven Poe. 2003. 'Sometimes You Just Have to Leave: Domestic Threats and Forced Migration, 1964–1989'. *International Interactions* 29 (1): 27–55.

Dawson, Graham. 2007. *Making Peace with the Past? Memory, Trauma and the Irish Troubles*. Manchester: Manchester University Press.

Dawson, Graham. 2017. 'The Meaning of "Moving On": From Trauma to the History and Memory of Emotions in "Post-Conflict" Northern Ireland'. *Irish University Review* 47 (1): 82–102.

De Baroid, Ciaran. 2000. *Ballymurphy and the Irish War*. London: Pluto Press.

De Vroome, Thomas and Frank van Tubergan. 2014. 'Settlement Intentions of Recently Arrived Immigrants and Refugees in the Netherlands'. *Journal of Immigrant and Refugee Studies* 12 (1): 47–66.

Demmers, Jolle. 2017. *Theories of Violent Conflict: An Introduction*. London and New York: Routledge.

Department of Justice, Equality and Law Reform. 2003. 'The Remembrance Commission and Scheme of Acknowledgement, Remembrance, and Assistance for Victims in this Jurisdiction of the Conflict in Northern Ireland'. Policy document. http://www.justice.ie/en/JELR/RembCommOverview.pdf/Files/RembCommOverview.pdf (accessed 1 August 2022).

Devlin, Paddy. 1993. *Straight Left: An Autobiography*. Belfast: Blackstaff Publications.

Doná, Giorgia. 2007. 'The *Microphysics* of Participation in Refugee Research'. *Journal of Refugee Studies* 20 (2): 210–29.

Donnan, Hastings. 2005. 'Material Identities: Fixing Ethnicity in the Irish Borderlands'. *Identities: Global Studies in Culture and Power* 12 (1): 69–105.

Donnan, Hastings and Simpson, Kirk. 2007. 'Silence and Violence among Northern Ireland Border Protestants'. *Ethnos* 72 (1): 5–28.

Duthie, Roger. 2011. 'Transitional Justice and Displacement'. *International Journal of Transitional Justice* 5 (2): 241–61.

Duthie, R., and P. Seils. 2016. *The Case for Action on Transitional Justice and Displacement: Strategies During and After Conflict*. New York: International Center for Transitional Justice.

East Belfast Historical and Cultural Society. 2000. *Hands Across the Water. Belfast–Liverpool: The Refugee Crisis, 1971. The Untold Story*. Belfast: East Belfast Historical and Cultural Society.

Eastmond, Marita. 2007. 'Stories as Lived Experience: Narratives in Forced Migration Research'. *Journal of Refugee Studies* 20 (2): 248–64.

Ellis, Donald. G. 2006. *Transforming Conflict: Communication and Ethnopolitical Conflict*. Oxford: Rowman and Littlefield Publishers.

Ellison, G. and Smyth, J. 2000. *The Crowned Harp: Policing Northern Ireland*. London: Pluto.

Enloe, Cynthia H. 2014. *Bananas, Beaches and Bases: Making Feminist Sense of International Politics*. Berkeley: University of California Press.

Erdal, Marta Bivand and Ceri Oeppen. 2018. 'Forced to Leave? The Discursive and Analytical Significance of Describing Migration as Forced and Voluntary'. *Journal of Ethnic and Migration Studies* 44 (6): 981–98.

Fairey, Tiffaney and Rachel Kerr. 2020. 'What Works? Creative Approaches to Transitional Justice in Bosnia and Herzegovina'. *International Journal of Transitional Justice* 14 (1): 142–64.

Farrington, Christopher. 2004. 'Models of Civil Society and Their Implications for the Northern Ireland Peace Process'. IBIS Working Papers 43 (Dublin).

Ferguson, Neil, Mark Burgess, and Ian Hollywood. 2010. 'Who are the Victims? Victimhood Experiences in Postagreement Northern Ireland'. *Political Psychology* 31 (6): 857885.

Ferry, Finola, Edel Ennis, Brendan Bunting, Samuel Murphy, David Bolton, and Siobhan O'Neill. 2011. 'Troubled Consequences: A Report on the Mental Health Impact of the Civil Conflict in Northern Ireland'. Report for the Commission for Victims and Survivors (Belfast).

Ferry, Finola, Edel Ennis, Brendan Bunting, Samuel Murphy, David Bolton, and Siobhan O'Neill. 2017. 'Exposure to Trauma and Mental Health Service Engagement Among Adults Who Were Children of the Northern Ireland Troubles of 1968 to 1998'. *Journal of Traumatic Stress* 30: 593–601.

Ferstman, C. 2017. 'Reparations, Assistance and Support'. In *Victim Participation in International Criminal Justice*, edited by Kinga Tibori-Szabó and Megan Hirst, 385–411. The Hague: Asser Press. https://link.springer.com/chapter/10.1007/978-94-6265-177-7_13.

Firchow, P. 2017. 'Do Reparations Repair Relationships? Setting the Stage for Reconciliation in Colombia'. *International Journal of Transitional Justice* 11 (2): 315–38. https://doi.org/10.1093/ijtj/ijx010.

Firchow, P. and Mac Ginty, R. 2013. 'Reparations and Peacebuilding: Issues and Controversies'. *Human Rights Review* 14 (3): 231–39. https://link.springer.com/article/10.1007/s12142-013-0275-1.

García-Godos, J. 2008. 'Victim Reparations in Transitional Justice – What is at Stake and Why'. *Nordisk tidsskrift for menneskerettigheter* 26: 111–202. https://heinonline.org/HOL/LandingPage?handle=hein.journals/norjhur26&div=11&id=&page=.

Ghorashi, Halleh. 2005. 'Agents of Change or Passive Victims: The Impact of Welfare States (the Case of the Netherlands) on Refugees'. *Journal of Refugee Studies* 18 (2): 181–98.

Giddens, Anthony. 1991. *Modernity and Self-Identity: Self and Society in the Late Modern Age*. Cambridge: Polity Press.

Gilligan, Chris. 2008. 'Community Responses to Disaster: Northern Ireland 1969 as a Case Study'. In *Handbook of Community Movements and Local Organizations*, edited by Ram A. Cnaan and Carl Milofsky, 311–28. New York: Springer.

Gilmartin, Niall. 2019. *Female Combatants after Armed Struggle: Lost in Transition?* New York: Routledge.

Gilmartin, Niall. 2021. '"Ending the Silence": Addressing the Legacy of Displacement in Northern Ireland's "Troubles"'. *International Journal of Transitional Justice* 15 (1): 108–27.

Graham, Laura K. 2016. *Beyond Social Capital: The Role of Leadership, Trust and Government Policy in Northern Ireland's Victim Support Groups*. London: Palgrave Macmillan.

Greiff, Pablo de. 2006. 'Justice and Reparations'. In *The Handbook of Reparations*, edited by Pablo de Greiff, 451–72. Oxford: Oxford University Press.

Griffiths, J. H. 1975. 'Paramilitary Groups and Other Community Action Groups in Northern Ireland Today'. *International Review of Community Development* 33 (4): 189–206.

Gubrium, Jaber F. and James A. Holstein. 2001. *Handbook of Interview Research: Context and Method*. London: Sage.

Hackett, Claire and Bill Rolston. 2009. 'The Burden of Memory: Victims, Storytelling and Resistance in Northern Ireland'. *Memory Studies* 2 (3): 355–76.

Haddad, Emma. 2008. *The Refugee in International Society: Between Sovereigns*. Cambridge: Cambridge University Press.

Hamber, Brandon and Gráinne Kelly. 2016. 'Practice, Power and Inertia: Personal Narrative, Archives and Dealing with the Past in Northern Ireland'. *Journal of Human Rights Practice* 8: 25–44.

Hamber, Brandon and Patricia Lundy. 2020. 'Lessons from Transitional Justice? Toward a New Framing of a Victim-Centered Approach in the Case of Historical Institutional Abuse'. *Victims and Offenders* 15 (6): 744–70. https://doi.org/10.1080/1 5564886.2020.1743803.

Hanley, Brian. 2018. *The Impact of the Troubles on the Republic of Ireland, 1968–79: Boiling Volcano?* Manchester: Manchester University Press.

Hanley, Brian and Scott Millar. 2009. *The Lost Revolution: The Story of the Official IRA and the Workers' Party*. Dublin: Penguin Ireland.

Hansson, Ulf and McLaughlin, Helen. 2018. 'Protestant Migration from the West Bank of Derry / Londonderry 1969–1980'. Report for the Pat Finucane Centre (Derry).

Hart, Peter. 1998. *The IRA and Its Enemies: Violence and Community in Cork, 1916–1923*. Oxford: Oxford University Press.

Hayes, B. C., and I. McAllister. 2013. *Conflict to Peace: Politics and Society in Northern Ireland Over Half a Century*. Manchester: Manchester University Press.

Hayner, Priscilla B. 2001. *Unspeakable Truths: Facing the Challenge of Truth Commissions*. New York and London: Routledge.

Healey, R. L. 2006. 'Asylum-seekers and Refugees: A Structuration Theory Analysis of Their Experiences in the UK'. *Population, Space and Place* 12 (4): 257–71.

Hearty, K. 2020. 'Problematising Symbolic Reparation: "Complex Political Victims", "Dead Body Politics" and the Right to Remember'. *Social & Legal Studies* 29 (3): 334–54.

Heimerl, Daniela. 2005. 'The Return of Refugees and Internally Displaced Persons: From Coercion to Sustainability?' *International Peacekeeping* 12 (3): 377–90.

Hennessey, Thomas. 2005. *Northern Ireland: The Origins of the Northern Ireland Troubles*. Dublin: Gill & Macmillan.

Hennessey, Thomas. 2007. *The Evolution of the Troubles 1970–72*. Dublin: Irish Academic Press.

Horowitz, Donald L. 2000. *Ethnic Groups in Conflict*. Berkeley: University of California Press.

Hourmat, Margarida. 2016. 'Victim-Perpetrator Dichotomy in Transitional Justice: The Case of Post-Genocide Rwanda'. *Narrative and Conflict: Explorations in Theory and Practice* 4 (1): 43–67.

Howe, S. 2000. *Ireland and Empire: Colonial Legacies in Irish History and Culture.* Oxford: Oxford University Press.

Hoyt, William, John Toohey, and Lord Mark Saville. 2010. 'Report of the Bloody Sunday Inquiry: v. 1-10'. House of Commons papers (London).

Hughes B. 2017. 'Catholics Ordered out of Belfast Shared Housing in Sectarian Threat'. *The Irish News*, 28 September. https://www.irishnews.com/news/2017/11/07/news/rise-in-people-presenting-themselves-as-homeless-due-to-paramilitary-intimidation-1181044/ (accessed 15 September 2021).

Jankowitz, Sarah. 2017. 'Sociopolitical Implications of Exclusive, Intergroup Perceptions of Victims in Societies Emerging from Conflict'. *Peacebuilding* 5 (3): 289–304.

Jankowitz, Sarah E. 2018. *The Order of Victimhood: Violence, Hierarchy, and Building Peace in Northern Ireland.* London: Palgrave Macmillan.

Jeffery, Laura. 2010. 'Forced Displacement, Onward Migration and Reformulations of "Home" by Chagossians in Crawley, UK'. *Journal of Ethnic and Migration Studies* 36 (7): 1099–117.

Jenne, E. K. 2016. 'The Causes and Consequences of Ethnic Cleansing'. In *The Routledge Handbook of Ethnic Conflict*, edited by Karl Cordell and Stefan Wolff, 112–21. New York: Routledge.

Kaldor, Mary. 2012. *New and Old Wars: Organised Violence in a Global Era.* Cambridge: Polity.

Kerr, Rachel and Eirin Mobekk. 2007. *Peace and Justice: Seeking Accountability after War.* Cambridge: Polity.

Kilmurray, Avila. 2016. *Community Action in a Contested Society: The Story of Northern Ireland.* Oxford: Peter Lang Ltd, International Academic Publishers.

Kingsley, Paul. 1989. *Londonderry Revisited.* Belfast: Belfast Publications.

Korac, Maja. 2001. 'Cross-Ethnic Networks, Self-Reception System and Functional Integration of Refugees from the Former Yugoslavia in Rome'. *Journal of Migration and Integration* 2 (1): 1–26.

Kunz, E. F. 1973. 'The Refugee in Flight: Kinetic Models and Forms of Displacement'. *The International Migration Review* 7 (2): 125–46.

Kutz, C. 2004. 'Justice in Reparations: The Cost of Memory and the Value of Talk'. *Philosophy & Public Affairs* 32 (3): 277–312. https://escholarship.org/content/qt46w3t4do/qt46w3t4do.pdf.

Laing, R. D. 2010 [1960]. *The Divided Self: An Existential Study in Sanity and Madness.* London: Penguin Books.

Laplante, L. J. 2007. 'On the Indivisibility of Rights: Truth Commissions, Reparations, and the Right to Develop'. *Yale Hum. Rts. & Dev. Law Journal* 10: 141–77. https://heinonline.org/HOL/LandingPage?handle=hein.journals/yhurdvl10&div=6&id=&page=.

Laplante, L. J. 2014. 'The Plural Justice Aims of Reparations'. In *Transitional Justice Theories*, edited by S. Buckley-Zistel, T. K. Beck, C. Braun, and F. Mieth, 66–84. https://www.corteidh.or.cr/tablas/r32526.pdf#page=79.

Lawther, Cheryl. 2014. *Truth, Denial and Transition: Northern Ireland and the Contested Past.* New York: Routledge.

Lawther, Cheryl and Luke Moffett. 2021. 'Lives, Landscapes and the Legacy of the Past'. *Dealing with the Legacy of Conflict in Northern Ireland through Engagement & Dialogue* (March): 126–37.

Lederach, John Paul. 1997. *Building Peace: Sustainable Reconciliation in Divided Societies.* Washington, DC: United States Institute of Peace Press.

Leonard, Madeleine. 2004. 'Bonding and Bridging Social Capital: Reflections from Belfast'. *Sociology* 38 (5): 927–44.

Lewis, Anthony. 1971. 'Weary, Fearful Refugees from Ulster Crowd into Ireland'. *The New York Times*, 13 August. https://www.nytimes.com/1971/08/13/archives/weary-fearful-refugees-from-ulster-crowd-into-ireland.html (accessed 15 October 2021).

Liggett, Michael. 2004. *Glenard: Surviving Fear*. Dublin: Sásta.

Little, Adrian. 2004. *Democracy and Northern Ireland: Beyond the Liberal Paradigm?* New York: Palgrave Macmillan.

Loescher, Gil. 1992. *Refugee Movements and International Security*. Adelphi Papers. London: Brassey's.

Loescher, Gill and James Milner. 2005. 'Security Implications of Protracted Refugee Situations'. *The Adelphi Papers* 45 (375): 23–34.

Lu, C. 2018. 'Reconciliation and Reparations'. *The Oxford Handbook of Ethics of War*, edited by Seth Lazar and Helen Frowe, 538–56. https://www.oxfordhandbooks.com/view/10.1093/oxfordhb/9780199943418.001.0001/oxfordhb-9780199943418-e-17.

Lundy, Patricia and Mark McGovern. 2008. 'Whose Justice? Rethinking Transitional Justice from the Bottom Up'. *Journal of Law and Society* 35 (2): 265–92.

MacKenzie, Catriona and Christopher McDowell. 2007. 'Beyond "Do No Harm": The Challenge of Constructing Ethical Relationships in Refugee Research'. *Journal of Refugee Studies* 20 (2): 299–319.

Marks, S. 1978. 'The Myths of Reparations'. *Central European History* 11 (3): 231–55. http://www.jstor.org/stable/4545835.

Marlowe, Jay. 2017. *Belonging and Transnational Refugee Settlement: Unsettling the Everyday and the Extraordinary*. New York: Routledge.

McAleese, Mary. 2020. *Here's the Story: A Memoir*. London: Sandycove.

McCann, Michael. 2019. *Burnt Out: How the Troubles Began*. Dublin: Mercier Press.

McCarron, J J. 2006. 'Civil Society in Northern Ireland: A New Beginning?' Report for the Northern Ireland Council for Voluntary Action (Belfast).

McClements, Freya. 2021. 'Northern Ireland's Refugees 50 years on: "I can still see him standing there waving"'. *The Irish Times*, 7 August. https://www.irishtimes.com/life-and-style/northern-ireland-s-refugees-50-years-on-i-can-still-see-him-standing-there-waving-1.4632825 (accessed 15 February 2022).

McConville M. 2017. 'Paramilitary Intimidation has Driven almost 500 People from their Homes'. *The Irish News*, 7 November. https://www.irishnews.com/news/2017/11/07/news/rise-in-people-presenting-themselves-as-homeless-due-to-paramilitary-intimidation-1181044/ (accessed 15 September 2021).

McEvoy, Kieran. 2007. 'Beyond Legalism: Towards a Thicker Understanding of Transitional Justice'. *Journal of Law and Society* 34 (4): 411–40.

McEvoy, Kieran and Kirsten McConnachie. 2012. 'Victimology in Transitional Justice: Victimhood, Innocence and Hierarchy'. *European Journal of Criminology* 9 (5): 527–38.

McGrattan, Cillian. 2016. 'The Stormont House Agreement and the New Politics of Storytelling in Northern Ireland'. *Parliamentary Affairs* 69: 928–46.

McKay, Susan. 2000. *Northern Protestants: An Unsettled People*. Belfast: Blackstaff Press.

McKay, Susan. 2021. *Northern Protestants: On Shifting Ground*. Newtownards: Blackstaff Press.

McKee, Brian. 2020. *Ardoyne '69: Stories of Struggle and Hope*. Dublin: Orpen Press.

McKittrick, David and David McVea. 2001. *Making Sense of the Troubles*. London: Penguin.

Miller, K. E., M. Kulkarni, & H. Kushner. 2006. 'Beyond Trauma-Focused Psychiatric Epidemiology: Bridging Research and Practice with War-Affected Populations'. *American Journal of Orthopsychiatry* 76 (4): 409–22.

Mills, C. Wright. 1999 [1959]. *The Sociological Imagination*. New York: Oxford University Press.

Misztal, Barbara A. 2003. *Theories of Social Remembering*. Maidenhead: Open University Press.

Mitzen, Jennifer. 2018. 'Feeling at Home in Europe: Migration, Ontological Security, and the Political Psychology of EU Bordering'. *Political Psychology* 39 (6): 1373–87.

Moffett, L. 2015. 'Reparations for "Guilty Victims": Navigating Complex Identities of Victim–Perpetrators in Reparation Mechanisms'. *International Journal of Transitional Justice* 10 (1): 146–67. https://academic.oup.com/ijtj/article-abstract/10/1/146/2356877.

Moffett, L. 2017. 'Transitional Justice and Reparations: Remedying the Past?' In *Research Handbook on Transitional Justice*, edited by C. Lawther, L. Moffett, and D. Jacobs, 377–400. Cheltenham: Edward Elgar Publishing. http://www.e-elgar.com/shop/research-handbook-on-transitional-justice.

Moffett, L., C. Lawther, K. McEvoy, C. Sandoval, and P. Dixon. 2019. *Alternative Sanctions Before the Special Jurisdiction for Peace: Reflections on International Law and Transitional Justice*. Belfast: QUB Human Rights Centre.

Moffett, Luke, Cheryl Lawther, Kevin Hearty, Andrew Godden, and Robin Hickey. 2020. 'No Longer Neighbours'. In *The Impact of Violence on Land, Housing and Redress in the Northern Ireland Conflict*, 1–56. Belfast: Queens University Belfast.

Moon, C. 2012. '"Who'll Pay Reparations on My Soul?" Compensation, Social Control and Social Suffering'. *Social & Legal Studies* 21(2): 187–99. https://journals.sagepub.com/doi/abs/10.1177/0964663911433670.

Moore, Will H. and Stephen M. Shellman. 2004. 'Fear of Persecution: Forced Migration, 1952–1995'. *Journal of Conflict Resolution* 48 (5): 723–745.

Moore, Will H. and Stephen M. Shellman. 2006. 'Refugee or Internally Displaced Person? To Where Should One Flee?' *Comparative Political Studies* 39 (5): 599–622.

Moore, Will H. and Stephen M. Shellman. 2007. 'Whither Will They Go? A Global Analysis of Refugee Flows 1955–1995'. *International Studies Quarterly* 51 (4): 811–34.

Moorthy, Shweta and Robert Brathwaite. 2019. 'Refugees and Rivals: The International Dynamics of Refugee Flows'. *Conflict Management and Peace Science* 36 (2): 131–48.

Mulroe, Patrick. 2017. *Bombs, Bullets and The Border. Policing Ireland's Frontier: Irish Security Policy, 1969–1978*. Newbridge: Irish Academic Press.

Mulvenna, Gareth. 2016. *Tartan Gangs and Paramilitaries: The Loyalist Backlash*. Liverpool: Liverpool University Press.

Murtagh, Brendan 1996. *Community and Conflict in Rural Ulster*. Coleraine: University of Ulster.

National Archives of Ireland. 1971. '2002/8/513 Note on Social Welfare Benefits Paid to Refugees from Northern Ireland in the Republic of Ireland'. Edited by Department of the Taoiseach. (Dublin).

National Archives of Ireland. 1973. '2004/21/494. Department of Defence: Memorandum for the Government on Arrangements for Catering for the Needs of Refugees from Northern Ireland in the Republic of Ireland'. (Dublin).

ní Dochartaigh, Kerri. 2021. *Thin Places*. Edinburgh: Canongate Books.

Ó Dochartaigh, Niall. 2005. *From Civil Rights to Armalites: Derry and the Birth of the Irish Troubles*. Basingstoke: Palgrave Macmillan.

Ó Dochartaigh, Niall. 2021. *Deniable Contact: Back-Channel Negotiation in Northern Ireland*. New York: Oxford University Press.

Oakley, Ann. 1981. 'Interviewing Women: A Contradiction in Terms'. In *Doing Feminist Research*, edited by Helen Roberts. 30–61. London: Routledge.

O'Leary, Brendan and John McGarry. 1995. *Explaining Northern Ireland: Broken Images*. Oxford: Blackwell.

O'Rawe, Mary. 2003. 'Truth and Justice'. In *Recognition & Reckoning: The Way Ahead on Victims Issues*, edited by B. Hamber and R. Wilson, 52–54. Belfast: Democratic Dialogue.

Pappe, I. 2007. *The Ethnic Cleansing of Palestine*. New York: Simon & Schuster.

Parry, Jacqueline. 2020. 'Constructing Space for Refugee Voices in National Peacebuilding Processes'. *Peacebuilding* 8 (2): 159–77.

Patterson, Henry. 2010. 'Sectarianism Revisited: The Provisional IRA Campaign in a Border Region of Northern Ireland'. *Terrorism and Political Violence* 22 (3): 337–56.

Patterson, Henry. 2013. *Ireland's Violent Frontier: The Border and Anglo-Irish Relations During the Troubles*. New York: Palgrave.

Petrovic, D. 1994. 'Ethnic Cleansing – An Attempt at Methodology'. *European Journal of International Law* 5: 342–59.

Poole, M. and Doherty, P. 2010. *Ethnic Residential Segregation in Northern Ireland*. Coleraine: University of Ulster.

Portes, Alejandro. 2014. 'Downsides of Social Capital'. *PNAS* 111 (52): 18407–08. https://doi.org/10.1073/pnas.1421888112.

Power, J. and Shuttleworth, I. 1997. 'Intercensal Population Change in the Belfast Urban Area 1971–91: The Correlates of Population Increase and Decrease in a Divided Society'. *International Journal of Population Geography* 3: 91–108.

Pradier, A., M. Rubin, and H. van der Merwe. 2018. 'Between Transitional Justice and Politics: Reparations in South Africa'. *South African Journal of International Affairs* 25 (3): 301–21. https://www.tandfonline.com/doi/abs/10.1080/10220461.2018.1514528.

Prince, Simon and Geoffrey Warner. 2019. *Belfast and Derry in Revolt: A New History of the Start of the Troubles*. Newbridge, Ireland: Irish Academic Press.

Putnam, Robert D. 2000. *Bowling Alone: The Collapse and Revival of American Community*. New York: Touchstone.

Puvimanasinghe, Teresa, Linley A. Denson, Martha Augoustinos, and Daya Somasundaram. 2015. 'Narrative and Silence: How Former Refugees Talk about Loss and Past Trauma'. *Journal of Refugee Studies* 28 (1): 69–92.

Reed, Richard. 2015. *Paramilitary Loyalism: Identity and Change*. Manchester: Manchester University Press.

Roht-Arriaza, N. 2004. 'Reparations Decisions and Dilemmas'. *Hastings Int'l & Comp. L. Rev.* 27: 157–219. http://repository.uchastings.edu/faculty_scholarship/691.

Roht-Arriaza, N. 2014. 'Reparations and Economic, Social, and Cultural Rights'. *Justice and Economic Violence in Transition*: 109–38. https://papers.ssrn.com/sol3/papers.cfm?abstract_id=2177024.

Roht-Arriaza, N. and K. Orlovsky. 2009. 'A Complementary Relationship: Reparations and Development'. Research brief for the International Center for Transitional Justice, https://www.ictj.org/sites/default/files/ICTJ-Development-Reparations-Research Brief-2009-English.pdf.

Rubio-Marin, R. and P. de Greiff. 2007. 'Women and Reparations'. *International Journal of Transitional Justice* 1 (3): 318–37. https://academic.oup.com/ijtj/article-abstract/1/3/318/2356926.

Ryder, Chris. 1989. *The RUC: A Force Under Fire*. London: Methuen.

Ryder, Chris. 2000. *Inside the Maze: The Untold Story of the Northern Ireland Prison Service*. London: Methuen Publishing.

Said, Edward. 2001. *Reflections on Exile and Other Literary and Cultural Essays*. London: Granta Books.

Samers, Michael and Michael Collyer. 2017. *Migration*. London and New York: Routledge.

Saunders, Natasha. 2017. *International Political Theory and the Refugee Problem*. London: Routledge.

Scarman, Justice. 1972. 'Violence and Civil Disturbances in Northern Ireland in 1969: Report of Tribunal of Inquiry'. https://cain.ulster.ac.uk/hmso/scarman.htm (accessed 1 August 2022).

Sheeran, Robin. 2021. 'The Troubles: When Belfast Children Fled the City'. BBC News NI, 30 August. https://www.bbc.co.uk/news/uk-northern-ireland-58193536.amp (accessed 15 February 2022).

Shirlow, Peter. 2001. 'Fear and Ethnic Division.' *Peace Review* 13: 67–74. doi:10.1080/10402650120038161.

Shirlow, Peter. 2003. 'Ethno-sectarianism and the Reproduction of Fear in Belfast'. *Capital & Class* 27 (2): 77–93.

Shirlow, Peter. 2014. 'Rejection, Shaming, Enclosure, and Moving On: Variant Experiences and Meaning Among Loyalist Former Prisoners'. *Studies in Conflict & Terrorism* 37 (9): 733–46.

Shirlow, Peter. 2018. 'Truth Friction in Northern Ireland: Caught between Apologia and Humiliation'. *Parliamentary Affairs* 71: 417–37.

Shirlow, Peter, Brian Graham, Amanda McMullan, Brendan Murtagh, Gillian Robinson and Neil Southern. 2005. 'Population Change and Social Inclusion Study. Derry/Londonderry'. Research report for the Office of the First Minister and Deputy First Minister (Belfast).

Shirlow, Peter and Kieran McEvoy. 2008. *Beyond the Wire: Former Prisoners and Conflict Transformation in Northern Ireland*. London: Pluto Press.

Shirlow, Peter and Brendan Murtagh. 2006. *Belfast: Violence, Segregation and the City*. London: Pluto Press.

Shuttleworth, I., P. J. Barr, and M. Gould. 2013. 'Does Internal Migration in Northern Ireland Increase Religious and Social Segregation? Perspectives from the Northern Ireland longitudinal Study (NILS) 2001–2007'. *Population, Space and Place* 19 (1): 72–86.

Shuttleworth, I. and D. Lloyd. 2009. 'Are Northern Ireland's Communities Dividing? Evidence from Geographically Consistent Census of Population data, 1971–2001'. *Environment and Planning A* 41: 213–29.

Side, K. 2015. 'Visual and Textual Narratives of Conflict-related Displacement in Northern Ireland'. *Identities* 22 (4): 486–507.

Side, Katherine. 2018. '"Ungenerous, Though Not Mean": The Scheme for the Purchase of Evacuated Dwellings in Belfast, Northern Ireland'. In *Boundaries, Passages, Transitions: Essays in Irish Literature, Culture & Politics in Honour of Werner Huber*, edited by Hedwig Schwall, 25–39. Trier: Wissenschaftlicher Verlag Trier.

Silverman, David. 2006. *Interpreting Qualitative Data* (3rd ed). London: Sage.

Silverman, David. 2010. *Doing Qualitative Research*. London: Sage.

Smithey, Lee A. 2012. *Unionists, Loyalists, and Conflict Transformation in Northern Ireland*. Oxford: Oxford University Press.

Smyth, Marie. 1996. 'Urban Regeneration and Sectarian Division with Specific Reference to Segregation and the Situation of Enclave Communities: A Commentary on Urban Regeneration in Derry-Londonderry 1996–1999'. Report for Templregrove Action Research (Derry and Londonderry).

Smyth, Marie. 2007. *Truth Recovery and Justice after Conflict: Managing Violent Pasts.* London: Routledge.

Spencer, Graham. 2008. *The State of Loyalism in Northern Ireland.* Basingstoke: Palgrave MacMillan.

Southern, Neil. 2007. 'Protestant Alienation in Northern Ireland: A Political, Cultural and Geographical Examination'. *Journal of Ethnic and Migration Studies* 33 (1): 159–80.

Steele, Abbey. 2009. 'Seeking Safety: Avoiding Displacement and Choosing Destinations in Civil Wars'. *Journal of Peace Research* 46 (3): 419–29.

Steele, Abbey. 2011. 'Electing Displacement: Political Cleansing in Apartado, Colombia'. *Journal of Conflict Resolution* 55 (3): 423–45.

Stewart, A.T. Q. 1997. *The Narrow Ground: Aspects of Ulster, 1609–1969.* Belfast: Blackstaff Press.

Straus, Scott. 2015. *Making and Unmaking Nations: The Origins and Dynamics of Genocide in Contemporary Africa.* London: Cornell University Press.

Strauss, Anselm and Juliet Corbin. 1990. *Basics of Qualitative Research Techniques and Procedures for Developing Grounded Theory.* London: Sage.

Suchkova, M. 2011. 'The Importance of a Participatory Reparations Process and its Relationship to the Principles of Reparation'. Report for the Essex Transitional Justice Network. https://biblioteca.corteidh.or.cr/tablas/r26685.pdf (accessed 1 August 2022).

Taylor, Helen. 2015. *Refugees and the Meaning of Home: Cypriot Narratives of Loss, Longing and Daily Life in London.* New York: Palgrave MacMillan.

Teitel, Ruti, T. 2003. 'Transitional Justice Genealogy'. *Harvard Human Rights Journal* 16: 69–94.

Tickner, J. Ann. 1992. *Gender in International Relations: Feminist Perspectives on Achieving Global Security.* New York: Columbia University Press.

Todd, Jennifer. 2018. *Identity Change After Conflict: Ethnicity, Boundaries and Belonging in the Two Irelands.* Basingstoke: Palgrave Macmillan.

Todd, Jennifer and Joseph Ruane. 1996. *The Dynamics of Conflict in Northern Ireland: Power, Conflict and Emancipation.* Cambridge: Cambridge University Press.

United Nations. nd. 'Ethnic Cleansing'. https://www.un.org/en/genocideprevention/ethnic-cleansing.shtml (accessed 1 August 2022).

United Nations High Commissioner for Refugees (UNHCR). 2010. 'Convention and Protocol Relating to the Status of Refugees'. https://www.unhcr.org/3b66c2aa10 (accessed 1 August 2022).

United Nations Office for the Coordination of Humanitarian Affairs (UNOCHA) 1998. 'Guiding Principles on Internal Displacement. E/CN.4/1998/53/Add.2'. http://www.unocha.org/sites/dms/Documents/GuidingPrinciplesDispl.Pdf (accessed 1 August 2022).

Val-Garijo, F. 2009. 'Reparations for Victims as a Key Element of Transitional Justice in the Middle East Occupied Territories: A Legal and Institutional Approach'. *Int'l Stud. J.* 6: 39–62. https://cadmus.eui.eu/bitstream/handle/1814/14040/ISJ%20Val-Garijo_EN.pdf;sequence=2.

Van Hear, N. 1998. *New Diasporas.* London: UCL Press.

Verdeja, E. 2006. 'A Normative Theory of Reparations in Transitional Democracies'. *Metaphilosophy* 37 (3–4): 449–68. https://onlinelibrary.wiley.com/doi/epdf/10.1111/j.1467-9973.2006.00440.x.

Vullnetari, Julie. 2012. 'Beyond "Choice or Force": Roma Mobility in Albania and the Mixed Migration Paradigm'. *Journal of Ethnic and Migration Studies* 38 (8): 1305–21.

Walker, M. U. 2015. 'Transformative Reparations? A Critical Look at a Current Trend in Thinking about Gender-Just Reparations'. *International Journal of Transitional Justice* 10 (1): 108–25. https://academic.oup.com/ijtj/article-abstract/10/1/108/2356876.

Walsh, Andrew. 2015. *Belfast '69: Bombs, Burnings and Bigotry*. Dublin: Fonthill Publishing.

Weidmann, Nils B. 2009. 'Geography as Motivation and Opportunity: Group Concentration and Ethnic Conflict'. *Journal of Conflict Resolution* 53 (4): 526–43.

Wenar, L. 2006. 'Reparations for the Future'. *Journal of Social Philosophy* 37 (3): 396–405. https://onlinelibrary.wiley.com/doi/abs/10.1111/j.1467-9833.2006.00344.x.

White, Robert W. 2017. *Out of the Ashes: An Oral History of The Provisional Irish Republican Movement*. Newbridge, Ireland: Merrion Press.

Whiting, Matthew. 2019. *Sinn Féin and the IRA: From Revolution to Moderation*. Edinburgh: Edinburgh University Press.

Wilson, R. 2016. 'Northern Ireland Peace Monitoring Report'. Report for the Community Relations Council (Belfast).

Wolff, Stefan. 2007. *Ethnic Conflict: A Global Perspective*. Oxford: Oxford University Press.

Zetter, Roger. 2007. 'More Labels, Fewer Refugees: Remaking the Refugee Label in an Era of Globalization'. *Journal of Refugee Studies* 20 (2): 172–92.

Index